COMBINED COMPANION — Unit 18

Preparing Business Taxation Computations (Finance Act 2006)

For exams in June 2007 and December 2007

First edition February 2005
Third edition August 2006

ISBN 0 7517 2729 6 (Previous ISBN 0 7517 1643 X)

British Library Cataloguing-in-Publication Data
A catalogue record for this book is available from the British Library

Published by

BPP Professional Education
Aldine House,
Aldine Place,
London, W12 8AW

Printed in Great Britain by Ashford Colour Press Ltd
Unit 600
Fareham Reach
Fareham Road
Gosport
Hampshire
PO13 0FW

All our rights reserved. No part of this publication may be reproduced, stored in a retrieval system or transmitted, in any form or by any means, electronic, mechanical, photocopying, recording or otherwise, without the prior written permission of BPP Professional Education.

©
BPP Professional Education
2006

CONTENTS

Introduction (v)
Standards of competence and performance criteria (vii)
Assessment strategy (xiii)
Tax rates and allowances (xvii)

Course Companion

1	Introduction	3
2	Computing trading income	11
3	Capital allowances	27
4	Taxing unincorporated businesses	47
5	Relieving trading losses	57
6	Partnerships	63
7	Capital gains tax for sole traders	75
8	Chargeable gains: additional aspects	87
9	Shares	95
10	Deferring taxation of capital gains	109
11	Computing profits chargeable to corporation tax	117
12	Computing corporation tax payable	129
13	Corporation tax losses	143
14	National insurance	153
15	Administration and payment of income tax, CGT and Class 4 NICs	159
16	Administration and payment of corporation tax	171
	Answers to chapter activities	185
	How much have you learned? – answers	207

Revision Companion

		Questions	Answers
Chapter activities			
1	Introduction	223	357
2	Computing trading income	225	359
3	Capital allowances	229	361
4	Taxing unincorporated businesses	233	365
5	Relieving trading losses	237	369
6	Partnerships	239	371
7	Capital gains tax for sole traders	241	375
8	Chargeable gains: additional aspects	243	379
9	Shares	245	383
10	Deferring taxation of capital gains	249	393
11	Computing profits chargeable to corporation tax	253	397
12	Computing corporation tax payable	259	401
13	Corporation tax losses	261	405
14	National insurance	263	409
15	Administration and payment of income tax, CGT and Class 4 NICs	265	411
16	Administration and payment of corporation tax	267	413
Practice exams			
Practice Exam 1 (December 2003 paper)		269	417
Practice Exam 2 (June 2004 paper)		283	423
Practice Exam 3 (December 2004 paper)		301	429
Practice Exam 4 (June 2005 paper)		317	435
Practice Exam 5 (December 2005 paper)		335	441
Index		449	

INTRODUCTION

This is the third edition of BPP's Combined Companion for AAT Unit 18: Preparing Business Taxation Computations. It has been carefully designed to enable students to practise all aspects of the requirements of the Standards of Competence and performance criteria, and ultimately be successful in their exam.

There is a Course Companion section containing these key features:

- clear, step by step explanation of the topic
- logical progression from one topic to the next
- numerous illustrations and practical examples
- interactive activities within the text itself, with answers supplied
- a bank of questions of varying complexity again with answers supplied.

The Revision Companion section contains:

- graded activities corresponding to each chapter of the Course Companion, with answers
- five practice exams with answers. The December 2003, June 2004, December 2004, June 2005 and December 2005 papers are included. BPP have written their own answers to these exams.

introduction

UNIT 18 STANDARDS OF COMPETENCE AND PERFORMANCE CRITERIA

The structure of the standards of Unit 18

The Unit commences with a statement of the knowledge and understanding which underpin competence in the Unit's elements.

The Unit of Competence is then divided into elements of competence describing activities which the individual should be able to perform.

Each element includes:

a) A set of performance criteria. This defines what constitutes competent performance.

b) A range statement. This defines the situations, contexts, methods etc in which competence should be displayed.

The elements of competence for Unit 18: Preparing Business Taxation Computations are set out below. Knowledge and understanding required for the Unit as a whole are listed first, followed by the performance criteria and range statements for each element.

standards of competence: Unit 18

UNIT 18 PREPARING BUSINESS TAXATION COMPUTATIONS

What is the unit about?

This unit is about preparing tax computations for businesses and completing the relevant tax returns. There are four elements.

The first element requires you to prepare capital allowances computations, including adjustments for private use by the owners of a business.

In the second element you must prepare assessable business income computations for partnerships and self-employed individuals. This includes identifying the National Insurance Contributions payable.

The third element is concerned with preparing capital gains computations for companies and unincorporated businesses.

The final element requires you to prepare Corporation Tax computations for UK resident companies.

Throughout the unit you must show that you take account of current tax law and HM Revenue and Customs (HMRC) practice and make submissions within statutory timescales. You also need to show that you consult with HMRC in an open and constructive manner, give timely and constructive advice to business clients and maintain client confidentiality.

Knowledge and understanding

To perform this unit effectively you will need to know and understand:

The business environment

1. The duties and responsibilities of the tax practitioner (Elements 18.1, 18.2, 18.3 & 18.4)
2. The issues of taxation liability (Elements 18.1, 18.2, 18.3 & 18.4)
3. Relevant legislation and guidance from HMRC (Elements 18.1, 18.2, 18.3 & 18.4)

Taxation principles and theory

4. Basic law and practice relating to all issues covered in the range and referred to in the performance criteria (Elements 18.1, 18.2, 18.3 & 18.4)

5. Availability and types of capital allowance:
   - first year allowance
   - writing down allowance
   - balancing allowance and charge (relevant to industrial buildings and plant and machinery including computers, motor vehicles and short life assets) (Element 18.1)

6. Treatment of capital allowances for unincorporated businesses including private use adjustments (Element 18.1)

7. Adjustment of trading profits and losses for tax purposes (Element 18.2)

standards of competence: Unit 18

8   Regulations relating to disallowed expenditure such as business entertaining, bad debt write-offs and provisions, private expenditure and capital expenditure (Element 18.2)

9   Basis of assessment of unincorporated businesses (Element 18.2)

10 Basic allocation of income between partners (Element 18.3)

11 Identification of business assets disposed of including part disposals (Element 18.3)

12 Calculation of gains and losses on disposals of business assets including indexation allowance (Element 18.3)

13 Capital gains exemptions and reliefs on business assets including rollover relief and taper relief but excluding retirement relief (Element 18.3)

14 Rates of tax payable on gains on business assets disposed of by individuals (Element 18.3)

15 The computation of profit for Corporation Tax purposes including income, capital gains and charges (Element 18.4)

16 Calculation of Corporation Tax payable by starting, small, large and marginal companies including those with associated companies (Element 18.4)

17 Set-off of trading losses incurred by companies (Element 18.4)

18 Calculation of National Insurance Contributions payable by self-employed persons and employers of not contracted-out employees (Elements 18.2 & 18.4)

19 Self assessment including payment of tax and filing of returns for unincorporated businesses and companies (Elements 18.2 & 18.4)

The organisation

20 How the taxation liabilities of an organisation are affected by its legal structure and the nature of its business transactions (Elements 18.1, 18.2, 18.3 & 18.4)

21 The organisation's legal structure and its business transactions (Elements 18.1, 18.2, 18.3 & 18.4)

standards of competence: Unit 18

Element 18.1 Prepare capital allowances computations

Performance criteria | **Chapter(s)**

In order to perform this element successfully you need to:

- Classify expenditure on capital assets in accordance with the statutory distinction between capital and revenue expenditure — 2, 3
- Ensure that entries and calculations relating to the computation of capital allowances for a company are correct — 3
- Make adjustments for private use by business owners — 2, 3
- Ensure that computations and submissions are made in accordance with current tax law and take account of current HMRC practice — 15
- Consult with HMRC staff in an open and constructive manner — 15, 16
- Give timely and constructive advice to clients on the maintenance of accounts and the recording of information relevant to tax returns — 15
- Maintain client confidentiality at all times — 15

Range statement

Performance in this element relates to the following contexts:

- Self-employed individuals – Partnerships

Element 18.2 Compute assessable business income

Performance criteria | **Chapter(s)**

In order to perform this element successfully you need to:

- Adjust trading profits and losses for tax purposes — 2, 5
- Make adjustments for private use by business owners — 2, 3
- Divide profits and losses of partnerships amongst partners — 6
- Apply the basis of assessment for unincorporated businesses in the opening and closing years — 4–6
- Identify the due dates of payment of Income Tax by unincorporated businesses, including payments on account — 15
- Identify the National Insurance Contributions payable by self-employed individuals — 14
- Complete correctly the self-employed and partnership supplementary pages to the Tax Return for individuals, together with relevant claims and elections, and submit them within statutory time limits — 15

	Chapter(s)
■ Consult with HMRC staff in an open and constructive manner	15, 16
■ Give timely and constructive advice to clients on the maintenance of accounts and the recording of information relevant to tax returns	15
■ Maintain client confidentiality at all times	15

Range statement

Performance in this element relates to the following contexts:

- Sole traders – Partnerships

Element 18.3 Prepare capital gains computations

Performance criteria   **Chapter(s)**

In order to perform this element successfully you need to:

	Chapter(s)
■ Identify and value correctly any chargeable assets that have been disposed of	7–9
■ Identify shares disposed of by companies	9
■ Calculate chargeable gains and allowable losses	7–9
■ Apply reliefs, deferrals and exemptions correctly	7, 10
■ Ensure that computations and submissions are made in accordance with current tax law and take account of current HMRC practice	15
■ Consult with HMRC staff in an open and constructive manner	15, 16
■ Give timely and constructive advice to clients on the maintenance of accounts and the recording of information relevant to tax returns	15
■ Maintain client confidentiality at all times	15

Range statement

Performance in this element relates to the following contexts:

- Chargeable assets that have been:

  Sold
  Gifted
  Lost
  Destroyed

- Reliefs:

  Rollover relief
  Relief for gifts

Element 18.4 Prepare Corporation Tax computations

Performance criteria   Chapter(s)

In order to perform this element successfully you need to:

- Enter adjusted trading profits and losses, capital allowances, investment income and capital gains in the Corporation Tax computation — 11

- Set-off and deduct loss reliefs and charges correctly — 13

- Calculate Corporation Tax due, taking account of marginal relief — 12

- Identify and set-off Income Tax deductions and credits — 16

- Identify the National Insurance Contributions payable by employers — 14

- Identify the amount of Corporation Tax payable and the due dates of payment, including payments on account — 16

- Complete Corporation Tax returns correctly and submit them, together with relevant claims and elections, within statutory time limits — 16

- Consult with HMRC staff in an open and constructive manner — 15, 16

- Give timely and constructive advice to clients on the maintenance of accounts and the recording of information relevant to tax returns — 15

- Maintain client confidentiality at all times — 15

Range statement

Performance in this element relates to the following contexts:

- Loss reliefs relating to:

    Trade losses – Non-trade losses

ASSESSMENT STRATEGY

This Unit is assessed by exam based assessment only.

Exam based assessment

An exam based assessment is a means of collecting evidence that you have the essential knowledge and understanding which underpins competence. It is also a means of collecting evidence across the range of contexts for the standards, and of your ability to transfer skills, knowledge and understanding to different situations. Thus, although exams contain practical tests linked to the performance criteria, they also focus on the underpinning knowledge and understanding. You should, in addition, expect each exam to contain tasks taken from across a broad range of the standards.

Format of exam

There will be a three hour exam in two sections.

Section 1:   Element 18.2 (taxation of sole traders and partnerships)
Section 2:   Element 18.4 (taxation of limited companies)

Elements 18.1 and 18.3 can appear in either section.

There will be an additional 15 minutes reading time.

Further guidance

The Standard is divided into four elements. Element 18.1 is called Prepare capital allowances computations, Element 18.2 is called Compute assessable business income, Element 18.3 is called Prepare capital gains computations and Element 18.4 is called Prepare Corporation Tax computations.

Element 18.1 is not to be seen in isolation. It has an impact on both Element 18.2 and 18.4. This is because both 18.2 and 18.4 require the calculation of trading (Schedule D Case I/II) profits or losses, and capital allowances need to be deducted as an allowable expense.

Specific areas that need to be covered are:

1) Awareness of the kind of expenditure on which capital allowances will be available: What is plant and machinery? What is an industrial building? When is expenditure for capital purposes and when is it for revenue purposes?

2) The ability to calculate capital allowances on: Plant and machinery. This includes special rules on: Motor vehicles; Short life assets; Computers; First year allowances; Private use assets (unincorporated businesses only); Industrial buildings allowance (this only includes buildings that have continuously been used for industrial purposes).

These calculations need to be made for both unincorporated and incorporated businesses. The rules governing opening, continuing and ceasing organisations need to be considered.

assessment strategy

Writing down allowances, balancing allowances and balancing charges are required.

Students must consider the rationale behind these calculations, so that they can provide a written explanation of the calculations, for instance, when dealing with client queries.

The purpose of Element 18.2 is to demonstrate the ability to calculate trading (Schedule D Case I/II) profits or losses.

Firstly, students should be able to determine whether trading is taking place, for instance, through the use of the badges of trade.

In calculating the adjusted trading (Schedule D Case I/II) profit or loss of the business, a sound knowledge is required of how to adjust the accounting profit or loss. Only a few of the adjustments required are specifically mentioned in the Knowledge and Understanding. This list should be viewed as being indicative, rather than exhaustive. Part of these adjustments is the ability to correctly identify, and adjust for, private usage of expenditure as shown in the accounting profit and loss account.

If the trade is being carried on by a partnership, students need to be able to determine how profits are to be split between the partners according to the rules laid down by HMRC. This includes changes in the profit-sharing agreement or a change in the composition of the partnership, such as when a partner joins or leaves the business.

For both a sole trader and a partnership, a sound knowledge is required of the rules for opening, continuing and closing years of trade. This includes overlap profits. However, the rules for the change of accounting date are excluded. Such calculations will be expected in round tax months, not in days.

Once determined, students need to demonstrate understanding of the use of the profit or loss in the inclusion of the income tax return. The dates for submission of the return and payment of income tax must be considered, together with the implications of making a late filing of the return. However, the completion of the actual income tax return and completion of the income tax computation is assessable under Unit 19.

If the trading (Schedule D Case I/II) figure results in a loss, students must have knowledge of the ways in which such a loss can be relieved. S385, s380, s381 and s388 ICTA 1988 should all be covered, but detailed and complex loss relief provisions will not be assessed. Excluded from this are losses for partnerships.

For National Insurance Contributions, knowledge of both Class 2 and Class 4 is required.

Element 18.3 deals with the calculation of capital gains for businesses only. This includes chargeable disposals by individuals and companies of business assets, and of the business itself. Disposal of private assets held by individuals is assessable under Unit 19. Taper relief is therefore included where an individual disposes of a business asset, but the treatment of capital gains for a partnership is excluded.

Capital gains computations may include:

Shares and securities, including rights issues and bonus issues, FA 1985 pool and matching rules
Chattels
Part disposal of assets
Improvement expenditure
Indexation allowance
Tapering relief as appropriate to individuals

A capital gain computation will not be required on any assets acquired before 31 March 1982.

In addition, students should have an understanding of business reliefs, including rollover relief and relief for gifts. Students should be able to demonstrate knowledge about the conditions for such reliefs and be able to complete basic calculations. Complex calculations will not be required, for example assets with non-business use or depreciating assets. Calculations on partial reinvestment or gift relief will be straight forward. The capital tax implications for leases are also excluded.

Under Element 18.4, the student must be able to compute the trading (Schedule D Case I) profit or loss of a company using the same rules for capital allowances and adjustment of profit as detailed in Elements 18.1 and 18.2 respectively. A capital gains computation from Element 18.3 may also be included in a full Corporation Tax computation. For periods of accounts, students should be able to understand how those shorter or longer than twelve months affect the CT computation.

If the company has made a loss, knowledge is expected of how to deal with that loss under s393 (1) and s393A (1) ICTA 1988. This includes computational aspects of loss relief, together with the ability to provide clients with advice on the best option to take for the most tax effective way of handling the loss, albeit in a simple way. Students should be able to deal with company losses other than trading (Schedule D Case I), such as capital losses and property business (Schedule A).

When determining the amount of Corporation Tax payable, the following knowledge is required: pre FY06: the impact of the starting rate and the use of upper and lower limits for small company rate purposes, FY06 onwards: the use of the marginal relief calculation, together with the impact of associated companies on the limits for the marginal relief, the deduction of income tax and the calculation of Mainstream Corporation Tax payable.

The FA 2004 introduced new rules for non company distributions. As this was abolished in the FA 06, this is no longer examinable.

Students should be able to state the due date of payment and be able to explain the self-assessment rules. Translation of these figures to the short version of Form CT600 may also be required.

For National Insurance Contributions, students should be able to compute the NIC payable by companies for their employees who are not contracted out. This includes a basic understanding of the definition of earnings, on which the NIC will be based.

Excluded topics from this element are: close companies and close investment holding companies, investment companies, groups and consortium structures, group capital gains tax, overseas aspects, including double tax relief, calculation of property business (Schedule A) rental income (assessable under Unit 19).

Typical tasks in the first section

- Trading (Schedule D Case I/II) computation, leading to either a profit or a loss. This could be for either a sole trader or a partnership
- Set-off of income tax losses for individuals
- Capital allowances computation for industrial buildings and/or plant and machinery
- Capital gains computation for business asset disposals for an individual
- National Insurance Contributions for the self-employed
- Opening and closing rules for unincorporated businesses, including overlap profits
- Completion of the supplementary pages to the Tax Return for individuals

assessment strategy

Typical tasks in the second section

- Trading (Schedule D Case I) computation, leading to either a profit or a loss
- Set-off of trading (Schedule D Case I) losses, restricted to a scenario involving four years
- Capital allowances computation for industrial buildings and/or plant and machinery
- Capital gains computation for limited companies
- Calculation of the Corporation Tax payable, including small company marginal relief, MCT and the dates of payment
- National Insurance Contributions for the employees of companies
- Completion of the Corporation Tax returns

It is not anticipated that students will be required to compute certain topics more than once during the examination. For instance, capital allowances for industrial buildings and plant and machinery will only be assessed once in either Section 1 or Section 2. The same principle applies for capital gains, although it may be appropriate to assess the disposal of a business in Section 1 and the disposal of shares in Section 2.

TAX RATES AND ALLOWANCES

A Income tax

1 Rates

	2006/07		2005/06	
	£	%	£	%
Starting rate	1 – 2,150	10	1 – 2,090	10
Basic rate	2,150 – 33,300	22	2,091 – 32,400	22
Higher rate	33,301 and above	40	32,401 and above	40

Savings (excl. Dividend) income is taxed at 20% if it falls in the basic rate band. Dividend income in both the starting rate and the basic rate bands is taxed at 10%. Dividend income within the higher rate band is taxed at 32.5%.

2 Allowances

	2006/07	2005/06
	£	£
Personal allowance	5,035	4,895

3 Capital allowances

	%
Plant and machinery	
Writing down allowance	25
First year allowance (acquisitions after 2 July 1998)	40
First year allowances for small enterprises (1 April 2004 to 31 March 2005 or 6 April 2004 to 5 April 2005 and 1 April 2006 to 31 March 2007 or 6 April 2006 to 5 April 2007)	50
First year allowance (information and communication technology equipment – period 1 April 2000 to 31 March 2004, energy/water saving equipment)	100
Industrial buildings allowance	
Writing down allowance:	4

B Corporation tax

1 Rates

Financial year	Full rate %	Small companies rate %	Starting rate	Starting rate marginal relief fraction	Lower limit for starting rate £	Upper limit for starting rate £	Small companies' rate marginal relief	Lower limit for SCR £	Upper Limit for SCR £
2003	30	19	0	19/400	10,000	50,000	11/400	300,000	1,500,000
2004	30	19	0	19/400	10,000	50,000	11/400	300,000	1,500,000
2005	30	19	0	19/400	10,000	50,000	11/400	300,000	1,500,000
2006	30	19	n/a	n/a	n/a	n/a	11/400	300,000	1,500,000

2 Marginal relief

$(M - P) \times I/P \times$ Marginal relief fraction

C Capital gains tax

1 Annual exemption (individuals)

	£
2005/06	8,500
2006/07	8,800

2 Taper relief

Number of complete years after 5 April 1998 for which asset held	Business assets % of gain chargeable
0	100
1	50
2	25
3	25
4	25
5	25
6	25
7	25
8	25

D National insurance (not contracted out rates) 2006/07

Class 1 contributions

Employer

Earnings threshold	£5,035 (£97 pw)
Employer contributions	12.8% on earnings above earnings threshold

Class 1A contributions

Rate	12.8%

Class 2 contributions

Rate	£2.10 pw
Small earnings exception	£4,465 pa

Class 4 contributions

Main rate between LEL and UEL	8%
Additional rate above UEL	1%
Lower earnings limit	£5,035
Upper earnings limit	£33,540

COURSE COMPANION UNIT 18

chapter 1: INTRODUCTION

chapter coverage

In this opening chapter we will consider the various methods through which a business can be operated. We then see that the tax law governing businesses is included in both legislation and a body of law known as case law.

Finally, we briefly consider how to calculate an individual's income tax liability. You may need to be aware of this when dealing with business losses or when computing an individual's income tax liability. However, detailed income tax computations are not tested in Unit 18 and will not be covered in this Course Companion. You will deal with income tax computations if you study Unit 19.

The topics that we shall cover are:

- methods of operating a business
- relevant legislation and guidance from HMRC
- calculating an individual's income tax liability

KNOWLEDGE AND UNDERSTANDING AND PERFORMANCE CRITERIA COVERAGE

knowledge and understanding

- The issues of taxation liability (Elements 18.1, 18.2, 18.3, 18.4)
- Relevant legislation and guidance from HMRC (Elements 18.1, 18.2, 18.3, 18.4)
- Basic law and practice (Elements 18.1, 18.2, 18.3, 18.4)

Performance criteria

This is an introductory chapter and there are no specific performance criteria applicable to it.

METHODS OF OPERATING A BUSINESS

A person wishing to operate a business could do so:

a) As a sole trader (i.e. a self employed individual), or
b) in partnership with other self employed individuals, or
c) through a limited company

Business taxes

Sole traders and partnerships are unincorporated businesses. This means that there is no legal separation between the individual(s) carrying on the business and the business itself. As a result the individual(s) concerned must pay income tax on any income arising from the business and capital gains tax on any gains arising on the disposal of business assets. As a general rule, income is a receipt that is expected to recur (such as business profits), and a gain is a one off profit on the disposal of a capital asset (eg the profit on the sale of a factory used in the business).

Companies are incorporated businesses. This means they are taxed as separate legal entities independently of their owners. Companies must pay corporation tax on their total profits. Total profits include income arising from all sources and gains arising on the disposal of any assets.

All businesses, ie sole traders, partnerships and companies, must pay employer's national insurance contributions (NICs). These NICs are related to the earnings of employees of the business. In addition, the self employed, ie sole traders and partners, must pay NICs on their business profits. We will look at the calculation of NICs in Chapter 14 in this Course Companion.

You will study income tax and capital gains tax in the first part of this Course Companion. These taxes are normally examined in Section One of the exam. Corporation tax is normally examined in Section Two of the exam. You will study corporation tax in the second part of this Course Companion.

Payment and administration of tax

Both companies and individuals must submit a regular tax return and pay any tax due by the due date. The due dates for submitting returns and paying tax differs for individuals and companies and will be looked at in Chapters 15 and 16 of this Course Companion.

RELEVANT LEGISLATION AND GUIDANCE FROM HMRC

student notes

Most of the rules governing the above taxes are laid down in various Acts of parliament. These Acts are collectively known as the Tax Legislation. The existing Acts may be amended each year in the annual Finance Act. This Course Companion includes the provisions of the Finance Act 2006. The Finance Act 2006 will be examined in June 2007 and December 2007.

To help taxpayers, HM Revenue and Customs (HMRC), which administers tax in the UK, publish a wide range of guidance material on how they interpret the various Acts. Much of this information can be found on HMRC's website www.hmrc.gov.uk. However, none of HMRC's guidance material has the force of law. Although, you may like to have a look at this website, you should find all you need for exam purposes within this Course Companion.

Sometimes there may be a disagreement between HMRC and a taxpayer as to how a certain part of the tax legislation should be interpreted. In this case either the taxpayer or HMRC may take the case to court.

Cases decided by the court provide guidance on how legislation should be interpreted and collectively form a second source of tax law known as case law. You will not be expected to quote the names of decided cases in your exam but you may need to know the principle decided in a case. Where relevant this will be mentioned within this Course Companion.

CALCULATING AN INDIVIDUAL'S INCOME TAX LIABILITY

As well as income from his business, an individual may receive various other types of income, such as bank and building society interest, rental income and/or dividends.

All of an individual's income must be added together to arrive at what is called STATUTORY TOTAL INCOME. All individuals are entitled to a personal allowance. The personal allowance is deducted from statutory income to arrive at TAXABLE INCOME. The personal allowance effectively represents an amount of income that an individual may receive tax free.

Activity 1

An individual has the following income in 2006/07.

	£
Business profits	16,000
Building society interest	6,000
Dividends	8,750

His personal allowance is £5,035. What is his total taxable income?

student notes

The first step in calculating the income tax liability is to divide the total taxable income into three bands:

a) the first £2,150 of income; this is called income in the **starting rate band**

b) the next £31,150 of income; this is income in the **basic rate band**

c) the remaining income over the **higher rate threshold** of £33,300

The rate of tax applied to the income in each band depends on whether the income is non-savings income, savings (excluding dividend) income or dividend income.

There is only one set of income tax bands used for all three types of income. These bands must be allocated to income in the following order:

a) **non-savings income**
b) **savings** (excluding dividend) **income**
c) **dividend income**

Non-savings income in the starting rate band is taxed at 10%. Next any non-savings income in the basic rate band is taxed at 22%, and finally non-savings income above the higher rate threshold is taxed at 40%.

Savings (excl dividend) income is dealt with after non-savings income. If any of the starting or basic rate bands remain **after taxing non-savings income** they can be used here. Savings (excl dividend) income is taxed at 10% in the starting rate band. If savings (excl dividend) income falls within the basic rate band it is taxed at 20% (not 22%). Once income is above the higher rate threshold, it is taxed at 40%.

Lastly, tax dividend income. If dividend income falls within the starting or basic rate bands, it is taxed at 10% (never 20% or 22%). If, however, the dividend income exceeds the basic rate threshold of £33,300, it is taxed at 32.5%.

How it works

Zoë has total taxable income of £34,000. Of this £19,000 is non-savings income, £12,000 is interest and £3,000 is dividend income.

What is Zoë's income tax liability for 2006/07?

Solution

	£
Income tax	
Non savings income	
£2,150 × 10%	215
£16,850 × 22%	3,707
£19,000	
Savings (excl. dividend) income	
£12,000 × 20%	2,400
Dividend income	
£2,300 × 10%	230
£700 × 32.5%	228
3,000	
Tax liabilities	6,780

Activity 2

An individual has total taxable income of £50,000 for 2006/07. All of his income is non-savings income. What is the total income tax liability?

CHAPTER OVERVIEW

- A business may be operated by a sole trader, partnership or company

- Individuals trading as sole traders or in partnerships suffer income tax and capital gains tax

- Companies suffer corporation tax

- All businesses must pay NICs related to their employees' earnings. Sole traders and partners must pay NICs on their business profits

- Companies and individuals must submit regular tax returns

- All of an individual's income is added together to arrive at statutory total income

- A personal allowance is deducted from statutory total income to arrive at taxable income

- Taxable income is taxed at one of five rates, depending on which rate band it falls into and the type of income it is

> **KEY WORDS**
>
> **Statutory total income** is the total of an individual's income from all sources
>
> **Taxable income** is an individual's statutory total income minus his personal allowance

HOW MUCH HAVE YOU LEARNED?

1   Name two UK taxes suffered by a company.

2   Name three UK taxes that may be suffered by a sole trader.

3   The total of all of an individual's income is called _____

4   Arun has the following income in 2006/07:

   Non savings income   £20,000
   Savings (excl. dividends) income   £12,000
   Dividend income   £10,000

   What is Arun's income tax liability for 2006/07?

chapter 2:
COMPUTING TRADING INCOME

chapter coverage

We start this chapter by looking at the factors that HMRC consider when deciding whether a trade is being carried on. We then look at the detailed rules that determine how taxable trading profits are arrived at. The tax rules for calculating trading profits are identical to those for calculating profits from a profession or vocation so references to taxable trading profits can also be taken to refer to the taxable profits arising from a profession or vocation.

The topics that we shall cover are:

- is a trade being carried on?
- calculating trading profits
- allowable and disallowable expenditure

KNOWLEDGE AND UNDERSTANDING AND PERFORMANCE CRITERIA COVERAGE

knowledge and understanding

- Basic Law and Practice (Elements 18.1, 18.2, 18.3, 18.4)
- Adjustment of trading profits and losses for tax purposes (Element 18.2)
- Regulations relating to disallowed expenditure such as business entertaining, bad debt write-offs and provisions, private expenditure and capital expenditure (Element 18.2)

Performance criteria

- Classify expenditure on capital assets in accordance with the statutory distinction between capital and revenue expenditure
- Adjust trading profits and losses for tax purposes
- Make adjustments for private use by business owners

student notes

IS A TRADE BEING CARRIED ON?

It is important to know whether an individual is trading or not. If he is trading, the profits of that trade are subject to income tax. However, if a trade is not being carried on, any profit arising on the sale of an item may be exempt from tax or it may be subject to capital gains tax.

For example, a person who buys and sells stamps may be trading as a stamp dealer. Alternatively, stamp collecting may be a hobby of that person. In this case he is probably not trading.

For historical reasons, taxable trading profits were known as Schedule D Case I profits, but this terminology has now been abolished (except in relation to companies). In this Course Companion we will refer to these profits as taxable trading profits, but you may still meet the term Schedule D Case I profits elsewhere.

The badges of trade

It is necessary to look at a number of factors known as the BADGES OF TRADE when deciding if a trade is being carried on. The badges of trade each provide evidence as to whether a trade is being carried on. The overall weight of the evidence determines the final decision. The badges of trade are:

The subject matter

Some items are commonly held as an investment, for example, works of art and antiques. However, where the subject matter of a transaction is such that it would not normally be held as an investment (for example, 1,000,000 rolls of toilet paper), it is presumed that any profit on resale is a trading profit.

The frequency of transactions

A series of similar transactions indicates trading. Conversely, a single transaction is unlikely to be considered as a trade.

The length of ownership

The purchase and sale of items soon afterwards indicates trading. Conversely, if items are held for a long time before sale there is less likely to be a trade.

Supplementary work and marketing

If work is done to make an asset more marketable, or steps are taken to find purchasers, there is likely to be a trade. For example, when a group of accountants bought, blended and recasked a quantity of brandy they were held to be taxable on a trading profit when the brandy was later sold.

A profit motive

If an item is bought with the intention of selling it at a profit, a trade is likely to exist.

The way in which an asset was acquired

If goods are acquired unintentionally, for example, by gift or inheritance, their later sale is unlikely to constitute trading.

The taxpayer's intentions

Where objective criteria clearly indicate that a trade is being carried on, the taxpayer's intentions are irrelevant. If, however, a transaction (objectively) has a dual purpose, you should consider the taxpayer's intentions. An example of a transaction with a dual purpose is the acquisition of a site partly as premises from which to conduct another trade, and partly with a view to possible development and resale of the site.

How it works

Tim is employed by an NHS trust as a medical consultant. In his spare time he buys and sells stamps. Tim regards this as a hobby and his only intention in acquiring stamps is to add them to his collection.

Tim attends stamp auctions several times a year to acquire stamps. Stamps are usually bought in lots of several stamps. Most stamps he adds to his collection and does not intend to sell. Stamps that he does not want to add to his collection he sells soon after purchase, usually at a profit. Discuss whether or not Tim is trading with reference to the badges of trade.

We need to consider each of the badges of trade in turn:

The subject matter Many people collect stamps as a hobby whilst stamp dealers trade in the purchase and sale of stamps. In this case this badge of trade does not help to decide the question either way.

The frequency of transactions Tim regularly attends stamp auctions to buy stamps and some stamps are sold soon after they are acquired. This frequency of purchasing and selling stamps may suggest that Tim trades in stamps.

The length of ownership The fact that most stamps are added to Tim's collection and not sold suggests that Tim is not trading.

Supplementary work and marketing Tim does no supplementary work to the stamps and it is assumed that he does no marketing of the stamps he sells. As a result there is no indication that Tim is trading.

A profit motive Although Tim buys and immediately sells some stamps at a profit, his main intention is to find stamps for his collection. This indicates that he is not trading.

The manner in which stamps were acquired The fact that the stamps were bought rather than inherited or received by way of gift could indicate that Tim is trading.

It is the overall balance of the above evidence that determines whether a trade exists. On these facts it appears that Tim is not trading. Any profit on the sale of stamps could, however, be subject to capital gains tax.

CALCULATING TRADING PROFITS

If a taxpayer is trading it is important to be able to work out taxable trading profits.

The starting point is to take the net profit in the profit and loss account prepared by the trader. The trader arrives at this profit by taking income and deducting various trading expenses. However, the trader is unlikely to follow tax rules in arriving at this profit as, for example there are some costs for which HMRC will not allow a tax deduction even though the taxpayer quite legitimately deducts them for accounting purposes.

There are four types of adjustment that need to be made to accounting profit to arrive at taxable profit:

1) Add back expenditure that has been deducted in the accounts but which is not allowable for tax purposes. This is called DISALLOWABLE (OR NON DEDUCTIBLE) EXPENDITURE. We will look at various types of disallowable expenditure below.

2) Deduct income that has been included as income in the accounts but which is not taxable trading income. Examples are capital receipts (which may be subject to capital gains tax), income that is exempt from tax altogether or investment income (which is taxed separately to trading income).

3) Deduct items that have not been deducted in the accounts but which tax law allows as a deduction from taxable trading profits. An example is capital allowances. Depreciation cannot be deducted in computing taxable profits but capital allowances, calculated in the

way laid down by the taxes legislation, are deductible instead. We will look at the calculation of capital allowances later in this Course Companion.

4) Add income that must be taxed as trading income but which is not included in the accounts. An example, is where the trader takes goods from his business for his own use. For tax purposes you should treat the trader as though he sold those goods for their market value. It is unlikely that the trader will have recorded this sale at market value in his accounts so an adjustment needs to be made.

Activity 1

Pratish trades as a car mechanic. His most recent accounts show a profit of £38,000. In arriving at this figure he deducted entertaining expenses of £2,000 and depreciation of £4,000. These amounts are not allowable for tax purposes. Capital allowances of £3,500 are available for tax purposes. Calculate the taxable trading profit.

ALLOWABLE AND DISALLOWABLE EXPENDITURE

You may see allowable and disallowable expenditure referred to as deductible and non deductible expenditure. The two sets of terms are interchangeable.

The basic rule is that expenditure is allowable if it is revenue expenditure that is incurred WHOLLY AND EXCLUSIVELY FOR TRADE PURPOSES. If not, the expenditure is disallowable.

Revenue expenditure

The distinction between capital and revenue expenditure can be a difficult one to make. The cost of repairing an asset is revenue expenditure but the cost of improving it is capital expenditure. The cost of repairs needed to put a newly acquired asset into a usable state is disallowable capital expenditure. However, the cost of repairs needed to remedy normal wear and tear on a newly acquired asset is allowable.

How it works

The cost of repairs needed to make a newly acquired ship seaworthy before using it is disallowable capital expenditure. However, if the ship had been seaworthy on acquisition the cost of making normal repairs would be allowable. This point was decided in a very famous case called Law Shipping Co Ltd v CIR.

You are not expected to remember case names for exam purposes.

computing trading income

student notes

> **Activity 2**
>
> A taxpayer bought a cinema that was usable on acquisition. However, the cinema was fairly dilapidated and various repairs were immediately carried out. Is this repair expenditure allowable?

Wholly and exclusively for trade purposes

There is a case where a lady barrister incurred expenditure on black clothing to be worn in court. The expenditure was not deductible because it was not incurred exclusively for trade purposes. The expenditure had the dual purpose of allowing the barrister to be warmly and properly clad.

Strictly, expenditure incurred partly for private purposes and partly for business purposes has a dual purpose and is not deductible. However, HMRC normally allow taxpayers to apportion the expenditure between the part that is wholly for business purposes and therefore is deductible and the part that is wholly for private purposes and therefore not deductible.

How it works

A sole trader, who runs his business from home incurs £500 on heating and lighting bills. 30% of these bills relate to the business use of his house. £500 has been deducted in arriving at the accounts profit. How much should be added back in the calculation of taxable trading profits?

The amount relating to business use is allowable. 70% × £500 = £350 must be added back to the accounts profit.

> **Activity 3**
>
> Pratish deducts his total motor expenses of £600 in calculating his accounts profit. 60% of Pratish's motoring is for business purposes and 40% is for private purposes. What amount of the motoring expenses must be added back to the accounts profit in calculating taxable trading profit?

Charitable donations

Donations to charity are not incidentally incurred in any trade. This means that they are not incurred for trade purposes and are therefore normally disallowable. However, where a donation is made to a small local charity, HMRC will allow the donation on the grounds that, in these circumstances, the donation is made to benefit the trade (through developing local goodwill etc).

computing trading income

Activity 4

Nitin, a greengrocer deducts the following donations in computing his accounting profit:

£100 to Oxfam
£280 to a small local charity

What is the total amount of the donations that must be added back in computing taxable trading profits?

student notes

The treatment of various other items

The table below details various types of allowable and disallowable expenditure. Both unincorporated businesses (individuals and sole traders) and incorporated businesses (companies) may have trading income. The rules for computing taxable trading income for companies are slightly different to those for calculating taxable trading income for individuals/partnerships. Although this part of the Course Companion is mainly concerned with unincorporated businesses, for completeness, we mention where the rules for companies differ at relevant points in the table below.

Allowable expenditure	Disallowable expenditure	Comments
	Fines and penalties	HMRC usually allow parking fines incurred in parking an employer's car whilst on the employer's business. Fines relating to proprieters are, however, never allowed. Similarly, a company would not be able to deduct fines relating to directors
Costs of registering trade marks and patents		
Incidental costs of obtaining loan finance		This deduction does not apply to companies because they get a deduction for the cost of borrowing in a different way. We look at companies later in this text
	Depreciation or amortisation	In specific circumstances a company can deduct these amounts, but this is outside the scope of Unit 18

computing trading income

student notes

Allowable expenditure	Disallowable expenditure	Comments
	Any salary or interest paid to a sole trader or partner	
	The private proportion of any expenses incurred by a proprietor	The private proportion of an employee's expenses is, however, deductible
Specific bad debt provisions (against a particular trade debt, for example)	General bad debt provisions	Specific provisions against employee bad debts are not allowable
	Patent and copyright royalties	Patent and copyright royalties paid by a company for trade purposes are deductible
Staff entertaining	Non staff (eg customer) entertaining	
Gifts for employees Gifts to customers costing not more than £50 per donee per year if they carry a conspicuous advertisement for the business and are not food, drink, tobacco or vouchers exchangeable for goods Gifts to a small local charity if they benefit the trade	All other gifts including those made under the gift aid scheme	The gift aid scheme is a scheme under which tax relief is given on gifts. It is not assessable in unit 18
Subscriptions to a professional or trade association	Political donations	Exceptionally, if it can be shown that political expenditure is incurred for the survival of the trade, then it is allowable
Legal and professional charges relating directly to the trade.	Legal and professional charges relating to capital or non trading items	Deductible items include: ■ charges incurred defending the taxpayer's title to fixed assets ■ charges connected with an action for breach of contract ■ expenses of the renewal (not the original grant) of a lease for less than 50 years; ■ charges for trade debt collection ■ normal charges for preparing accounts and assisting with the self assessment of tax liabilities

computing trading income

Allowable expenditure	Disallowable expenditure	Comments
Accountancy expenses arising from an enquiry	Accountancy expenses relating to specialist consultancy work	Expenses are not allowed if an enquiry reveals discrepancies and additional liabilities, which arise as a result of negligent or fraudulent conduct. Where, however, the enquiry results in no addition to profits, or an adjustment to the profits for the year of enquiry only and that assessment does not arise as a result of negligent or fraudulent conduct, the additional accountancy expenses are allowable
Interest on loans taken out for trade purposes	Interest on overdue tax	These rules are for unincorporated businesses. Companies have different rules for the cost of borrowing. We look at these later in this Course Companion
Costs of seconding employees to charities or educational establishments		
Expenditure incurred in the seven years prior to the commencement of a trade		Provided expenditure is of a type that would have been allowed had the trade started. Treat as an expense on the first day of trading
Removal expenses (to new business premises)		Only if not an expansionary move
Travelling expenses on the trader's business	Travel from home to the trader's place of business	
Redundancy payments		If the trade ceases, the limit on allowability is 3 × the statutory amount (in addition to the statutory amount
Where car costing over £12,000 is leased: $$\frac{£12,000 + P}{2P} \times R$$ Where R = annual rental P = Cost of car		Learn this formula

student notes

computing trading income

student notes

How it works

An example of a disallowable provision is a general bad debt provision. Any increase in the general bad debt provision must be added back to accounts profit to arrive at taxable profits. Similarly, a decrease in the general bad debt provision must be deducted from the accounts profits. A specific bad debt provision is however allowable. Let's have a look at the following example of a bad debt account:

BAD AND DOUBTFUL DEBTS ACCOUNT

The account below results in a credit to profit and loss of £28. All the debts are trade debts. What adjustment should be made to net profit?

2006	£	£	2006	£	£
31 December			1 January		
Bad debts written off			Provisions b/d		
J Jones	67		General	150	
A Smith	119		Specific	381	
		186			531
Provisions c/d			31 December		
General	207		Bad debts recovered		90
Specific	200				
		407			
Profit and loss account		28			
		621			621
			2007		
			1 January		
			Provisions b/d		407

Solution

Every adjustment shown is either taxable or tax deductible except for the increase in general provision from £150 to £207. Thus £57 is added to the accounts profit to arrive at taxable profit.

Activity 5

A sole trader has accounts profit of £180,000 after charging legal expenses as follows:

	£
Expenses relating to purchase of new offices	7,000
Expenses relating to employee service contracts	2,000
Expenses relating to the renewal of a 25 year lease	1,500

What amount of the above expenses must be added back in computing taxable trading profits?

Activity 6

A sole trader charged the following expenses in computing his accounts profit:

	£
Fine for breach of Factories Act	1,000
Cost of specialist tax consultancy work	2,000
Redundancy payments	10,000
Salary for himself	15,000

The redundancy payments were made for trade purposes as a result of reorganisation of the business. The trade is continuing.

What is the total amount of the above expenses that must be added back in computing taxable trading profit?

Activity 7

Sana runs her business from home. Sana has deducted all of her heating and lighting bills of £800 in computing her accounts profit. 30% of the heating and lighting bills relate to be business. What amounts must be added back in computing taxable trading profits?

Activity 8

The entertainment account of Green and Co showed:

	£
Staff tennis outing for 30 employees	1,800
2,000 tee shirts with firm's logo given to race runners	4,500
Advertising and sponsorship of an athletic event	2,000
Entertaining customers	7,300
Staff Christmas party (30 employees)	2,400

What amount must be added back in arriving at taxable trading profits?

computing trading income

Activity 9

Here is the profit and loss account of S Pring, a trader.

	£	£
Gross operating profit		30,000
Rental income received		860
		30,860
Wages and salaries	7,000	
Rent and rates	2,000	
Depreciation	1,500	
Specific bad debts written off	150	
Provision against a fall in the price of raw materials	5,000	
Entertainment expenses	750	
Patent royalties	1,200	
Bank interest	300	
Legal expenses on acquisition of new factory	250	
		(18,150)
Net profit		12,710

a) Salaries include £500 paid to Mrs Pring who works full time in the business.

b) No staff were entertained.

c) The provision of £5,000 is a general provision charged because of an anticipated trade recession.

Compute the taxable trading profit.

computing trading income

CHAPTER OVERVIEW

The badges of trade indicate whether or not a trade is being carried on

The main disallowable items that you must add back in computing taxable trading profits are:

- entertaining (other than staff entertaining)
- depreciation (deduct capital allowances instead)
- any increase in a general provision (eg bad debts)
- fines
- legal fees relating to capital items
- wages or salary paid to a business owner
- the private proportion of any expenses

Deduct non trading income/capital profits included in the accounts from the accounts profit to arrive at taxable trading profit

KEY WORDS

Badges of trade indicate whether or not a trade is being carried on

Disallowable expenditure is expenditure that cannot be deducted in computing taxable trading profit

Expenditure wholly and exclusively for trade purposes is expenditure that is incidental to the trade and which does not have a dual purpose

computing trading income

HOW MUCH HAVE YOU LEARNED?

1. Which of the following expenses is deductible in computing taxable trading profits?

   Legal fees incurred on the acquisition of a factory to be used for trade purposes
   Legal fees incurred on pursuing trade debtors

2. A sole trader incurs the following expenditure on entertaining and gifts

	£
Staff entertaining	700
50 christmas food hampers given to customers	240
Entertaining customers	900
	1,840

   How much of the above expenditure is allowable for tax purposes?

3. Which of the following expenses would be disallowed, and which allowed, in the adjustment of profits computation for a trade?

   a) Parking fines incurred by the proprietor of the business.

   b) Parking fines incurred by an employee whilst on the employer's business.

   c) Legal costs incurred in relation to acquiring a lease of property for the first time.

   d) Legal costs incurred in relation to the renewal of a lease for 20 years.

   e) Gifts of calendars to customers, costing £4 each and displaying an advertisement for the trade concerned.

   f) Gifts of bottles of whisky to customers, costing £12 each.

4. Herbert, a self-employed carpenter, makes various items of garden furniture for sale. He takes a bird table from stock and sets it up in his own garden. The cost of making the bird table amounts to £80, and Herbert would normally expect to achieve a mark-up of 20% on such goods.

   What adjustment is to be made to the accounts for tax purposes, assuming that no entry has been made in the accounts in respect of the sale of the bird table?

5 Set out below is the bad debts account of Kingfisher, a sole trader:

BAD AND DOUBTFUL DEBTS

	£		£
Bad debts written off		1.4.06	
		Provisions b/fwd	
		General	2,500
Specific trade debtor	1,495	Specific (trade)	1,875
		Bad debt recovered	275
		Specific trade debtor	
31.3.07			
Provisions c/fwd			
General	1,800		
Specific (trade)	2,059	Profit & Loss account	704
	5,354		5,354

What amount must be added to or deducted from Kingfisher's accounts profit to arrive at taxable trading profit?

6 Trude works from home as a self employed hairdresser. She incurs £450 on heating and lighting bills and this amount is deducted in her accounts. 20% of this expenditure relates to the business use of her home. How much of the expenditure is disallowable for tax purposes?

chapter 3:
CAPITAL ALLOWANCES

chapter coverage 📖

You saw in the last chapter that depreciation is not an allowable expense when computing taxable trading profits. Instead capital allowances may be deducted. However, as capital allowances are not automatically available on all assets owned and depreciated by a trader we start this chapter by learning when expenditure on plant and machinery qualifies for capital allowances. We then see how to calculate those allowances. Finally, we learn that expenditure on industrial buildings may also qualify for allowances and we learn how to compute industrial buildings allowances.

The topics that we shall cover are:

- ✍ expenditure qualifying for capital allowances
- ✍ allowances on plant and machinery
- ✍ expenditure qualifying for industrial buildings allowances
- ✍ allowances on industrial buildings

KNOWLEDGE AND UNDERSTANDING AND PERFORMANCE CRITERIA COVERAGE

knowledge and understanding

- Availability and types of capital allowances: first year allowances; writing down allowances; balancing allowance and charge (relevant to industrial buildings and plant and machinery including computers, motor vehicles and short life assets) (Element 18.1)
- Treatment of capital allowances for unincorporated businesses including private use adjustments (Element 18.1)

Performance criteria

- Classify expenditure on capital assets in accordance with the statutory distinction between capital and revenue expenditure
- Ensure that entries and calculations relating to the computation of capital allowances for a company are correct
- Make adjustments for private use by business owners

capital allowances

student notes

EXPENDITURE QUALIFYING FOR CAPITAL ALLOWANCES

Expenditure on plant and machinery qualifies for capital allowances. For this purpose machinery is given its ordinary everyday meaning. Plant, however, is harder to define.

The main definition of PLANT is that plant is apparatus that performs a function in the business. Apparatus that is merely part of the setting is not plant. The following table gives examples of what is and what is not plant:

Items that are plant	Items that are not plant	Comments
Moveable office partitioning	Fixed office partitioning	Fixed partitioning is part of the setting in which a business is carried on. However, moveable partitioning performs a function in the trade and capital allowances are available on it.
Special display lighting in retail premises	General lighting used in retail premises	Special lighting performs a function in the trade so capital allowances are available on it
Decorative assets (eg lights, decor and murals) used in hotels etc where the function of those items is to create a certain ambience		

The following items also qualify as plant:

- Cars, vans, lorries etc
- Furniture
- Computers

ALLOWANCES ON PLANT AND MACHINERY

The general pool

Most expenditure on plant and machinery is put into a pool known as the general pool.

A WRITING DOWN ALLOWANCE (WDA) is given on the general pool **at the rate of 25% a year** (on a reducing balance basis). The WDA is calculated on the value of pooled plant, after adding the current period's additions and taking out the current period's disposals.

How it works

On 1 April 2006 Panikah has a balance on his general pool of plant and machinery of £28,000. In the year to 31 March 2007 he bought a car for £10,000. He also sold a machine for £2,000. Calculate the capital allowances available for the year.

The general pool must be constructed as follows:

	General pool £	Allowances
B/f	28,000	
Addition	10,000	
Less disposal	(2,000)	
	36,000	
WDA @ 25%	(9,000)	9,000
C/f	27,000	

Activity 1

Nathan has a balance of £10,000 brought forward on 1 April 2006 on his general pool of plant and machinery. In the year to 31 March 2007 he bought an asset for £8,000 and disposed of an asset for £6,000.

Calculate the capital allowances available on the general pool.

Disposals

As you have seen above, the most common disposal value at which assets are entered in a capital allowances computation is the sale proceeds. However, there is an overriding rule that the capital allowances disposal value cannot exceed the original purchase price of the asset. Try applying this rule in the following activity.

Activity 2

On 1 April 2006, a sole trader had a balance on his general pool of £47,000. Plant which had cost £7,000 was sold for £14,000 on 1 August. Calculate the capital allowances available on this general pool for the year to 31 March 2007.

capital allowances

student notes

Periods that are not 12 months long

WDAs are 25% × months/12:

a) For unincorporated businesses where the PERIOD OF ACCOUNT is longer or shorter than 12 months. The period of account is the period for which the business prepares its accounts

b) For companies where the accounting period is shorter than 12 months (a company's accounting period for tax purposes is never longer than 12 months): Remember that we will be studying companies in detail later in this Course Companion. We will see what is meant by an accounting period then.

How it works

Melissa had a tax written down value brought forward on her general pool of plant and machinery on 1 April 2006 of £40,000.

She prepared accounts for the nine months to 31 December 2006. Compute Melissa's capital allowances for this period, assuming there were no disposals or additions.

	£
B/f	40,000
WDA × 25% × 9/12	(7,500)
	32,500

Melissa's capital allowances for the period are £7,500.

Activity 3

Gotaum had a tax written down value brought forward on his general pool of plant and machinery on 1 January 2007 of £20,000. He prepared accounts for the three months to 31 March 2007. During this period he bought a car for £4,000.

Compute Gotaum's capital allowances, assuming there were no disposals in the period.

First year allowances

We saw above how to compute writing down allowances on the general pool of plant and machinery. We will now look at another type of allowance: the FIRST YEAR ALLOWANCE (FYA).

capital allowances

FYAs of between 100% and 40% may be available in the period that expenditure is incurred. The rate of FYA depends on the size of the business and the type of expenditure as follows:

Type of expenditure	Small sized businesses	Medium sized businesses
Computer equipment purchased in the four year period to 31 March 2004.	100% FYA	40% FYA
Energy saving and water efficient plant*	100% FYA	100% FYA
Cars with CO_2 emissions not exceeding 120 g/km (low emission cars)*	100% FYA	100% FYA
Other expenditure on plant and machinery (except cars) before or after the one year periods below.	40% FYA	40% FYA
Other expenditure on plant and machinery in the one year period commencing 1 April 2004 (companies) or 6 April 2004 (unincorporated businesses) and in one year period commencing 1 April 2006 (companies) or 6 April 2006 (unincorporated businesses).	50% FYA	40% FYA

* These 100% FYA are also available to large businesses.

In your examination you will be told if a business is small or medium sized. You will also be given the rates of FYA in the tax tables in your exam.

Calculation of FYAs

First year allowances are given in the place of writing down allowances. For subsequent years a WDA is given on the balance of expenditure at the normal rate. You should therefore have a separate column for FYA but transfer the balance of the expenditure to the general pool at the end of the first period.

How it works

Joe, a sole trader, had a balance on his general pool of plant and machinery of £8,000 on 1 April 2006. In October 2006 he bought new plant for £6,000.

Calculate the total capital allowances claimable for the year to 31 March 2007. Joe's business is a medium sized business for capital allowance purposes.

student notes

capital allowances

student notes

Solution

	FYA @ 40% £	General pool £	Allowances £
B/f		8,000	
WDA @ 25%		(2,000)	2,000
		6,000	
Additions			
Qualifying for FYA	6,000		
FYA @ 40%	(2,400)		2,400
Transfer balance to pool		3,600	
C/f/allowances		9,600	4,400

As Joe's business is medium sized for capital allowance purposes, FYA are available at 40%.

Activity 4

Amarjat, a sole trader, had a balance on his general pool of £60,000 on 1 June 2005. In the year to 31 May 2006 the following occurred:

Date	Cost £
31.12.05 (Low emission car)	2,000
1.5.06 (Machine)	5,000

Amarjat's business is a small business for FYA purposes.

Show the capital allowances available in the year to 31 May 2006.

Periods that are not 12 months long

FYAs always given in full in the period that expenditure is incurred. It is irrelevant whether the period concerned is twelve months or not. FYAs are not scaled up or down by reference to the length of the period.

How it works

On 1 July 2006 Jed, a sole trader, had a balance of £20,000 on his general pool of plant and machinery. He bought new plant for £10,000 on 15 October 2006.

Jed's business is a small business for capital allowance purposes.

Jed prepared accounts for the six months to 31 December 2006. What capital allowances are available for this period?

capital allowances

Solution

	FYA @ 50% £	General pool £	Allowances £
B/f		20,000	
WDA @ 25% × 6/12		(2,500)	2,500
		17,500	
Addition	10,000		
FYA @ 50%	(5,000)		5,000
Transfer balance to pool		5,000	
C/f/allowances		22,500	7,500

Writing down allowances are pro-rated in a short period but first year allowances are not.

Activity 5

Debbie, a hairdresser, had a general pool brought forward on 1 April 2006 of £36,000. The only addition in the nine month period to 31 December 2006 were hairdryers costing £20,000.

Debbie's business is a small business for capital allowance purposes.

What are the maximum capital allowances that Debbie will be entitled to claim in the nine month period to 31 December 2006?

The cessation of a business

When a business stops trading no FYAs or WDAs are given in the final period of account (unincorporated businesses) or accounting period (companies – see later in this Course Companion).

Additions in the final period are added to the pool in the normal way. Similarly, any disposal proceeds (limited to cost) of assets sold in the final period are deducted from the balance of qualifying expenditure. If assets are not sold they are deemed to be disposed of on the final day of trading for their market value. This means that you must deduct the market value from the pool.

If, after the above adjustments, a balance of qualifying expenditure remains in the pool then a balancing allowance equal to this amount is given. The balancing allowance is deducted from taxable trading profits. If on the other hand the balance on the pool has become negative, a balancing charge equal to the negative amount is given. The balancing charge increases taxable trading profits.

student notes

capital allowances

student notes

How it works

The balance of expenditure on Raj's general pool of plant and machinery was £40,000 on 30 June 2006. Raj stopped trading on 31 December 2006. All assets in the general pool were sold on 31 December 2006 for £25,000. Calculate the balancing allowance or balancing charge arising in the final period. All assets sold were sold for less than cost.

Solution

	£
B/F	40,000
Less disposal proceeds	(25,000)
	15,000
Balancing allowance	(15,000)

The balancing allowance is deducted in arriving at taxable trading profits. Note that there are no FYAs or WDAs in the final period of trading.

Assets which are not pooled

We have seen above how to compute capital allowances on the general pool of plant and machinery. However, some special items are not put into the general pool. A separate record of allowances must be kept for each such asset. Assets which are not pooled are:

a) cars costing more than £12,000.

b) assets not wholly used for business purposes (such as cars with private use by the proprietor of an unincorporated business);

c) short-life assets for which an election has been made (see below).

We will look at each of these assets in turn.

Cars costing more than £12,000

These cars are not put into the general pool because the maximum WDA is £3,000 a year. The limit is £3,000 × months/12:

a) For short or long periods of account of unincorporated businesses
b) For short accounting periods of companies

FYAs are not available on cars (except for certain low emission cars – see above). You will be told in your exam if a car is a low emission car. Note that a van is *not* a car. A van is dealt with in the same way as any other type of plant and machinery.

capital allowances

How it works

Jack started trading on 1 September 2004, making up accounts to 31 December 2004 and each 31 December thereafter. On 1 November 2004 he bought a car for £14,000. What are the capital allowances for the first three periods of account?

	Expensive car £	Allowances £
4 m/e 31 December 2004		
Addition	14,000	
WDA (£3,000 × 4/12)	(1,000)	(1,000)
	13,000	
y/e 31 December 2005		
WDA (max £3,000)	(3,000)	3,000
	10,000	
y/e 31 December 2006		
WDA @ 25%	(2,500)	2,500
	7,500	

Activity 6

Hermione prepared accounts for the ten months to 31 March 2005 and annually thereafter. She bought a car for use in her business on 12 January 2005 for £15,000. Show the capital allowances available on the car for the three periods of account to 31 March 2007.

Assets used partly for private purposes

An asset (for example, a car) that is used partly for private purposes by a sole trader or a partner is never put in the general pool. You should put the asset in a pool of its own and then make all calculations on full cost but claim only the business use proportion of the allowances.

An asset with some private use by an employee (not a proprietor), however, suffers no restriction. The employee may be taxed on a benefit, so the business is entitled to full capital allowances on such assets. Similarly, there is never any private use restriction in a company's capital allowance computation (we look at companies later in this Course Companion).

student notes

capital allowances

student notes

How it works

On 1 August 2004 a sole trader, who has been in business for many years making up accounts to 31 December, buys a car for £7,000. The private use proportion is 10%. What are the capital allowances for the three years to 31 December 2006?

Solution

	Private used car £		Allowances 90% £
Y/e 31 December 2004			
Purchase price	7,000		
WDA 25% of £7,000 = £1,750	(1,750) × 90%		1,575
	5,250		
Y/e 31 December 2005			
WDA @ 25%	(1,312) × 90%		1,181
	3,938		
Y/e 31 December 2006			
WDA @ 25%	(984) × 90%		886
C/f	2,954		

Note that full allowances are deducted in the private use asset column but the allowances (in the allowances column) to be deducted in computing taxable trading profits are restricted to the business proportion of the allowances.

Activity 7

Pippa, a sole trader, uses a computer in her business. However, the computer is kept at home and she also uses the computer 20% of the time for private purposes. The computer was bought on 29 May 2006 for £10,000. Pippa prepares annual accounts to 30 June each year. Show the capital allowances available on the computer in the year to 30 June 2006. Pippa's business is a small business for FYA purposes.

Short life assets

A SHORT LIFE ASSET is an asset that a trader expects to dispose of within four years of the end of the period of acquisition.

A trader can make a DEPOOLING ELECTION to be keep such an asset in its own pool. For an unincorporated business, the time limit for electing is the 31 January which is 22 months after the end of the tax year in which the period of account of the expenditure ends. (For a company, it is two years after the end of the accounting period of the expenditure.)

If the asset is disposed of within four years of the end of the period of account or accounting period in which it was bought a balancing charge or allowance is made on its disposal. However, if the asset is not disposed of within this period it is transferred to the general pool at the end of that period.

Short life asset treatment cannot be claimed for:

- Motor cars
- Plant used partly for private purposes

These items are not put in the general pool in any case.

How it works

Nisar bought a computer on 1 March 2003 for £22,000 and elected for de-pooling. His accounting year end is 30 June. Calculate the capital allowances due if:

a) The asset is scrapped for £650 in August 2006.
b) The asset is scrapped for £1,200 in August 2007.

Nisar's business is a medium sized enterprise for FYA purposes.

Solution

a)

	FYA £	De-pooled Asset £
Year ended 30 June 2003		
Cost – 1 March 2003	22,000	
FYA @ 40%	(8,800)	
		13,200
Year ended 30 June 2004		
WDA 25%		(3,300)
		9,900
Year ended 30 June 2005		
WDA 25%		(2,475)
		7,425
Year ended 30 June 2006		
WDA @ 25%		(1,856)
		5,569
Year ended 30 June 2007		
Disposal proceeds		(650)
Balancing allowance		4,919

b) If the asset is still in use at 30 June 2007, a WDA of 25% × £5,569 = £1,392 would be claimable in year ended 30 June 2007.

student notes

The unrelieved expenditure of £5,569 – £1,392 = £4,177 would be added to the general pool at the beginning of year ended 30 June 2008. The disposal proceeds of £1,200 would be deducted from the general pool in the year ended 30 June 2008 capital allowance computation.

EXPENDITURE QUALIFYING FOR INDUSTRIAL BUILDINGS ALLOWANCES

The second type of capital allowance that you may meet in Unit 18 is an INDUSTRIAL BUILDINGS ALLOWANCE (IBA).

Qualifying buildings

The main types of building that qualify for IBAs are:

- Factories
- Staff welfare buildings (such as workplace nurseries and canteens but not directors' restaurants) if the premises in which the trade is carried on is an industrial building

Dwelling houses, shops, showrooms and offices do not normally qualify for IBAs.

Eligible expenditure

IBAs are computed on the amount of eligible cost of an industrial building. The eligible cost is:

- The original cost of a building if built by the trader, or
- The purchase price if the building was acquired from a person trading as a builder.

If the building was acquired other than from a person trading as a builder, the eligible cost is the lower of the purchase price and the original cost incurred by the person incurring the construction expenditure.

Where an industrial building includes some non industrial parts (e.g. offices) the whole cost qualifies for IBAs, provided that the cost of the non-qualifying part is not more than 25% of the total expenditure. If the non-qualifying part of the building does cost more than 25% of the total, that part of the cost must be excluded from the IBA computation.

The cost of land does not qualify for IBAs but expenditure incurred in preparing land for building does qualify.

Professional fees, for example architects' fees, incurred in connection with the construction of an industrial building also qualify for IBAs.

How it works

Owen buys a new factory direct from the builder, at a cost of £250,000. The purchase price is allocated:

	£	£
Land		50,000
Preparation of land		5,000
Construction:		
Factory	150,000	
Administrative offices	30,000	
Staff canteen	15,000	
		195,000
		250,000

What is the qualifying expenditure for industrial buildings allowance purposes?

Solution

		£
Preparation of land		5,000
Construction costs: factory	150,000	
Canteen	15,000	
Offices	30,000	
		195,000
		200,000

The cost of non-qualifying parts (administrative offices) is less than 25% of total construction costs and is therefore treated as qualifying. The cost of land does not qualify.

Activity 8

Bal purchased an industrial building for £1,250,000. This cost was made up of:

	£
Factory	1,000,000
Land	250,000
	1,250,000

The cost attributable to offices within the factory was £150,000.

What is the expenditure qualifying for industrial buildings allowances?

student notes

ALLOWANCES ON INDUSTRIAL BUILDINGS

An industrial buildings allowance (IBA) is given for the period in which an industrial building is first brought into use provided it is in industrial use on the last day of the period concerned. The date that the building is brought into use is irrelevant. What matters is that the building is in industrial use on the last day of the period concerned.

The IBA is 4% of the eligible expenditure incurred by the taxpayer.

The allowance is calculated on a straight line basis (in contrast to WDAs on plant and machinery which are calculated on the reducing balance), starting when the building is brought into use.

Buildings always have a separate computation for each building. They are never pooled.

How it works

Carey, who makes accounts up to 30 April each year, buys a new industrial building on 31 January 2006. It is taken into industrial use on 1 June 2006 and continues to be so used throughout 2007.

Assuming the qualifying cost of the building is £180,000, show the IBAs available for the year to 30 April 2006 and the year to 30 April 2007.

Solution

No IBAs are available in the year to 30 April 2006 as the building was not in industrial use on that date. In the year to 30 April 2007 IBAs of 4% × £180,000 = £7,200 are available.

Activity 9

Smith bought a factory for £1,200,000 and started to use it for industrial purposes on 1 December 2006. What are the IBAs for the year to 31 December 2006?

The IBA is 4% × months/12 if the period concerned is not 12 months long. Note that IBAs are apportioned only when the period concerned is not 12 months long. If the period is 12 months long, IBAs are not apportioned. Students often try to apportion IBAs according to the date within the period that a building is brought into use. This is incorrect.

Activity 10

Jones bought a factory for £1,000,000 and started to use it for industrial purposes on 1 January 2007. What IBAs are available in the 9 month period to 31 March 2007?

Disposals of industrial buildings

The 'tax life' of an industrial building is 25 years (hence the 4% straight line IBA) after it is first used. If a building is disposed of after the end of its 25 year tax life then, there are no IBA implications for either the trader disposing of the building or the trader buying it.

If a building is sold within its 25 year life, there will be IBA implications for both the seller and the buyer. The seller will have a balancing charge or balancing allowance calculated as follows:

	£
Cost	X
Less allowances previously given	(X)
Residue before sale	X
Less proceeds (limited to cost)	(X)
Balancing (charge)/allowance	(X)

The buyer obtains annual straight line IBAs for the remainder of the building's 25 year tax life. This life is calculated to the nearest month. The buyer's allowances are given on the lower of his purchase price and the original cost of the building.

How it works

Abdul, a businessman who prepares accounts to 31 October, bought an industrial building for £300,000 on 1 August 1999. He brought it into use as a factory immediately. On 31 July 2006 he sold it for £320,000 to Nigel, whose accounting date is 31 December and who brought the building into industrial use immediately.

Show the IBAs available to both Abdul and Nigel.

student notes

Solution

Abdul

	£
Cost 1 August 1999	300,000
Year ended 31 October 1999 to 31 October 2005	
WDA 7 × 4% × £300,000	(84,000)
Residue before sale	216,000
Year ended 31 October 2006	
Proceeds (limited to cost)	(300,000)
Balancing charge	(84,000)

Note. Where proceeds exceed original cost the balancing charge is always equal to the allowances previously given.

Nigel

Lower of:

Purchase price, £320,000
Original cost, £300,000

ie £300,000

The tax life of the building ends on 1 August 1999 + 25 years = 31 July 2024

The date of Nigel's purchase was 31 July 2006. The unexpired life was therefore 18 years.

Nigel's allowances are, therefore, $\frac{300,000}{18}$ = £16,667 per annum

Activity 11

Mr Khan bought a factory for £400,000 on 31 December 2004 and brought it into immediate industrial use. Mr Khan prepares accounts to 31 March each year. On 30 June 2006 Mr Khan sold the building to Mr Jones for £500,000. Mr Jones prepares accounts to 30 June each year. Show the IBAs available to both Mr Khan and Mr Jones.

Where a building is sold for less than original cost the balancing allowance/charge is equal to the difference between the net cost of the building and the allowances previously given. The net cost of the building is the sale proceeds – original cost.

You will see this in the following activity.

Activity 12

On 1 June 2004 Raj bought an industrial building for £500,000 and brought it into immediate industrial use. Raj prepares accounts to 30 September each year. On 1 December 2005 he sold the building for £400,000. Show the IBAs available to Raj.

Show the IBAs available to the purchaser of the building, assuming the purchaser continues to use the building for industrial purposes.

capital allowances

CHAPTER OVERVIEW

- Assets that perform a function in the trade are generally plant. Assets that are part of the setting are not plant

- Most expenditure on plant and machinery goes into the general pool and qualifies for a 25% writing down allowance (WDA) on the reducing balance every 12 months

- WDAs are time apportioned in short or long periods

- First year allowances (FYAs) may be available on certain expenditure

- FYAs are never reduced or increased for short or long periods of account

- Private use assets by sole traders and partners have restricted capital allowances

- An election can be made to de-pool short life assets. If a de-pooled asset is not sold within four years of the end of the period of acquisition, the value of the short life asset at the end of that period is transferred to the general pool

- Factories and certain staff welfare buildings may qualify for IBAs

- IBAs are 4% a year on straight line basis. Pro rate IBAs in short or long periods

- IBAs are only available if a building is in industrial use at the end of the period concerned

- The tax life of an industrial building is 25 years, after that there are no allowances available

- The purchaser of a second hand building is entitled to IBAs over the remainder of the building's life. The allowances are given on the lower of the purchase price of the building and the original cost.

KEY WORDS

Plant is apparatus that performs a function in the business. Apparatus that is merely part of the setting is not plant

A **first year allowance** may be available in a period in which expenditure is incurred on plant and machinery

An **industrial buildings allowance** is a capital allowance given on industrial buildings

A **short life asset** is an asset that a trader expects to dispose of within four years of the end of the period of acquisition

A **de-pooling election** is an election not to put an asset into the general pool of plant and machinery

A **writing down allowance** is a capital allowance of 25% per annum given on the general pool of plant and machinery

The **period of account** is the period for which a business prepares its accounts

HOW MUCH HAVE YOU LEARNED?

1. An item of plant is acquired for £2,000 and sold five years later for £3,200. What is deducted from the pool as proceeds when the disposal is made?

2. Nitin who prepares accounts to 30 June year each year, had a balance on his general pool of £22,500 on 1 July 2005. In the year to 30 June 2006 he sold one asset and bought one asset as follows:

Disposal proceeds on sale on 1.5.06 (less than cost)	£7,800
Addition (eligible for FYA of 40%)	£2,300

   What is the maximum of capital allowances available for year ended 30 June 2006?

3. An individual starts to trade on 1 July 2006, making up accounts to 31 December, and buys a car costing £8,000 on 15 July 2006. He buys plant costing £5,000 on 1 September 2006. FYAs are available at 40% on this expenditure.

   What capital allowances are available in the first period of account to 31 December 2006?

4. Abdul ceased trading on 31 December 2006 drawing up his final accounts for the year to 31 December 2006.

   The following facts are relevant:

Pool balance at 1.1.06	£12,500
Addition – 31.5.06	£20,000
Disposal proceeds (in total – proceeds not exceeding cost on any item) – 31.12.06	£18,300

   What balancing charge or allowance arises for the year to 31 December 2006?

5. Raj, a sole trader who makes up accounts to 30 April each year, buys a Volvo estate car for £30,000 on 31 March 2006. 60% of his usage of the car is for business purposes.

   What capital allowance is available to Raj in respect of the car for y/e 30 April 2006?

6. Jerome starts to trade on 1 May 2006 and prepares accounts annually to 30 June. He purchases a new industrial building for £100,000 on 1 June 2006 bringing it into use immediately. What IBAs are available in the year to 30 June 2006?

7. What allowance is available for year ended 31 December 2006 in the following circumstances:

   a) to Abel – who purchased a new industrial building on 3 November 2006 from the builder: qualifying cost £320,000. Abel brought the building into immediate industrial use.

   b) to Beckwith – who purchased a second-hand industrial building on 1 October 2006, which was first used by the original owner on 1 October 1993: original cost of building £128,000; cost to Beckwith £225,000.

chapter 4:
TAXING UNINCORPORATED BUSINESSES

chapter coverage

Individuals must pay tax for tax years. In this chapter we see what is meant by a tax year and we learn how to arrive at the trading profits to be taxed in each tax year.

The topics that we shall cover are:

- continuing businesses
- the start of trading
- the cessation of trading
- overlap profits

KNOWLEDGE AND UNDERSTANDING AND PERFORMANCE CRITERIA COVERAGE

knowledge and understanding

- Basis of assessment for unincorporated businesses (Element 18.2)

Performance criteria

- Apply the basis of assessment for unincorporated businesses in opening and closing years

CONTINUING BUSINESSES

Traders can produce their business accounts to any date in the year they choose. However, income tax is charged for tax years. This means that a mechanism is needed to link the taxable profits arising from a particular set of accounts to a tax year. This mechanism is known as the basis of assessment, and the period whose profits are assessed in a tax year is called the BASIS PERIOD.

The TAX YEAR, FISCAL YEAR or YEAR OF ASSESSMENT runs from 6 April in one year to 5 April in the next year. For example, 2006/07 runs from 6 April 2006 to 5 April 2007.

The basis of assessment for a continuing business is the period of account ending in a tax year. The profits resulting from those accounts are taxed in that tax year. This is known as the CURRENT YEAR BASIS OF ASSESSMENT.

How it works

If a trader prepares accounts to 30 April each year, the profits of the year to 30 April 2006 will be taxed in 2006/07. This is because the year to 30 April 2006 ends in 2006/07.

Activity 1

Talet, a dressmaker, prepares accounts to 30 September each year. What is her basis period for 2006/07?

THE START OF TRADING

Special rules are needed to find the basis period in the first three years of a new business.

The first tax year

The tax year in which a trade starts is the first year in which profits will be taxed.

How it works

If a trade starts on 15 May 2006 the first tax year in which profits are taxed is 2006/07.

This rule ensures that profits are taxed right from the start of a business.

The basis period for the first tax year runs from the date the trade starts to the next 5 April (or to the date of cessation if the trade does not continue until the end of the tax year). If accounts are not prepared to the end of the first tax year you will need to time apportion taxable profits arising from one or more periods of account. For exam purposes all time apportionment should be made on a monthly basis.

How it works

Sasha starts a trade on 1 December 2006. She prepares her first accounts for the ten months to 30 September 2007. The taxable profits arising as a result of these accounts are £60,000. What are Sasha's taxable profits for 2006/07?

2006/07 is the tax year in which Sasha's trade starts, so the first year in which profits are taxed is 2006/07. The basis period for 2006/07 runs from 1 December 2006 to 5 April 2007. Taxable profits of £60,000 × 4/10 = £24,000 arise in this period and will be taxed in 2006/07.

The second tax year

Finding the basis period or the second tax year is tricky because there are three possibilities:

a) If the accounting date falling in the second tax year is less than 12 months after the start of trading, the basis period is the first 12 months of trading.

b) If the accounting date falling in the second tax year is at least 12 months after the start of trading, the basis period is the 12 months to that accounting date.

c) If there is no accounting date falling in the second tax year, because the first period of account is a very long one which does not end until a date in the third tax year, the basis period for the second tax year is the year itself (from 6 April to 5 April).

student notes

Some students find the following flowchart helpful in determining the basis period for the second year:

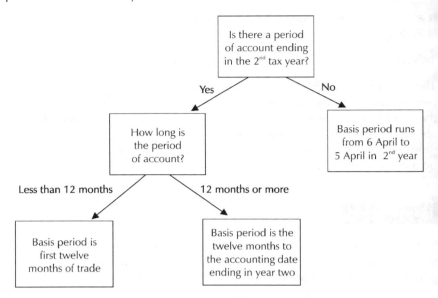

You can now use the flowchart to see if it helps you with the following examples:

How it works (accounting date in second year less than 12 months after the start of trade)

Janet starts trading on 1 July 2006. She prepares accounts for the ten months to 30 April 2007 and annually thereafter.

Janet's basis periods for the first two tax years of her business are:

Year	Basis period	
2006/07	1.7.06 – 5.4.07	(commencement to next 5 April)
2007/08	Year to 30.06.07	(first 12 months)

How it works (accounting date in second year at least 12 months after the start of trade)

John starts trading on 1 July 2006. He prepares accounts for the fifteen months to 30 September 2007.

John's basis periods for the first two tax years are:

Year	Basis period	
2006/07	1.7.06 – 5.4.07	(commencement to following 5 April)
2007/08	Year to 30.9.07	(12 months ended in second tax year)

How it works (no accounting date in second tax year)

Abduls starts trading on 1 January 2006 and prepares accounts for the sixteen months to 30 April 2007.

Abdul's basis periods for the first two years are:

Year	Basis period	
2005/06	1.1.06 – 5.4.06	Commencement to 5 April
2006/07	6.4.06 – 5.4.07	Tax year

Note that it was important to take care here and realise that the first tax year was 2005/06. This is because 1 January 2006 falls in 2005/06.

The third tax year

Finding the basis period in the third tax year is easier than the second year. The basis period in the third year is always the 12 months to the end of the period of account ending in that year.

How it works

On 1 January 2006, Shamimma started trading. She prepares accounts to 31 December each year. What are the basis periods for the first three years of trading?

2005/06	1.1.06 – 5.4.06	Commencement to 5 April
2006/07	year to 31 December 2006	accounting date in second year
2007/08	year to 31 December 2007	12 month period ending in year

Now you can try an activity in which you must time apportion profits to the first three tax years. Remember that time apportionment for exam purposes is done on a monthly basis.

Activity 2

Kumar starts to trade on 1 June 2005, with the following results.

Period	Profit
	£
1.6.05 – 31.5.06	12,000
1.6.06 – 31.5.07	21,000

Show the profits to be taxed in each year of assessment from 2005/06 to 2007/08.

student notes

student notes

THE CESSATION OF TRADING

You have seen the special basis period rules that apply in the first three years of a business. There are also special rules that apply in the last tax year that a business is carried on.

The basis period for the final year normally runs from the end of the basis period for the previous year to the date of cessation.

Exceptionally, if a trade starts and ceases in the same tax year, the basis period for that year is the whole lifespan of the trade. If the final year is the second year, the basis period runs from 6 April at the start of the second year to the date of cessation.

Activity 3

Malcolm has been trading for many years. His results for the last four periods of account before he ceased trading on 31 January 2008 are:

y/e 30.6.05	£12,000
y/e 30.6.06	£8,000
y/e 30.6.07	£6,000
p/e 31.01.08	£5,000

Show the taxable profits for the years 2005/06 to 2007/08 inclusive before considering any overlap relief (see below).

OVERLAP PROFITS

You may have noticed above that the basis periods in the first three tax years of a new business may overlap with each other. This results in profits in the early years of a trade being taxed more than once.

Profits which have been taxed more than once are called OVERLAP PROFITS.

Some profits may be taxed twice because the basis period for the second tax year includes some or all of the period of trading in the first tax year or because the basis period for the third tax year overlaps with that for the second tax year.

How it works

Canning started a trade on 1 January 2005 and has the following results:

	£
1.1.05 – 30.6.05	28,500
1.7.05 – 30.6.06	48,000
1.7.06 – 30.6.07	70,000

Show the taxable profits for the first four tax years and the overlap profits that arise.

Solution

The taxable profits are as follows.

Year	Basis period	Working	Taxable profits £
2004/05	1.1.05 – 5.4.05	£28,500 × 3/6	14,250
2005/06	1.1.05 – 31.12.05	£28,500 + £48,000 × 6/12	52,500
2006/07	1.7.05 – 30.6.06		48,000
2007/08	1.7.06 – 30.6.07		70,000

Overlap profits are:

	£
1.1.05 – 5.4.05	14,250
1.7.05 – 31.12.05	24,000
	38,250

Activity 4

Harriet starts a trade on 1 March 2005, and has the following results.

Period	Profit £
1.3.05 – 30.6.06	32,000
1.7.06 – 30.6.07	36,800

Show the taxable profits for the first four tax years and any overlap profits that arise.

taxing unincorporated businesses

student notes

When the trade ceases overlap profits are deducted from the final year's taxable profits. This means that over the life of a business total taxable profits should equal actual profits.

Activity 5

Rex trades from 1 May 2003 to 31 January 2008, with the following results.

Period	Profit £
1.5.03 – 30.4.04	15,000
1.5.04 – 30.4.05	9,000
1.5.05 – 30.4.06	10,500
1.5.06 – 30.4.07	16,000
1.5.07 – 31.1.08	950
	51,450

Show the profits to be taxed in each year from 2003/04 to 2007/08, and the total taxable profits.

CHAPTER OVERVIEW

- The profits of a period of account ending in a tax year are normally taxed in that year

- In the first tax year, the basis period is the date the business starts to the following 5 April

- There are three possibilities in the second tax year:

    - If a period of account of 12 months or more ends in the second tax year, the basis period for the second tax year is the 12 months to the end of that period of account

    - If a period of account of less than 12 months ends in the second tax year, the basis period for the second tax year is the first 12 months from the start of trading

    - If no period of account ends in the second year, the basis period for that year is 6 April to 5 April in the year

- The basis period for the third tax year is the 12 months to the end of the period of account ending in that year

- The basis period in the final year of a business runs from the end of the previous basis period to the date that the trade stops

- When a trade ceases overlap profits are deducted from the final year's taxable profits

> **KEY WORDS**
>
> **Overlap profits** are the profits that are taxed more than once when a business starts
>
> The **tax year**, **fiscal year** or **year of assessment** is the year from 6 April in one year to 5 April in the next year
>
> The **current year basis of assessment** taxes the profits of the period of account ending in a tax year in the that year

HOW MUCH HAVE YOU LEARNED?

1. Oliver starts to trade on 1 May 2006. He makes his first set of accounts up to 31 December 2006 and annually thereafter.

   Set out the basis periods for the first three tax years and the overlap period of profits.

2. Explain how overlap profits may be relieved.

3. Barlow stops trading on 31 December 2006 having been in business since January 2000. Previously he has always made accounts up to 31 May. Overlap profits on commencement were £10,000.

   Results for the last few years (as adjusted for tax) are:

	Profits £
Period to 31.12.06	15,000
Year ended 31.5.06	25,000
Year ended 31.5.05	32,000
Year ended 31.5.04	18,000

   Compute the taxable profits for the final three years of trading.

4. Amarjat started trading on 1 February 2006. He prepared his first accounts to 30 June 2007. Taxable profits for this 17 month period were £34,000. Show the taxable profits for 2005/06, 2006/07 and 2007/08. State what overlap profits arise.

5. Susi started to trade on 1 December 2005. Her first accounts were prepared to 30 June 2006. Taxable profits for the first two periods of account were:

   Period to 30 June 2006 £70,000
   Year to 30 June 2007 £60,000

   Compute the taxable profits for the first three tax years and the overlap profits arising.

chapter 5:
RELIEVING TRADING LOSSES

chapter coverage

So far in this Course Companion we have seen how to compute taxable trading profits. Sometimes the result of this computation is a loss rather than a profit. In this chapter we will cover the various methods by which a taxpayer may obtain relief for such a loss.

The topic that we shall cover is:

- losses in a continuing business

KNOWLEDGE AND UNDERSTANDING AND PERFORMANCE CRITERIA COVERAGE

knowledge and understanding

- Issues of tax liability (Elements 18.1 to 18.4)
- Adjustment of trading profits and losses for tax purposes (Element 18.2)
- Basis of assessment for unincorporated businesses (Element 18.2)

Performance criteria

- Adjust trading profits and losses for tax purposes
- Apply the basis of assessment for unincorporated businesses in opening and closing years

LOSSES IN A CONTINUING BUSINESS

As you know, the starting point for computing a business' trading results is to take the profit or loss in the accounts and adjust it for tax purposes. If this adjusted figure is negative then there is a trading loss rather than a taxable profit. This has two implications:

a) The loss is a loss of the tax year for which the period of account concerned formed the basis period. However, the amount taxable in that tax year is Nil. It is not the negative amount.

b) The amount of the trading loss is equal to the tax adjusted negative figure. The taxpayer has a choice as to how this is relieved as explained below.

How it works

If a trader makes a loss of £5,000 in the year to 31 December 2006, the 2006/07 taxable profits based on that period will be £nil. There will be a trading loss in 2006/07 of £5,000. The taxpayer can choose to relieve the 2006/07 loss in the ways discussed below.

The alternative ways in which a trading loss can be relieved are as follows:

a) The loss can be carried forward to reduce taxable trading profits arising from the same trade in future years. If this option is chosen the loss must be used as quickly as possible. If the following year's taxable profits are less than the amount of the loss, then those profits will be reduced to Nil and the balance of the loss carried forward to relieve in future years. The loss can be carried forward indefinitely until it is relieved. This relief is often known as s385 RELIEF

b) The loss can be used to reduce (or eliminate) statutory total income in the tax year of the loss. You should recall from chapter one that statutory total income is the total of a taxpayer's income from all sources. Consequently statutory total income may include rental income, employment income, interest and dividends.

c) Whether or not option b) is chosen, the loss can be set against statutory total income in the tax year preceding the tax year of the loss.

A taxpayer does not have to set a loss off under either b) or c) above if he does not wish to do so. If he does wish to make either of these set offs he must make a claim to do so. Claims to set off a loss must be made by the 31 January which is 22 months after the end of the tax year of the loss: thus by 31 January 2009 for a loss in 2006/07.

If a taxpayer has sufficient loss to set off under both b) and c) he can choose to make one or both of the set offs. He can also choose the order of the set offs. However, once a claim is made all of the available loss must be set off. Partial claims are not possible.

Set offs under b) and c) are often known as s380 RELIEFS.

Any loss remaining after any claims under b) and c) above have been made is automatically carried forward to set off under a) against the first available trading profits.

How it works

Ahmed, a sole trader, has the following taxable trading profits/(loss):

	£
Year to 30 September 2005	10,000
Year to 30 September 2006	(59,000)
Year to 30 September 2007	20,000

His only other income is rental income of £15,000 a year. Discuss how Ahmed could relieve the loss of £59,000.

Solution

The loss of £59,000 is a loss of 2006/07. This loss could be set against statutory total income of £25,000 (£10,000 + £15,000) in 2005/06 and/or against statutory total income of £15,000 in 2006/07. If both of these claims are made, the loss not relieved of £19,000 is automatically set against the taxable trading profits of £20,000 arising in 2007/08.

Ahmed does not have to claim to set the loss against other income in 2005/06 and/or 2006/07. Any loss not set off under these provisions is added to the loss carried forward to set off against taxable trading profits in future years.

The disadvantage of setting a loss against statutory total income in the year of the loss and/or in the preceding year is that personal allowances may be wasted. You will recall that every individual has a personal allowance that he can set against his statutory total income. Income of up to the personal allowance is effectively tax free income so there is no benefit in setting losses against that amount of income.

How it works

Sase has a loss in her period of account ending 31 December 2006 of £13,000. In the year to 31 December 2005 she made a profit of £5,000. Her other income is £9,000 a year and she wishes to claim loss relief for the year of loss and then for the preceding year. Show her taxable income for each year, and comment on the effectiveness of the loss relief.

student notes

Assume personal allowances were £5,035 in 2005/06 and in 2006/07.

Solution

The loss-making period ends in 2006/07, so the year of the loss is 2006/07.

	2005/06 £	2006/07 £
Income	14,000	9,000
Less s.380 relief	(4,000)	(9,000)
STI	10,000	NIL

In 2006/07, Sase's personal allowance will be wasted. If Sase claims loss relief in the year there is nothing she can do about this waste of relief. Sase could however make the 2005/06 claim and not the 2006/07 claim. This would leave STI of £1,000 in 2005/06 to set the personal allowance against.

Activity

In 2006/07 Niahla makes a loss of £30,000. Her statutory total income in 2006/07 totals £21,000, and her personal allowance for that year is £5,035. She has no other source of income for any other year. If she obtains loss relief as soon as possible, what loss is carried forward for s385 relief?

CHAPTER OVERVIEW

- A trading loss can be

  a) carried forward to set against the first available profits of the same trade

  b) set against statutory total income in the tax year the of the loss and/or in the preceding tax year

  Any loss not set off under b) above is automatically carried forward for set off under a)

> **KEY WORDS**
>
> **S380 relief** sets a loss against statutory total income in the year of the loss and/or in the preceding year
>
> **S385 relief** sets a loss against taxable trading profits arising in the same trade in future years

relieving trading losses

HOW MUCH HAVE YOU LEARNED?

1. Harold, who has been in business for many years, makes a trading loss of £20,000 in the year ended 31 January 2007. In which year(s) may the loss be relieved, assuming s380 relief is claimed?

2. Trading losses can only be carried forward for offset in the six succeeding tax years. TRUE/FALSE?

3. Where losses are carried forward for s385 relief, against what sort of income may they be relieved?

4. Mallory, who has traded for many years, has the following tax adjusted results:

Year ended 30 April 2005	Profit	£10,000
Year ended 30 April 2006	Loss	£40,000
Year ended 30 April 2007	Profit	£25,000

   Mallory has other income of £9,000 each year. Explain how the loss in the year to 30 April 2006 can be relieved.

chapter 6:
PARTNERSHIPS

chapter coverage

You should recall that a partnership is a group of self employed individuals (partners) trading together. In this Chapter we will see how to compute a partnership's taxable trading profits and how these profits are divided between and taxed on the individual partners. We will look at situations where there is a change in the partnership profit sharing arrangements and where partners join or leave partnerships.

The topics that we shall cover are:

- computing taxable trading profits of partnerships
- dividing taxable trading profits between partners
- the tax positions of individual partners

KNOWLEDGE AND UNDERSTANDING AND PERFORMANCE CRITERIA COVERAGE

knowledge and understanding

- Basis of assessment for unincorporated businesses (Element 18.2)
- Basic allocation of income between partners (Element 18.2)

Performance criteria

- Divide profits and losses of partnerships amongst partners
- Apply the basis of assessment for unincorporated businesses in opening and closing years

student notes

COMPUTING TAXABLE TRADING PROFITS OF PARTNERSHIPS

A partnership is a group of self employed individuals who are trading together.

A partnership prepares a trading profit and loss account in exactly the same way as a sole trader would. This profit and loss account is the profit and loss account for the partnership business as a whole.

The net profit in the partnership profit and loss account must be adjusted for tax purposes in exactly the same way as you would adjust the net profit in the accounts of a sole trader. This means that you must add back disallowable items. You must deduct specifically deductible items that have not been deducted in the accounts (for example capital allowance) and also any income in the accounts that is not part of the taxable trading profit. Finally add any amounts taxable as trading profits that have not been included in the accounts. For example, the market value of any goods taken for own use.

A particular point worth noting is that any partners' salaries or interest on capital deducted in the accounts must be added back when computing taxable trading profits. These items are disallowable expenses because they are a form of drawings. They will be part of each partner's taxable trading profit as described below.

DIVIDING TAXABLE TRADING PROFITS BETWEEN PARTNERS

Once you have computed a partnership's taxable trading profit for a period of account you must divide it between the partners concerned.

The partners may agree to share profits in any way they wish. The agreed division will be set out in the partnership agreement and will always be stated for you in exam questions.

How it works

The Yellow partnership has tax adjusted profits of £40,000 for the year to 31 March 2007. The partners, Mr Blue and Mr Red have agreed to share profits equally.

For the year to 31 March 2007 each of the partners has taxable trading profits of £20,000.

Sometimes, rather than just divide profits between the partners in accordance with an agreed profit sharing ratio the partners may agree that some or all of the partners should:

a) be paid a 'salary' and/or
b) be paid interest on the capital they contributed to the partnership

In this case, your starting point in dividing a partnership's taxable profits between the partners should be to deal with any salary or interest on capital. Once you have done this you can divide the balance of any taxable trading profit between the partners in accordance with the profit sharing ratio.

How it works

Pearl and Ruby are in partnership. The partnership's taxable trading profits for the year ended 31 March 2007 were £110,000. The partnership agreement provides for Pearl to be paid a salary of £20,000 per annum and for Ruby to be paid a salary of £30,000 per annum. Any remaining profits are divided between Pearl and Ruby in the ratio 2:1. Calculate each partner's taxable profits for the year to 31 March 2007.

Solution

First allocate the partners' salaries and then divide the balance of the profit in accordance with the profit sharing ratio:

	Total £	Pearl £	Ruby £
Salary	50,000	20,000	30,000
Profit (£110,000 – £30,000 – £20,000)	60,000	40,000	20,000
	110,000	60,000	50,000

Pearl has taxable profits of £60,000 and Ruby has taxable profits of £50,000 for the year ended 31 March 2007.

Activity 1

Roger and Muggles are in partnership. Tax adjusted trading profits for the year to 31 December 2006 were £210,000. The partnership agreement states that profits should be divided between Roger and Muggles in the ratio 4:1 after paying a salary of £30,000 per annum to each of the partners. Show the taxable trading profits of each partner for the year to 31 December 2006.

partnerships

student notes

You should approach questions where the partnership agreement provides for interest on capital in exactly the same way. This means that you should allocate any interest on capital to the partners before dividing the balance of the profit in the agreed profit sharing ratio.

How it works

Sunita and Jim have been trading in partnership for several years. The partnership prepares accounts to 31 December each year and the taxable trading profits for the year to 31 December 2006 are £140,000. The partnership agreement provides for the following salaries, rates of interest on capital and share of remaining profits:

	Salary per annum £	Interest on capital %	Division of profit %
Sunita	45,000	3	50
Jim	25,000	3	50

The capital account balances of Sunita and Jim are £40,000 and £10,000 respectively. Show how the profits of the year to 31 December 2006 are allocated between the partners.

Solution

	Total £	Sunita £	Jim £
Salary	70,000	45,000	25,000
Interest on capital (3%)	1,500	1,200	300
Profits (£140,000 – 70,000 –1,500)	68,500	34,250	34,250
Taxable profits	140,000	80,450	59,550

Activity 2

James, Kieran and Jemmima are in partnership. For the year to 31 December 2006 taxable trading profits were £270,000. They contributed capital of £20,000 each to the partnership. The partnership agreement provides for interest on capital of 5% to each party and salaries of £35,000 to be paid to Kieran and Jemmima. James is not paid a salary. Remaining profits are divided between James, Kieran and Jemmima in the ratio 3:1:1.

Show how these profits for the year to 31 December 2006 are allocated between the partners.

Change in the profit sharing agreement

Sometimes the agreed profit sharing arrangements may change during a period of account. If this happens you should time apportion the profits to before and after the change and then divide them between the partners.

How it works

Jenny and Chris are in partnership. Taxable trading profits of the partnership for the year ended 31 March 2007 are £60,000. Until 30 September 2006 profits are shared equally. From 1 October 2006 Jenny and Chris agree that the profits should be shared in the ratio 2:1.

Show how the taxable trading profits of the year to 31 March 2007 are divided between Jenny and Chris.

Your first step should be to apportion the profits to the periods before and after the change in the profit sharing ratio:

1.4.06 – 30.9.06   6/12 × £60,000 = £30,000
1.9.06 – 31.3.07   6/12 × £60,000 = £30,000

Next divide these profits between the partners:

	Total £	Jenny £	Chris £
1.4.06 – 30.9.06	30,000	15,000	15,000
1.10.06 – 31.3.07	30,000	20,000	10,000
	60,000	35,000	25,000

For the year to 31 March 2007, Jenny's taxable trading profits are £35,000 and Chris' taxable trading profits are £25,000.

Activity 3

Hansel and Greta are in partnership. The partnership accounts are prepared to 30 June each year. The taxable trading profits for the year ended 30 June 2006 were £80,000. Until 31 March 2006 Hansel and Greta shared profits equally. From 1 April 2006 they shared profits in the ratio 4:1. Calculate the taxable profits for each partner for the year to 30 June 2006.

A change in the rate at which salaries or interest are paid during a period of account has similar implications. You should time apportion the profits before and after the change and deal with each period separately. Remember that the salaries and interest will need to be time apportioned too.

partnerships

student notes

THE TAX POSITIONS OF INDIVIDUAL PARTNERS

Once you have allocated taxable profits for a period of account between partners you must decide which tax year the profits are taxed in.

The current year basis of assessment applies to partnerships in the same way as it does to sole traders. For example, if a partnership prepares accounts to 30 June each year, the year to 30 June 2006 is the basis period for 2006/07 and a partner will be taxed on his share of the profits arising in the year ended 30 June 2006 in 2006/07.

Changes in partners

Sometimes the partners within a partnership change. If a new partner joins a partnership, the special opening year rules that we saw earlier in this Course Companion for sole traders apply to the new partner. The existing partners continue to be taxed using the current year basis of assessment.

Similarly, if a partner leaves a partnership the closing year rules apply to that partner as though he were a sole trader but the other partners continue to be taxed using the current year basis of assessment.

How it works: partner joining a partnership

Francis and Caroline have been in partnership for many years making up accounts to 31 December each year. Profits were shared equally until 1 June 2005, when Charles joined the partnership. From 1 June 2005 profits were shared in the ratio 2:2:1.

Profits adjusted for tax purposes are as follows.

Period	Taxable profit £
1.1.05 – 31.12.05	48,000
1.1.06 – 31.12.06	18,000
1.1.07 – 31.12.07	24,000

Show the taxable profits for each partner for 2005/06 to 2007/08.

Solution

We must first share the profits between the partners.

	Total £	Francis £	Caroline £	Charles £
Year ended 31.12.05				
1.1.05 – 31.5.05 (5/12)				
Profits 50:50	20,000	10,000	10,000	
1.6.05 – 31.12.05 (7/12)				
Profits 2:2:1	28,000	11,200	11,200	5,600
Total	48,000	21,200	21,200	5,600
Year ended 31.12.06				
Profits	18,000	7,200	7,200	3,600
Total for y/e 31.12.06	18,000	7,200	7,200	3,600
Year ended 31.12.07				
Profits	24,000	9,600	9,600	4,800
Total for y/e 31.12.07	24,000	9,600	9,600	4,800

The next stage is to work out the basis periods and hence the taxable profits for the partners in each tax year. The most important thing to remember at this stage is to deal with each of the partners separately.

Francis and Caroline are taxed on the current year basis of assessment throughout.

Year	Basis period	Francis £	Caroline £
2005/06	1.1.05 – 31.12.05	21,200	21,200
2006/07	1.1.06 – 31.12.06	7,200	7,200
2007/08	1.1.07 – 31.12.07	9,600	9,600

Charles joins the partnership in 2005/06 so the opening year rules apply to him from 2005/06.

Year	Basis period	Working	Taxable profits £
2005/06	1.6.05 – 5.4.06	£5,600 + 3/12 × £3,600	6,500
2006/07	1.1.06 – 31.12.06		3,600
2007/08	1.1.07 – 31.12.07		4,800

Charles has overlap profits of £900 to carry forward and relieve in the tax year in which he leaves the partnership.

partnerships

student notes

How it works: partner leaving a partnership

Dominic, Sebastian and India have traded in partnership sharing profits equally for many years. On 1 May 2006 India left the partnership. Profits continue to be shared equally. Accounts have always been prepared to 30 September and recent results have been:

	Profit £
Y/e 30.9.04	36,000
Y/e 30.9.05	81,000
Y/e 30.9.06	60,000

Each of the partners had overlap profits of £10,000 on commencement of the business. Show the taxable trading profits of each partner for 2004/05 to 2006/07.

Solution

Firstly allocate the profits of each period of account to the partners.

	Total £	Dominic £	Sebastian £	India £
Y/e 30.9.04	36,000	12,000	12,000	12,000
Y/e 30.9.05	81,000	27,000	27,000	27,000
Y/e 30.9.06				
1.10.05 – 30.4.06 (7/12)	35,000	11,667	11,667	11,666
1.5.06 – 30.9.06 (5/12)	25,000	12,500	12,500	–
	60,000	24,167	24,167	11,666

Dominic and Sebastian are taxed on the continuing basis of assessment throughout:

	Dominic £	Sebastian £
2004/05 (y/e 30.9.04)	12,000	12,000
2005/06 (y/e 30.9.05)	27,000	27,000
2006/07 (y/e 30.9.06)	24,167	24,167

India is treated as ceasing to trade in 2006/07.

	£
2004/05 (y/e 30.9.04)	12,000
2005/06 (y/e 30.9.05)	27,000
2006/07 (p/e 30.4.06 – overlap profits)	
(£11,666 – £10,000)	1,666

Activity 4

A partnership makes profits as follows.

	£
Year ended 31 October 2005	34,200
Year ended 31 October 2006	45,600

A partner joins on 1 June 2005 and is entitled to 30% of the profits. What are his taxable profits for 2005/06 and 2006/07 and what are his overlap profits carried forward?

Activity 5

X, Y and Z have traded partnership for many years sharing profits in the equally. On 1 July 2005 X retired. Y and Z continue trading, sharing profits in the ratio 3:2.

There were no unrelieved overlap profits on commencement of the business.

The profits of the partnership as adjusted for tax purposes are as follows.

	Profits £
Year to 31 March 2005	24,000
Year to 31 March 2006	14,000
Year to 31 March 2007	48,000

Task

Show the taxable profits for each partner for 2004/05 to 2006/07 inclusive.

CHAPTER OVERVIEW

- A partnership is a group of self employed individuals trading together

- Calculate tax adjusted profits for a partnership in the same way as you would calculate the tax adjusted profits of a sole trader

- Divide the tax adjusted profits of a period of account between the partners in accordance with their profit sharing arrangements during the period of account

- If profit sharing arrangements change during a period of account, time apportion profits to the periods before and after the change before allocating them to partners

- Once you have found a partner's profit for a period of account you can consider which tax year that profit is taxed in. A continuing partner in a continuing business is taxed using the current year basis of assessment

- The opening year rules apply to a partner joining the partnership. The closing year rules apply to a partner leaving the partnership

HOW MUCH HAVE YOU LEARNED?

1. The adjusted profit of a partnership is divided between the partners in accordance with the profit sharing agreement in existence during what period?

2. Dave and Joe are in partnership together and make a profit of £18,000 for the year to 31 December 2006. Up to 30 September 2006 they share profits and losses equally but thereafter they share 3:2. Show each partner's taxable profits for 2006/07.

3. Sunita and Jasmine are in partnership sharing profits equally after paying a salary of £5,000 to Sunita and a salary of £80,000 to Jasmine. Taxable profits for the year to 31 March 2007 were £200,000. Show the taxable profits of each of the partners for the year.

4. Barry and Steve have been in partnership for many years. Profits are shared equally. For the year ended 31 March 2006, the partnership made a profit of £60,000 and for the year ended 31 March 2007 the profit was £80,000. Show the profit taxable on Barry and Steve for 2006/07.

5. Abdul and Ghita have been in partnership for many years. On 1 September 2006, Sase joins the partnership and profits are shared 2:2:1. For the year to 31 August 2007, the partnership makes a profit of £120,000. Show the profits assessable on Sase in 2006/07 and 2007/08 and any overlap profits arising.

6. William, Ann and John have been in partnership for many years sharing profits equally. Accounts have always been prepared to 31 October each year. All partners had overlap profits of £5,000 on commencement. On 31 December 2006 William left the partnership. Profits continued to be shared equally. Recent results were:

	£
Y/e 31 October 2005	21,000
Y/e 31 October 2006	33,000
Y/e 31 October 2007	36,000

Show the taxable profits for each partner for 2005/06 to 2007/08.

chapter 7:
CAPITAL GAINS TAX FOR SOLE TRADERS

chapter coverage

In this chapter we see how to compute chargeable gains arising on the disposal of business assets by a sole trader. Chargeable gains arising on the disposal of non-business assets are not examinable in Unit 18 and are not considered here. You will study the computation of gains on non-business assets if you study Unit 19.

We will see how to set allowable losses and taper relief against chargeable gains and how to arrive at the net gains taxable in any particular tax year.

Many of the rules for computing chargeable gains on disposals by companies are similar to those for computing chargeable gains on disposals by individuals. The important differences are highlighted in this chapter. We will be studying companies later in this Course Companion.

The topics that we shall cover are:

- when does a chargeable gain arise?
- computing chargeable gains and allowable losses
- computing taxable gains in a tax year
- computing Capital Gains Tax payable

KNOWLEDGE AND UNDERSTANDING AND PERFORMANCE CRITERIA COVERAGE

knowledge and understanding

- Identification of business assets disposed of including part disposals (Element 18.3)
- Capital gains exemptions and reliefs on business assets including rollover relief and taper relief (Element 18.3)
- Calculation of gains and losses on disposals of business assets including indexation allowance (Element 18.3)
- Rates of tax payable on gains on business assets disposed of by individuals (Element 18.3)

Performance criteria

- Identify and value correctly any chargeable assets that have been disposed of
- Apply reliefs, deferrals and exemptions correctly
- Calculate chargeable gains and allowable losses

capital gains tax for sole traders

WHEN DOES A CHARGEABLE GAIN ARISE?

student notes

You saw in chapter one that, as a general rule, income is a receipt that is expected to recur (such as business profits), whereas a gain is a one off profit on the disposal of a capital asset (eg the profit on the sale of a factory used in the business). For the gain on the disposal of a capital asset to be a chargeable gain there must be a CHARGEABLE DISPOSAL of a CHARGEABLE ASSET by a CHARGEABLE PERSON.

Chargeable persons

Individuals, partnerships and companies are chargeable persons.

Disposals of chargeable assets by partnerships are not examinable in unit 18 so we do not consider them in this Course Companion. The disposal of assets by companies is considered later in this Course Companion.

Chargeable disposals

The following are the important chargeable disposals at Unit 18:

- Sales of assets or parts of assets
- Gifts of assets or parts of assets

A chargeable disposal occurs on the date of the contract (where there is one, whether written or oral), or the date of a conditional contract becoming unconditional.

The transfer of an asset on death is an EXEMPT DISPOSAL. On death the heirs inherit assets as if they bought them at death for their then market values. There is no capital gain or allowable loss on death.

Chargeable assets

All assets are chargeable assets unless they are specifically designated as exempt.

The following are the exempt assets that you need to be aware of:

- Motor vehicles suitable for private use
- Gilt-edged securities (when disposed of by individuals)
- Qualifying corporate bonds (QCBs) (when disposed of by individuals)
- Certain chattels (see later in this Course Companion)

77

student notes

Any gain arising on disposal of an exempt asset is not taxable and any loss not allowable.

The exempt asset most commonly appearing in exam questions is a car. You should not waste time computing a gain or loss on a car. All you need to do is state that the car is an exempt asset, so no gain or loss arises.

COMPUTING CHARGEABLE GAINS AND ALLOWABLE LOSSES

Whenever a chargeable asset is disposed of a calculation to determine the amount of any gain or loss is needed. The computation follows a standard format as shown below:

	£
Disposal consideration (or market value)	100,000
Less incidental costs of disposal	(1,000)
Net proceeds	99,000
Less allowable costs	(28,000)
Less enhancement expenditure	(1,000)
Unindexed gain	70,000
Less indexation allowance (if available)	(10,000)
Chargeable gain	60,000

We will now look at each of the items in the above pro-forma in turn.

Disposal consideration

Usually the disposal consideration is the proceeds of sale of the asset, but disposal is deemed to take place at market value:

a) where the disposal is by way of a gift

b) where the disposal is made for a consideration which cannot be valued

c) where the disposal is made to a connected person (see below)

Costs

The following costs are deducted in the above proforma:

a) **Incidental costs of disposal**

These are the costs of selling an asset. They may include advertising costs, estate agents fees, legal costs or valuation fees. These costs should be deducted separately from any other allowable cost (because they do not qualify for any indexation allowance; see below, if it was available on that disposal).

b) **Allowable costs**

These include:

i) the original purchase price of the asset

ii) costs incurred in purchasing the asset (estate agents fees, legal fees etc).

Acquisition costs may qualify for an indexation allowance (from the month of acquisition) if it is available on the disposal.

c) **Enhancement expenditure**

ENHANCEMENT EXPENDITURE is capital expenditure which enhances the value of the asset and is reflected in the state or nature of the asset at the time of disposal.

Enhancement expenditure may qualify for an indexation allowance from the month in which it becomes due and payable.

Activity 1

Joe, a sole trader, bought an office building from which to carry out his trade for £400,000. He immediately spent £6,000 on erecting fixed office partitioning. However, by the time Joe sold the building the fixed partitioning had been removed. Is the £6,000 deductible as enhancement expenditure?

The indexation allowance

Indexation was introduced to remove the inflationary element of a gain from taxation.

Individuals are entitled to an indexation allowance until April 1998, but not thereafter. This rule does not apply to companies. Companies are entitled to an indexation allowance until the date of disposal of an asset. We look at companies later in this Course Companion.

How it works

Mustaf bought a shop for use in his business 12 June 1986 and sold it on 1 March 2007.

Indexation allowance is available for the period June 1986 to April 1998 only.

To calculate an indexation allowance, you need an indexation factor calculated from the month the asset was acquired to the date the asset was sold or, for individuals, to April 1998. You will be given this indexation factor in the examination. You will not be expected to calculate it.

capital gains tax for sole traders

student notes

The indexation factor is multiplied by the cost of the asset to calculate the indexation allowance.

Similarly, indexation is available on enhancement expenditure incurred. This expenditure is multiplied by an indexation factor that runs from the date the expenditure was incurred to the date of sale or, for individuals, to April 1998.

How it works

A business asset was bought by an individual on 19 August 1984 for £10,000. Enhancement expenditure of £1,000 was incurred on 12 June 1996. The asset is sold for £20,500 on 20 February 2007. Calculate the chargeable gain arising on the sale of the asset. Assume indexation factors: August 1984 to April 1998 = 0.808; June 1996 to April 1998 = 0.063.

	£
Disposal proceeds	20,500
Less: purchase price	(10,000)
Less: enhancement expenditure	(1,000)
	9,500
Less: indexation on purchase price	
£10,000 × 0.808	(8,080)
indexation on enhancement expenditure	
£1,000 × 0.063	(63)
Chargeable gain	1,357

Activity 2

A sole trader bought a freehold factory in July 1995 for £100,000. He sold the factory for £200,000 in August 2006. What is the chargeable gain on sale? Assume indexation factors July 1995 – August 2006 = 0.319 and July 1995 – April 1998 = 0.091

The indexation allowance cannot create or increase an allowable loss. If there is a gain before the indexation allowance, the allowance can reduce that gain to zero, but no further. If there is a loss before the indexation allowance, there is no indexation allowance.

Activity 3

Sergio bought a business asset for £50,000 in August 1990 and sold it for £20,000 in January 2007. What is the allowable loss? Assume an indexation factor August 1990 – April 1998 = 0.269

capital gains tax for sole traders

COMPUTING TAXABLE GAINS IN A TAX YEAR

student notes

An individual pays capital gains tax on any TAXABLE GAINS arising in a tax year.

Taxable gains are the net chargeable gains (gains minus losses) of the tax year reduced by unrelieved losses brought forward from previous years, a taper relief and the annual exemption. We will look at each of these items in turn.

Annual exemption

All individuals are entitled to the annual capital gains exemption. For 2006/07 it is £8,800. It is the last deduction to be made in computing taxable gains and effectively means that for 2006/07 the first £8,800 of taxable gains are tax free.

Losses

Sometimes an allowable loss rather than a taxable gain arises. Once a loss has been calculated deal with it as follows:

a) firstly set it against gains arising in the same tax year until these are reduced to £Nil, then

b) set any remaining loss against net gains in the next tax year but only to reduce the net gains in the next year down to the amount of the annual exemption. (Companies do not have an annual exempt amount so no such restriction on the set off of losses applies to them: we cover companies later in this Course Companion.)

How it works

a) Tim has chargeable gains for 2006/07 of £25,000 and allowable losses of £19,000. As the losses are current year losses they must be fully relieved against the gains to produce net gains of £6,000, despite the fact that net gains are below the annual exemption.

b) Hattie has gains of £9,800 for 2006/07 and allowable losses brought forward of £6,000. Hattie restricts her loss relief to £1,000 so as to leave net gains of £(9,800 –1,000) = £8,800, which will be exactly covered by her annual exemption for 2006/07. The remaining £5,000 of losses will be carried forward to 2007/08.

c) Mildred has chargeable gains of £2,000 for 2006/07 and losses brought forward from 2005/06 of £12,000. She will leapfrog 2006/07 and carry forward all the brought forward losses to 2007/08. The gains of £2,000 are covered by the annual exemption for 2006/07.

student notes

Taper relief

After losses have been deducted from chargeable gains as described above taper relief may be applied. Taper relief is available to individuals. It is not available to companies.

Taper relief is more generous for business assets than for non-business assets. In Unit 18 you will only be expected to compute gains on the disposal of business assets. For this purpose, a business asset is, broadly:

a) an asset used for the purposes of a trade carried on by an individual or by a company within (c) below

b) an asset held for the purposes of any office or employment held by that individual with a person carrying on a trade

c) shares in: an unlisted trading company; a company in which the individual disposing of the shares is an officer or employee; company in which the individual holds at least 5% of the voting rights

The percentages of gains that remain chargeable after taper relief are set out below.

Business assets

Number of complete years after 5.4.98 for which asset held	% of gain chargeable
0	100
1	50
2 or more	25

The above percentages will be given in the tax tables at the beginning of the examination.

How it works

Pedro buys a business asset on 1 June 2005 and sells it on 1 July 2006. For the taper relief purposes Pedro held the asset for one complete year. This means that only 50% of the gain is chargeable after taper relief.

If the asset had been purchased in June 1997, only the complete years from April 1998 are counted, so there are eight complete years of ownership. 25% of the gain is chargeable after taper relief. In fact, all you need to identify is that there are at least two complete years of ownership for this rate of taper relief to apply.

Taper relief is applied to net chargeable gains after the deduction of current year and brought forward losses. The annual exemption is then deducted from the tapered gains. Remember that brought forward losses can only bring the gain before taper relief down to the amount of the annual exemption.

capital gains tax for sole traders

How it works

In 2006/07 a sole trader made a gain of £25,000. She had losses brought forward from previous years of £5,000. The asset sold had been held for one complete year for taper relief purposes.

The brought forward losses are set against the gain to give net chargeable gains before taper relief of £20,000.

Taper relief is then applied to give a gain after taper relief of 50% x £20,000 = £10,000.

Finally the annual exemption is deducted to give a taxable gain of £1,200 (£10,000 – £8,800)

Activity 4

Susannah sold a business asset in May 2006 realising a chargeable gain of £50,000 before taper relief. She had purchased the asset in May 1995. Susannah made no other disposals in 2006/07 but she had allowable losses of £6,000 brought forward from 2005/06. What is Susannah's taxable gains after the annual exemption for 2006/07?

The allocation of losses

Allocate losses to gains in the way that produces the lowest tax charge. This means that you should deduct losses from the gains attracting the lowest rate of taper relief (ie where the highest percentage of the gain remains chargeable).

Example: allocation of losses to gains

Abdul made the following capital losses and gains in 2006/07:

	£
Loss	15,000
Gains (before taper relief)	
Asset A (business asset:	
50% of gain chargeable after taper relief)	85,000
Asset B (business asset:	
25% of gain chargeable after taper relief)	20,000

student notes

83

capital gains tax for sole traders

student notes

The best use of the loss is to offset it against the gain on asset A:

	£	£
Gain – Asset A	85,000	
Less loss	(15,000)	
Gain after taper relief (£70,000 × 50%)		35,000
Gain – Asset B	20,000	
Gain after taper relief (£20,000 × 25%)		5,000
Gains after taper relief		40,000
Less annual exemption		(8,800)
Taxable gains		31,200

COMPUTING CAPITAL GAINS TAX PAYABLE

We have seen above how to compute an individual's taxable gains for a tax year. In chapter 1 we saw that the rate of tax on taxable income depends on which income tax band income falls into. This also effects the rate of CGT as taxable gains are chargeable to capital gains tax as if the gains were an extra slice of income for the tax year concerned. CGT is due at 10% in the starting rate band, at 20% in the basic rate band at 40% and when total taxable income and taxable gains exceed £33,300.

The rate bands are used first to cover income and then gains.

How it works

Sally had taxable income in 2006/07 of £23,900. She made taxable gains (ie gains after deduction of the annual exemption) in the year of £20,000.

Sally's taxable income uses all the starting rate band of £2,150. However, £9,400 (£33,300 – £23,900) of the basic rate band remains to be used by the taxable gains. The remaining gain is taxed at 40%.

Capital gains tax payable

	£
£9,400 × 20%	1,880
£10,600 × 40%	4,240
	6,120

Activity 5

In 2006/07, Mustafa, has the following income and net chargeable gains. Find the CGT payable.

	£
Business profits	40,000
Net chargeable gains	28,800

In 2006/07 Mustafa is entitled to a personal allowance of £5,035 and a capital gains annual exemption of £8,800. No taper relief is available

CHAPTER OVERVIEW

- A chargeable gain arises when there is a chargeable disposal of a chargeable asset by a chargeable person

- Enhancement expenditure can be deducted in computing a chargeable gain if it is reflected in the state and nature of the asset at the time of disposal

- Individuals are entitled to an indexation allowance until April 1998. Indexation cannot create or increase a loss

- Taxable gains are net chargeable gains for a year minus losses brought forward minus the annual exemption

- Losses brought forward can only reduce net chargeable gains down to the amount of the annual exemption

- Taper relief reduces gains for individuals after 5 April 1998

- Losses should be allocated to the gains that attract the lowest taper relief (i.e. where the highest % of the gain remains chargeable)

- Taper relief is applied to an individual's net gains after the set off of current and brought forward capital losses

- The annual exemption is deducted after the application of taper relief

- CGT may be payable at 10%, 20%, or 40%

- The rate bands are applied first to taxable income and then to taxable gains

- Companies are entitled to indexation until the date of disposal of an asset. They are not entitled to taper relief or an annual exemption

---

KEY WORDS

A **chargeable person** is an individual, partnership or company

A **chargeable asset** is any asset that is not an exempt asset

A **chargeable disposal** is a sale or gift of an asset

An **exempt disposal** is a disposal on which no chargeable gain or allowable loss arises

Enhancement expenditure is capital expenditure that enhances the value of the asset and is reflected in the state or nature of the asset at the time of disposal

Taxable gains are the net chargeable gains of a tax year, after deducting losses, taper relief and the annual exemption

HOW MUCH HAVE YOU LEARNED?

1. Which of the following constitute chargeable disposals for CGT:

    a) a gift of shares;
    b) the sale of a building?

2. Yvette buys a factory for use in her business as a sole trader on 9 August 2002 for £125,000. She sells the factory on 12 December 2006 for £160,000. Show her gain on sale, after taper relief.

3. Jameel bought a business asset in June 1990 for £30,000. He sold it for £60,000 in March 2007. No other disposals were made in 2006/07. Compute the gain arising after taper relief. Assume an indexation factor June 1990 to April 1998 of 0.283.

4. Philip has chargeable gains of £12,000 (no taper relief available) and allowable losses of £2,000 in 2006/07. Losses brought forward at 6 April 2006 amount to £7,000. What amount is liable to CGT in 2006/07? What are the losses carried forward?

5. Compute Martha's CGT liability for 2006/07, assuming she has:

    Taxable income £23,190
    Chargeable gains (before AE) £24,000

chapter 8:
CHARGEABLE GAINS: ADDITIONAL ASPECTS

chapter coverage

In this chapter we look at how to compute chargeable gains when part of a chargeable asset is disposed of. We also see how to compute gains and losses arising on the disposal of chattels. Finally we look at the special rules that apply when disposals are made to connected people or between spouses/civil partners.

The topics that we shall cover are:

- part disposals
- chattels
- connected persons
- spouses and civil partners

KNOWLEDGE AND UNDERSTANDING AND PERFORMANCE CRITERIA COVERAGE

knowledge and understanding

- Identification of business assets disposed of including part disposals (Element 18.3)
- Calculation of gains and losses on disposals of business assets including indexation allowance (Element 18.3)

Performance criteria

- Identify and value correctly any chargeable assets that have been disposed of
- Calculate chargeable gains and allowable losses

chargeable gains: additional aspects

student notes

PART DISPOSALS

Sometimes part, rather than the whole, of an asset is disposed of. For instance, one third of a piece of land may be sold. In this case we need to be able to compute the chargeable gain or allowable loss arising on the part of the asset disposed of.

The problem is that although we know what the disposal proceeds are for the part of the asset disposed of, we do not usually know what proportion of the cost of the whole asset relates to that part. The solution to this is that we use the following fraction to determine the cost of the part disposed of.

The fraction is:

$$\frac{A}{A+B} = \frac{\text{value of the part disposed of}}{\text{value of the part disposed of} + \text{market value of the remainder}}$$

A is the proceeds (or market value) before deducting incidental costs of disposal.

You will need to learn the above formula for use in your exam.

The above formula is used to apportion the cost of the whole asset. If, however, any expenditure was incurred wholly in respect of the part disposed of, it should be treated as an allowable deduction in full for that part and not apportioned. An example of this is incidental selling expenses, which are wholly attributable to the part disposed of.

How it works

Mr Heal bought four acres of building land for £264,000 in January 2005. He sold one acre of the land at auction in July 2006 for £200,000, before auction expenses of 15%. The market value of the three remaining acres is £460,000. Assume the land is a business asset. You are required to calculate Mr Heal's gain after taper relief.

Solution

The cost of the land being sold is:

$$\frac{200,000}{200,000+460,000} \times £264,000 = £80,000$$

	£
Disposal proceeds	200,000
Less: incidental costs of sale (15%)	(30,000)
Net proceeds	170,000
Less: cost (see above)	(80,000)
Gain before taper relief	90,000

Gain after taper relief (January 2005 – July 2006) = 1 year

50% × £90,000 = £45,000

Activity 1

Sergio bought a plot of land for use in his business for £50,000 in May 2004. In March 2007, he sold part of the land for £291,000, which was net of legal fees on the sale of £9,000. At that time, the value of the remaining land was £500,000. Calculate the chargeable gain arising on the disposal in March 2007 before taper relief.

CHATTELS

A CHATTEL is tangible movable property (i.e. property that can be moved, seen and touched). Examples are items such as furniture and works of art.

A WASTING CHATTEL is a chattel with an estimated remaining useful life of 50 years or less. An example would be a racehorse or a greyhound. Wasting chattels are exempt from CGT (so that there are no chargeable gains and no allowable losses). There is one exception to this, but this is not assessable in Unit 18.

Activity 2

Joe a sole trader bought a greyhound for use at client events in 2004 for £5,000. The greyhound was sold in December 2006 for £9,000. Calculate any chargeable gain arising.

There are special rules for calculating gains and losses on non-wasting chattels:

a) If a chattel is not a wasting asset, any gain arising on its disposal will still be exempt from CGT if the asset is sold for gross proceeds of £6,000 or less.

b) If sale proceeds exceed £6,000, the gain is limited to:

5/3 × (gross proceeds – £6,000).

chargeable gains: additional aspects

student notes

c) If sale proceeds are less than £6,000, and the cost is more than £6,000, any allowable loss is restricted to that which would arise if it were sold for gross proceeds of £6,000.

We will have a look at examples of each of these situations in turn.

How it works: gains on the disposal of non-wasting chattels

A sole trader purchased a painting to hang in his showrooms on 1 April 2003 for £3,000. On 1 January 2007 he sold the painting at auction.

Show the chargeable gain arising before taper relief if the sale proceeds were:

a) £3,600 net of the auctioneer's 10% commission
b) £7,200 net of the auctioneer's 10% commission

Solution

a) If the gross sale proceeds are £3,600 × 100/90 = £4,000 the gain arising on disposal of the chattel will be exempt

b) If the gross proceeds are £7,200 × 100/90 = £8,000 the gain arising on the disposal of the painting will be calculated as follows:

	£
Gross proceeds	8,000
Less: incidental costs of sale (10%)	(800)
Net proceeds	7,200
Less: cost	(3,000)
Gain before taper relief	4,200

Restricted to a maximum of 5/3 × £(8,000 – 6,000) = £3,333

Activity 3

On 1 May 2003 a sole trader purchased a non wasting chattel for £2,500. On 1 October 2006 he sold the chattel at auction for £8,100 (which was net of the auctioneer's 10% commission). Calculate the chargeable gain arising before taper relief.

How it works: losses

Sunita purchased a painting to hang in her office on 1 July 2005 for £7,000. She sold the painting in September 2006 at auction for £3,600 net of auctioneer's fees of 10%.

Compute the gain or loss arising.

Solution

Sunita obviously has a loss and therefore the allowable loss is calculated on deemed proceeds of £6,000. The costs of disposal can be deducted from the gross proceeds of £6,000.

	£
Deemed disposal proceeds	6,000
Less: incidental costs of disposal (£3,600 × 10/90)	(400)
	5,600
Less: cost	(7,000)
Allowable loss	(1,400)

Activity 4

Jeremy purchased a non wasting chattel on 1 June 2004 for £7,800 which he sold in October 2006 at auction for £3,825 (which was net of 15% commission). Compute the allowable loss arising.

CONNECTED PERSONS

If a disposal is made to a connected person the disposal is deemed to take place at the market value of the asset.

If an allowable loss arises on the disposal, it can be set only against gains arising in the same or future years from disposals to the same connected person and the loss can only be set off if he or she is still connected with the person making the loss.

For this purpose an individual is connected with:

- his relatives (brothers, sisters, ancestors and lineal descendants)
- the relatives of his spouse/civil partner
- the spouses/civil partners of his and his spouse's/civil partner's relatives

student notes

A company is connected with:

- a person who (alone or with persons connected with him) controls
- another company under common control

Companies are dealt with in detail later in this Course Companion.

SPOUSES AND CIVIL PARTNERS

Spouses and civil partners are taxed as two separate people. Each has an annual exemption, and losses of one spouse/civil partner cannot be set against gains of the other.

Disposals between spouses/civil partners do not give rise to chargeable gains or allowable losses. The disposal is said to be on a 'NO GAIN/NO LOSS BASIS. The acquiring spouse/civil partner takes the base cost of the disposing spouse/civil partner, plus any indexation allowance to the date of the disposal between them, or 6 April 1998, if earlier.

The acquiring spouse/civil partner normally takes over the taper relief position of the disposing spouse/civil partner. This means the acquiring spouse/civil partner is treated as acquiring the asset when the disposing spouse/civil partner did.

chargeable gains: additional aspects

CHAPTER OVERVIEW

- On the part disposal of an asset the formula A/A + B must be applied to work out the cost attributable to the part disposed of

- Wasting chattels are exempt assets for CGT purposes (eg racehorses and greyhounds)

- Non-wasting chattels are exempt if they are sold for gross proceeds of £6,000 or less. If gross proceeds exceed £6,000 any gain arising on the disposal of the asset is limited to 5/3 (Gross proceeds – £6,000)

- If the gross proceeds are less than £6,000 on the sale of a non wasting chattel, any loss otherwise arising is restricted by deeming the proceeds to be £6,000

- A disposal to a connected person takes place at market value

- For individuals, connected people are broadly brothers, sisters, ancestors, lineal descendants and their spouses/civil partners plus similar relations of a spouse/civil partner

- Losses on disposals to connected people can only be set against gains on disposals to the same connected person

- Disposals between spouses/civil partners take place on a no gain/no loss basis

> **KEY WORDS**
>
> A **no gain/no loss** disposal is a disposal on which no gain or loss arises
>
> A **chattel** is tangible movable property
>
> A **wasting chattel** is a chattel with an estimated remaining useful life of 50 years or less

chargeable gains: additional aspects

HOW MUCH HAVE YOU LEARNED?

1. Richard sells 4 acres of land in May 2006 out of a plot of 10 acres for £38,000. Costs of disposal amount to £3,000. The 10-acre plot cost £41,500 in 1987. The market value of the 6 acres remaining is £48,000.

   Compute the chargeable gain/allowable loss arising before taper relief, assuming an indexation allowance of 0.620 to April 1998.

2. Mustafa bought a non wasting chattel in 2005 for £5,500. Compute the gain arising before taper relief if he sells it in 2006 for

   a) £5,800 after deducting selling expenses of £180
   b) £8,200 after deducting selling expenses of £220

3. Simon bought a racehorse to use for business advertising for £4,500 in May 2004. He sold the racehorse for £9,000 in June 2006. Calculate the gain arising before taper relief.

4. Santa bought a painting to hang in his office for £7,000 in June 2005. He sold the painting in June 2006 for £5,000. Calculate the allowable loss arising.

5. A loss arising on a disposal to a connected person can be set against any gains arising in the same year or in subsequent years. TRUE/FALSE?

6. No gain or loss arises on a disposal to a spouse/civil partner. TRUE/FALSE?

chapter 9:
SHARES

chapter coverage

In this chapter we will see how to compute chargeable gains and allowable losses on the disposal of shares. We assume that all shares disposed of are business assets as the disposal of non-business assets is not examinable in Unit 18. For completeness in this chapter we will look at the rules for both individuals and companies.

This is a very important chapter as the computation of gains and losses on the disposal of shares is one of the examiner's favourite topics.

The topics that we shall cover are:

- the need for special rules
- disposals by individuals
- the FA 1985 pool
- bonus and rights issues
- the matching rules for companies

KNOWLEDGE AND UNDERSTANDING AND PERFORMANCE CRITERIA COVERAGE

knowledge and understanding

- Identification of business assets disposed of including part disposals (Element 18.3)
- Calculation of gains and losses on disposals of business assets including indexation allowance (Element 18.3)

Performance criteria

- Identify and value correctly any chargeable assets that have been disposed of
- Identify shares disposed of by companies
- Calculate chargeable gains and allowable losses

THE NEED FOR SPECIAL RULES

Shares present special problems when computing gains or losses on disposal. For instance, suppose that a taxpayer buys some shares in X plc on the following dates:

	No of shares	Cost £
5 July 1990	100	150
17 January 1995	100	375
2 May 1998	100	1,000

On 15 June 2006, he sells 220 of his shares for £3,300. To determine his chargeable gain, we need to be able to work out which shares out of his three original holdings were actually sold. Since one share is identical to any other it is not possible to work this out by reference to factual evidence.

As a result, it has been necessary to devise 'matching rules'. These allow HMRC, on a disposal, to identify which shares have been sold and so work out what the allowable cost (and therefore the gain) on disposal should be. These matching rules are considered in detail below.

It is very important that you understand the matching rules and that there are different matching rules for individuals and companies. These rules are very regularly examined and if you do not understand them you will not be able to get any of this part of a question right.

DISPOSALS BY INDIVIDUALS

For individuals the matching of the shares sold is in the following order:

a) shares acquired on the same day;

b) shares acquired in the following thirty days on a FIFO (first in, first out) basis;

c) shares acquired between 6 April 1998 and disposal on a LIFO (last in, first out) basis;

d) shares from the Finance Act 1985 (FA 1985 pool) pool.

The composition of the FA 1985 pool is explained in detail below.

How it works

George bought the following shares in Red Ltd:

Date	No of shares	Cost £
1 May 2006	9,000	18,000
4 September 2006	2,000	5,000
12 March 2007	5,000	12,000

He sold 10,000 shares on 20 February 2007 for £30,000.

You are required to show George's gain on sale before taper relief.

Solution

Matching:

12 March 2007	5,000 shares (following 30 days)
4 September 2006	2,000 shares (LIFO)
1 May 2006	3,000 shares (LIFO)
	10,000

Gains

	£	Gains £
12 March 2007 holding		
Proceeds 5/10 × £30,000	15,000	
Less: cost	(12,000)	
		3,000
4 September 2006 holding		
Proceeds 2/10 × £30,000	6,000	
Less: cost	(5,000)	
		1,000
1 May 2006 holding		
Proceeds 3/10 × £30,000	9,000	
Less: cost 3/9 × £18,000	(6,000)	
		3,000
Total gains		7,000

shares

student notes

Activity 1

Selina bought shares in Green Ltd on the following dates:

	No.	£
1 June 2002	4,000	6,000
1 May 2005	1,000	2,000
1 August 2006	1,500	3,000

On 1 March 2007 she sold 3,000 shares for £8,000. Compute the gain or loss arising on the sale before taper relief.

THE FA 1985 POOL

The FA 1985 pool for individuals includes shares acquired between 6 April 1982 and 5 April 1998.

The calculation of the FA 1985 pool value

To compute the value of the FA 1985 pool, set-up three columns of figures:

a) the number of shares;
b) the cost of the shares ignoring indexation;
c) the indexed cost of the shares. (ie cost plus indexation)

For historical reasons, your first step with a Finance Act 1985 pool should be to compute its value at 5 April 1985. To do this aggregate the indexed cost and number of shares acquired between 6 April 1982 and 5 April 1985 inclusive. In order to calculate the indexed cost of these shares, an indexation allowance, computed from the date of acquisition of the shares to April 1985, is added to the cost value.

How it works

Jackie bought 10,000 shares in X plc for £6,000 in August 1982 and another 10,000 for £9,000 in December 1984. Indexation factors are August 1982 – April 1985 0.157 December 1984 - April 1985 0.043.

Compute the value of the FA 1985 pool at 6 April 1985.

	No of shares	Cost £	Indexed cost £
August 1982 (a)	10,000	6,000	6,000
December 1984 (b)	10,000	9,000	9,000
	20,000	15,000	15,000
Index to April 1985			
£6,000 × 0.157 (a)			942
£9,000 × 0.043 (b)			387
Pool at 5 April 1985	20,000	15,000	16,329

Our second step should be to reflect all disposals and acquisitions of shares between 6 April 1985 and 5 April 1998 in the FA 1985 pool. Disposals/acquisitions of shares that decrease/increase the amount of expenditure within the FA 1985 pool are called OPERATIVE EVENTS.

You must reflect each operative event in the FA 1985 pool. However, prior to reflecting an operative event within the FA 1985 share pool, a further indexation allowance (sometimes described as an indexed rise) must be computed up to the date of the operative event you are looking at. You must look at each operative event in chronological order.

How it works

Following on from the above example, now assume that Jackie acquired 4,000 more shares on 1 January 1990 at a cost of £6,000.

Show the value of the FA 1985 pool on 1 January 1990 following the acquisition. Assume an indexation factor April 1985 – January 1990 0.261

Solution

	No of shares	Cost £	Indexed cost £
6 April 1985	20,000	15,000	16,329
Index to January 1990			
0.261 × £16,329			4,262
			20,591
January 1990 acquisition	4,000	6,000	6,000
	24,000	21,000	26,591

student notes

shares

student notes

If there are several operative events, the procedure described must be performed several times over. In the case of a disposal, following the calculation of the indexed rise, the cost and the indexed cost attributable to the shares disposed of are deducted from the cost and the indexed cost within the FA 1985 pool. This is computed on a pro-rata basis if only part of the holding is being sold.

How it works

Continuing the above example, suppose that Jackie now disposes of 12,000 shares on 9 January 1995 for £26,000.

Show the value of the FA 1985 pool on 10 January 1995 following the disposal. Compute the gain on the disposal. Assume an indexation factor January 1990 – January 1995 0.222.

Solution

	No of shares	Cost £	Indexed cost £
Value at January 1990	24,000	21,000	26,591
Indexed rise to January 1995 0.222 × £26,591			5,903
	24,000	21,000	32,494
Disposal	(12,000)	(10,500)	(16,247)
Pool c/f	12,000	10,500	16,247

The gain on the disposal is calculated as follows:

	£
Sale proceeds	26,000
Less: cost	(10,500)
	15,500
Less: indexation (£16,247 – £10,500)	(5,747)
Gain before taper relief	9,753

Note that the indexation is the difference for the shares sold between the indexed cost and the cost.

The above processes are repeated in the FA 1985 pool until, for individuals it closes on 6 April 1998. This means that if a disposal takes place after 5 April 1998, your final step should be to close the FA 1985 pool on 6 April 1998 by calculating an indexation allowance up to April 1998. No further indexation is available on the shares after this date.

shares

How it works

Continuing the above example, suppose that Jackie now disposes of 12,000 shares on 9 January 2007 for £40,000.

Compute the gain on the disposal. Assume indexation January 1995 to April 1998 = 0.114.

Solution

	No of shares	Cost £	Indexed cost £
Value at January 1995	12,000	10,500	16,247
Indexed rise 1.95 – 4.98			
0.114 × £16,247			1,852
Pool closes April 1998	12,000	10,500	18,099

Now that we have calculated the value of the FA 1985 pool at closure, we can calculate the chargeable gain or allowable loss arising on the disposal. The indexation allowance on the disposal is the difference between indexed cost of the shares being sold, and their cost. As usual, the indexation allowance cannot create or increase an allowable loss.

After calculating the value of the FA 1985 pool, the gain is then computed as follows:

	£
Disposal proceeds	40,000
Less: cost	(10,500)
Unindexed gain	29,500
Less: indexation allowance £(18,099 – 10,500)	(7,599)
Gain before taper relief	21,901

Activity 2

Abduljabbar bought 4,000 shares in Green plc on 1 February 1986 for £5,000. He bought another 2,000 shares in Green Plc for £5,000 on 4 January 1995. There were no further acquisitions or disposals of these shares until 2,000 shares were sold in January 2007 for £9,000. Calculate the chargeable gain arising on the sale after taper relief. Assume an indexation factor February 1986 – January 1995 = 0.511, January 1995 – April 1998 = 0.114

student notes

shares

student notes

BONUS AND RIGHTS ISSUES

Bonus issues

BONUS SHARES are additional shares given free to shareholders based on their current holding(s).

Bonus shares are treated as being acquired at the date of the original acquisition of the underlying shares giving rise to the bonus issue. This means that shares deriving from a post April 1998 acquisition are treated as part of that holding whilst shares deriving from the FA 1985 pool are treated as though they are part of that pool.

Since bonus shares are issued at no cost there is no need to adjust the original costs. Instead the number of shares purchased at particular times are increased by the bonus issue. There is no need to index the 1985 pool to the date of the bonus issue. The normal matching rules apply.

How it works

Calculate the gain arising on the sale of the following shares:

1 April 1992	Purchase of 1,000 shares
1 May 2004	Purchase of 3,000 shares
1 May 2005	Bonus issue of 1 for 4
1 December 2006	Sale of 5,000 shares.

Solution

a) Order of matching:

    i) 1 May 2004 purchase: then
    ii) FA 1985 pool;

The bonus shares are related to the holding that gave rise to them. Let's see how this works below:

b) Numbers of shares matched with:

i)
	No. of shares
1.5.04	3,000
Bonus (1 for 4)	750
	3,750
Disposal 1.12.06	(3,750)

102

		No. of shares
ii)	FA 1985 pool	
	1.4.92	1,000
	Bonus (1 for 4)	250
		1,250
	Disposal 1.12.06	(1,250)

Having identified the shares sold you can then calculate the chargeable gains/allowable losses arising. You can try this for yourself in the following activity.

Activity 3

Maria acquired shares in X Plc as follows:

	No.	£
19 August 1990	4,000	8,000
27 February 2002	6,000	15,000
5 March 2006	1 for 4 bonus issue	

On 1 May 2006 9,375 shares were sold for £20,000. Calculate the chargeable gains arising before taper relief. Assume an indexation factor August 1990 – April 1998 = 0.269

Rights issues

The difference between a bonus issue and a rights issue is that in a RIGHTS ISSUE the new shares are paid for. This results in an adjustment to the original cost.

Rights shares derived from shares in the 1985 pool go into that holding and those derived from post 5.4.98 holdings attach to those holdings. You should add the number and cost of each rights issue to each holding as appropriate.

For the purposes of calculating the indexation allowance for rights issues before April 1998, expenditure on a rights issue is taken as being incurred on the date of the issue and not on the acquisition date of the original holding.

The length of the period of ownership for taper relief purposes depends on the date of acquisition of the original holding not the date of acquisition of the rights shares.

shares

student notes

How it works

Richard acquired shares in Z Ltd as follows:

1 June 1992	Bought 10,000 shares for £8,000.
1 October 2005	Took up rights issue of 1 for 5 at £1.00 per share.
1 August 2006	Bought 10,000 shares for £12,000.
1 April 2007	Sold 15,000 shares for £21,000.

Compute the gain arising on the disposal after taper relief. Richard made no other disposals in 2006/07. Assume an indexation factor: June 1992 – April 1998 = 0.167

Post 6 April 1998 acquisition (1 August 2006)

Applying the matching rules for individuals the 10,000 shares bought after 6 April 1998 are treated as disposed of first:

	£
Disposal proceeds	
(10,000/15,000 × £21,000)	14,000
Less: cost	(12,000)
Gain before taper relief	2,000

No taper relief is due.

Gain after taper relief = £2,000

Next deal with the FA 1985 pool. All the rights issue shares attach to that pool:

	No of shares	Cost £	Indexed cost £
FA 1985 Pool			
1.6.92	10,000	8,000	8,000
Index to April 1998			
£8,000 × 0.167			1,336
Pool closes	10,000	8,000	9,336
Rights issue	2,000	2,000	2,000
	12,000	10,000	11,336
Disposal	5,000	4,167	4,723
	7,000	5,833	6,613

	£
Disposal Proceeds (5,000/15,000 × £21,000)	7,000
Less: cost	(4,167)
Indexation (4,723 – 4,167)	(556)
Gain before taper relief	2,277

...per relief is based on the length of ownership of the original shares (not the ...ghts shares)

...ain after taper relief (25% × £2,277) = £569

...otal gains after taper relief £569 + £2,000 = £2,569

Activity 4

Sarah acquired a shareholding in Y Ltd as follows:

1 August 1997	Bought 4,000 shares for £7,000
1 June 2004	Bought 2,000 shares for £6,000
1 June 2006	Took up rights issue 1 for 2 at £2.00 per share
1 December 2006	Sold 6,000 shares for £18,000

Compute the gain arising on the disposal, after taper relief (if applicable). Sarah made no other disposals in 2006/07. Assume an indexation factor August 1997 – April 1998 = 0.026.

THE MATCHING RULES FOR COMPANIES

The rules we have looked at so far in this chapter apply to disposals of shares by individuals. Very similar rules apply to disposals by companies, but with some differences.

For example, there are different matching rules for companies. The order of matching is:

a) shares acquired on the same day;

b) shares acquired in the previous nine days on a FIFO basis;

c) shares from the Finance Act 1985 pool (which starts on 1 April 1982 and continues beyond 6 April 1998)

You will see later in Course Companion that companies are entitled to indexation until the date of disposal of an asset but that they are not entitled to taper relief. This means that, for companies the FA 1985 pool continues beyond 6 April 1998. As there is no taper relief there is no need to deal with acquisitions after 6 April 1998 separately.

student notes

shares

student notes

How it works

S Ltd had the following transactions in the shares of B Ltd

May 1986	Purchased 2,000 shares for £4,000
May 2000	Took up one for two rights issue at £2.00 per share
October 2006	Sold all the shares for £12,000

Compute the chargeable gain or allowable loss arising on the sale in October 2006.

Indexation factors: May 2000 – October 2006 = 0.156; May 1986 – May 2000 = 0.745

	No of shares	Cost £	Indexed cost £
May 1986	2,000	4,000	4,000
Indexed rise to May 2000 £4,000 × 0.745			2,980
			6,980
Rights issue	1,000	2,000	2,000
	3,000	6,000	8,980
Indexed rise to October 2006 £8,980 × 0.156			1,401
	3,000	6,000	10,381

	£
Disposal proceeds	12,000
Less Cost	(6,000)
Less indexation (£10,381 – £6,000)	(4,381)
Chargeable gain	1,619

It is very important that you are confident in applying the rules above both for individuals and companies. It is important that you do not confuse the two sets of rules as this will mean that you lose a lot of marks.

CHAPTER OVERVIEW

- The matching rules for individuals are
    - Same day acquisitions
    - Next 30 days acquisitions on a FIFO basis
    - Acquisitions after 5.4.98 on a LIFO basis
    - Shares in the FA 1985 pool

- For individuals, the FA 1985 pool runs from April 1982 to April 1998

- The matching rules for companies are
    - Same day acquisitions
    - Previous nine days acquisitions
    - Shares in the FA 1985 pool

- The FA 1985 pool for companies runs to the date of disposal of the shares

- Bonus and rights shares are added to the shareholding to which they relate

- The difference between a bonus and a rights issue is that in a rights issue shares are paid for

- Indexation on rights issue shares runs from the date the rights were paid for. However, taper relief is based on the date the original shares were acquired

> **KEY WORDS**
>
> **Operative events** are disposals/acquisitions of shares that decrease/increase the amount of expenditure within the FA 1985 pool
>
> **Bonus shares** are shares that are issued free to shareholders based on original holdings
>
> **Rights issues** are similar to bonus issues except that in a rights issue shares must be paid for

HOW MUCH HAVE YOU LEARNED?

1. State how 5,000 shares sold by an individual on 7 November 2006 would be matched with acquisitions, if the acquisitions were made as follows:

	No of shares
30 September 1987	2,000
10 July 1989	1,000
15 June 1998	3,000

2. State how the above shares would be matched, if the shareholder was a company rather than an individual.

3. What is an 'operative event' in the FA 1985 pool?

4. The amount paid to acquire further shares on a rights issue ranks for indexation from the date on which the original shares were acquired. TRUE/FALSE?

5. What is the difference between a bonus issue and a rights issue?

6. Sasha sold all her shares in T Ltd on 1 September 2006 for £24,000. She had bought the shares on the following dates.

	No of shares	Cost £
1 September 1985	2,000	1,700
1 March 2006	2,000	6,000

   Calculate, before taper relief, the capital gains for 2006/07. Assume indexation factor September 1985 – April 1998 = 0.704

7. A Ltd acquired the following shares in X Ltd

	No of shares	Cost £
1 September 1985	1,000	5,000
28 July 2004	1,500	15,000

   A Ltd sold all the shares for £34,000 on 1 December 2006.

   Calculate the capital gain arising on the disposal.

   Indexation factors: September 1985 – July 2004 = 0.957; July 2004 – December 2006 = 0.061

Chapter 10:
DEFERRING TAXATION OF CAPITAL GAINS

chapter coverage

In this chapter we consider two circumstances in which the taxation of a gain may be deferred.

The basic principle is that a gain is deferred by deducting it from a base cost to be used to calculate a future gain. This lower base cost causes a larger gain to arise in the future. The deferred gain is often said to be 'held-over' or 'rolled-over'.

The topics that we shall cover are:

- replacement of business assets/Rollover relief
- gift relief

KNOWLEDGE AND UNDERSTANDING AND PERFORMANCE CRITERIA COVERAGE

knowledge and understanding

- Capital gains exemptions and reliefs on business assets including rollover relief and taper relief (Element 18.3)

Performance criteria

- Apply reliefs, deferrals and exemptions correctly

deferring taxation of capital gains

student notes

REPLACEMENT OF BUSINESS ASSETS/ROLLOVER RELIEF

A gain may be 'rolled-over' where it arises on the disposal of a business asset (the 'old' asset) if another business asset (the 'new' asset) is acquired.

The following conditions must be met.

- The old asset and the new asset must be used in a trade

- The old asset and the new asset must both be qualifying assets. Qualifying assets include:
    - Land and buildings used for the purpose of the trade
    - Fixed (that is, immovable) plant and machinery
    - Goodwill (for individuals only)

- Reinvestment of the proceeds of the old asset must take place in period beginning one year before and ending three years after the date of the disposal.

The new asset can be for use in a different trade from the old asset.

ROLLOVER RELIEF is available to both individuals and companies.

Deferral is obtained by deducting the gain on the old asset from the cost of the new asset. The gain deducted from the cost of the new asset is the gain before taper relief.

How it works

A freehold factory was purchased by a sole trader on 13 May 1998 for £60,000 and sold for £90,000 on 18 September 2006. A replacement factory was purchased on 6 December 2006 for £100,000. Rollover relief was claimed on the sale of the first factory.

Compute the revised base cost of the factory purchased in December 2006 taking account of the rolled over gain from the disposal in September 2006.

Solution

a) *Gain on sale September 2006*

	£
Disposal proceeds	90,000
Less: cost	(60,000)
Gain before taper relief	30,000

The gain before taper relief is eligible to be rolled over.

deferring taxation of capital gains

b) *Revised base cost of asset purchased in December 2006*

	£
Original cost	100,000
Less: rolled over gain	(30,000)
Revised base cost	70,000

Taper relief applies from 6 December 2006.

When the replacement asset is sold taper relief on that sale will only be given by reference to the holding period for that asset. Effectively, taper relief on the rolled over gain, for the period of ownership of the original asset, is lost.

How it works

Assume the replacement factory in the above example is sold in June 2008 for £110,000. Compute the gain arising after taper relief.

	£
Disposal proceeds	110,000
Less: revised base cost (see above)	(70,000)
Gain before taper relief	40,000

Taper relief of 50% is due as the replacement factory has been held for one complete year.

Gain after taper relief £20,000.

Activity 1

George bought a freehold factory for business use in August 2004 for £35,000. It was sold in March 2007 for £90,000. A replacement factory was purchased in April 2007 for £120,000. Compute the base cost of the replacement factory, taking into account any possible rolled over gain from the disposal in March 2007.

Activity 2

Louis bought office premises for £80,000 in July 2003. He sold them for £100,000 in May 2005. Louis bought a freehold factory for use in his business in June 2005 at a cost of £350,000. Louis sold the factory for £375,000 in September 2006. Louis made no other disposals and had no other capital assets in 2006/07.

Calculate the gain on sale of the factory, assuming rollover relief was claimed on the disposal of the office premises.

student notes

Sale proceeds not fully reinvested

If the proceeds of the sale of an asset are not fully reinvested in a new qualifying asset, an amount of the gain equal to the proceeds not reinvested is immediately chargeable. The balance of the gain can be rolled over.

How it works

Susannah realised a gain of £300,000 on the disposal of an office block used in her business. The office block was sold for £700,000. A new office block factory was bought for £600,000 in the following month.

The proceeds not reinvested are £100,000 so this amount of the gain is immediately chargeable. £200,000 of the gain can be rolled over and set against the base cost of the new office block. This means the base cost of the new office block is £(600,000 − 200,000) = £400,000.

> ### Activity 3
>
> A sole trader sold a factory in June 2006 for £670,000 realising a chargeable gain of £120,000. In September 2006 a replacement factory was bought for £650,000. Advise the sole trader as to whether a chargeable gain will arise on the sale of the first factory. Assume rollover relief is claimed where possible.

GIFT RELIEF

Individuals can claim GIFT RELIEF to defer a gain otherwise arising on the gift of a business asset. The gift is deemed to be made at market value. The deferred gain is the gain before taper relief.

The transferee is deemed to acquire the asset for its market value less the deferred gain. The transferee will start a new period for taper relief from the date of his acquisition.

How it works

John bought a business asset in 2004 for £20,000. On 1 May 2006 John gave the asset to Marie Louise. The market value of the asset on the date of the gift was £90,000.

Assuming gift relief is claimed, at what value is Marie Louise deemed to acquire the gift?

John is deemed to dispose of the asset for its market value of £90,000 so the gain arising on the gift is:

	£
Deemed disposal proceeds	90,000
Less: cost	(20,000)
Gain before taper relief	70,000

The gain before taper relief of £70,000 is deferred by setting it against the value of £90,000 at which Marie Louise is deemed to acquire the gift. Therefore Marie Louise is deemed to acquire the gift for £20,000 and this will be used as the base cost for future disposals.

Activity 4

Archie purchased business premises in July 2000 for £80,000. In December 2004 Archie gave the premises, then valued at £400,000, to Hugo and claimed gift relief. Hugo continued to run a business from the premises but decided to sell them in May 2006 for £675,000. Compute Hugo's chargeable gain on sale after taper relief.

Qualifying assets for gift relief purposes include:

a) Assets used in a trade carried on:

    i) by the donor, or
    ii) by the donor's personal company

b) Shares in:

    i) an unquoted trading company or
    ii) the donor's personal trading company.

A 'personal company' is one in which not less than 5% of the voting rights are controlled by the donor.

Activity 5

Deidre gives the following assets to Steve. Which, if any, are qualifying assets for the purposes of gift relief?

An antique painting

Quoted shares in a trading company of which Deidre controls 1%.

Unquoted trading company shares.

A freehold factory that Deidre has always used in her printing business.

Activity 6

Julie bought 10,000 shares in an unquoted trading company for £50,000 in July 2000. Julie gave her shares to Jack in May 2005 when they were worth £85,000. Jack sold the shares for £95,000 in December 2006.

Neither Julie nor Jack had made any other disposals in 2005/06 or 2006/07.

a) Calculate the gains arising if gift relief was not claimed

b) Calculate Jack's gain on sale after taper relief if gift relief was claimed on the gift from Julie

CHAPTER OVERVIEW

- Rollover relief can defer a gain when a qualifying business asset is replaced with another qualifying business asset

- Qualifying business assets for rollover relief include land and buildings, fixed plant and machinery and, for individuals, goodwill. Both the old and the new assets must be used for the purposes of a trade

> **KEY WORDS**
>
> **Rollover relief** can defer a gain when business assets are replaced
>
> **Gift relief** can defer a gain on a gift of business assets by an individual

- If sale proceeds are not fully reinvested an amount of the gain equal to the proceeds not reinvested is immediately chargeable. The remainder of the gain may be rolled over

- The rolled over gain is the gain before taper relief. It reduces the cost of the new asset

- The new asset must be acquired in the period commencing one year before and ending three years after the disposal

- Gift relief defers gains on the gift of business assets. The gain deferred is the gain before taper relief

- The transferee acquires the gift at its market value less the amount of the deferred gain

- Qualifying assets for gift relief include assets used in a trade by the donor or his personal company, unquoted shares in a trading company and shares in a personal trading company

- A personal company is a company in which the shareholder controls at least 5% of the voting rights

deferring taxation of capital gains

HOW MUCH HAVE YOU LEARNED?

1   L Ltd sold a factory on 10 November 2006. The company purchased the following assets:

Date of purchase	Asset
21 September 2005	Office block
15 February 2007	Freehold Factory
4 June 2008	Fork lift truck
8 December 2009	Freehold warehouse

    All of the above assets are used for the purpose of L Ltd's trade.

    Against which purchase may the company claim rollover relief in respect of the gain arising on disposal of the factory?

    A   Office block
    B   Factory
    C   Fork lift truck
    D   Warehouse

2   TJ Ltd bought land for £100,000 in March 2000. In March 2005, this land was sold for £400,000 and replacement land was bought for £380,000. The replacement land was sold in May 2006 for £500,000. Both pieces of land were used in TJ Ltd's trade.

    What is the chargeable gain arising in May 2006? Assume all available reliefs were claimed. Ignore indexation.

    A   £120,000
    B   £320,000
    C   £400,000
    D   £420,000

3   Provided both assets are used in Mr Astro's trade, a gain arising on the sale of freehold land and buildings can be rolled over against the cost of goodwill. TRUE/FALSE?

4   Freehold land and buildings are sold on 15 January 2007. By what date must replacement asset(s) be acquired if rollover relief is to be claimed?

5   Sara gave some jewellry to her daughter Emily. Can gift relief be claimed on this gift?

6   Tommy gave Sinbad a factory in June 2005 that had been used in his trade. The factory cost £50,000 in October 1999 and was worth £200,000 at the date of the gift. Sinbad sold the factory for £350,000 in May 2006. Show the gains arising if gift relief is claimed.

chapter 11:
COMPUTING PROFITS CHARGEABLE TO CORPORATION TAX

chapter coverage

In this chapter we see how to compute a company's profits chargeable to corporation tax. We also see that profits chargeable to corporation tax must be computed for accounting periods.

The topics that we shall cover are:

- profits chargeable to corporation tax
- long periods of account

KNOWLEDGE AND UNDERSTANDING AND PERFORMANCE CRITERIA COVERAGE

knowledge and understanding

- The computation of profit for corporation tax purposes including income, capital gains and charges (Element 18.4)

Performance criteria

- Enter adjusted trading profits and losses, capital allowances, investment income and capital gains in the corporation tax computation.

computing profits chargeable to corporation tax

student notes

PROFITS CHARGEABLE TO CORPORATION TAX

To arrive at the profits on which a company must pay tax you need to aggregate the company's various sources of income together with its chargeable gains. You should then deduct the amount of any gift aid donations paid. The resulting figure is known as the company's PROFITS CHARGEABLE TO CORPORATION TAX. The computation is shown in the following pro-forma:

	£
Trading profits (Schedule D Case I)	X
Interest (Schedule D Case III)	X
Rental income (Schedule A)	X
Other income (Schedule D Case VI)	X
Chargeable gains	X
Total profits	X
Less: Gift Aid donations paid	(X)
Profits chargeable to corporation tax (PCTCT)	X

Notice that dividends received from other companies are not included in the above computation. A company does not pay corporation tax on dividends received from other companies.

For historical reasons, income was classified into Schedules and, in some circumstances it was further divided into cases. This classification is becoming less important than it was in the past, so although we mention the Schedules and cases above, we will not usually use this terminology again in this Course Companion.

We will now look at each of the items in the above pro-forma in turn.

Trading profits

The trading profits of a company are, broadly, computed in the same way that the trading profits of a sole trader are computed. You should, therefore take the net profit in the company's accounts and adjust it for tax purposes in the same way as you would adjust a sole trader's accounts profit. We looked at this in Chapter 2.

One important difference is in the calculation of capital allowances. There is never a private use asset column in a company's capital allowance computation. This is because there is never any reduction of allowances to take account of any private use of an asset. The director or employee suffers a taxable benefit instead.

There may be a small difference in the name given to bad debts in a company's accounts. Where a company has followed International Accounting Standards in preparing its accounts, you will see bad debts referred to as impairment losses instead of bad debts.

computing profits chargeable to corporation tax

You may recall from Chapter 2 that royalties are not an allowable deduction when computing a sole trader's business profits. Similarly, royalties paid for non-trade purposes are not an allowable deduction for corporation tax purposes. Any such royalties paid may need to be added back in the computation of trading profits, but are deducted from other income. Non-trade royalties received will be included under other income in the computation of PCTCT. If they have been included in the accounts profit a deduction will need to be made to arrive at the tax adjusted profits.

For a company however, royalties that are paid/received for trade purposes should be included in trading profits on an accruals basis. This means that no adjustment to the accounts figure is needed if these items have been reflected in the accounts.

student notes

Activity 1

N Ltd makes up its accounts to 31 March each year. In the year to 31 March 2007, the profit and loss account showed the following:

	£	£
Gross trading profit (note)		514,000
General expenses	75,000	
Patent royalties paid (trade)	10,000	
		(85,000)
Net profit		429,000

Note. Gross trading profit includes:

	£
Non-trade copyright royalties received	4,000
Trade patent royalties received	10,000

The company had a pool of plant and machinery with a written down value of £15,000 as at 1 April 2006. On 1 December 2006, the company bought a car for £11,000. The car was used by a director of the company. It was agreed that 20% of the use of the car was private use by the director.

Show the profits chargeable to corporation tax for the year to 31 March 2007.

Interest

UK companies receive interest gross from banks and building societies. (i.e. no tax is deducted in advance from the amount received). Interest received from other UK companies (this includes debenture interest) is also received gross.

computing profits chargeable to corporation tax

student notes

Rental income

A company with rental income must pool the rents and expenses on all of its properties, to give a single profit or loss. Rental income is taxed on an accruals basis. You will not be expected to calculate rental income in Unit 18 (assessable under Unit 19). However, you may be given a profit or loss figure and required to deal with it in the corporation tax computation as appropriate

Chargeable gains

Companies do not pay capital gains tax. Instead their chargeable gains are included in the profits chargeable to corporation tax. A company's capital gains or allowable losses are computed in a similar way to individuals (see earlier in this Course Companion) but with a few major differences:

a) Indexation allowance calculations may include periods of ownership after 6 April 1998. Indexation is calculated to the month of disposal of an asset.

b) The FA 1985 pool for shares does not close at 5 April 1998: it runs to the month of disposal of the shares. This means that different matching rules are needed (see earlier in this Course Companion)

c) The taper relief does not apply

d) No annual exemption is available

Activity 2

P Ltd makes up accounts to 31 December each year. In the year to 31 December 2006, it had trading profits (adjusted for tax) of £200,000.

P Ltd sold the following assets:

March 2006   Factory for £350,000. Factory acquired in July 2000 for £225,000

October 2006 10,000 shares in Z plc for £100,000. P Ltd had acquired 8,000 shares in Z plc in April 1995 for £24,000 and a further 2,000 share in Z plc in January 2003 for £8,000

Show the profits chargeable to corporation tax for the year to 31 December 2006.

Indexation factors:

July 2000 to March 2006 = 0.141
April 1995 to January 2003 = 0.197
January 2003 to October 2006 = 0.107

computing profits chargeable to corporation tax

student notes

Gift aid donations

Charitable gifts of money qualify for tax relief under the gift aid scheme if they cannot be deducted as a trading expense (see Chapter 2).

For companies, gift aid donations paid are deducted in computing PCTCT as shown in the proforma above.

Sometimes a gift aid donation will have been deducted in computing the accounts profit. If this is the case, the amount deducted must be added back in computing taxable trading profits.

Income received/paid net of tax

Companies receive patent royalties from individuals net of 22% tax. This means that the individual withholds 22% tax and pays it over to HMRC on the company's behalf.

Income received net of tax is included within the corporation tax computation at its gross equivalent. For example £7,800 of patent royalties received net of tax would need to be grossed up by multiplying by 100/78 to include £10,000 within either trading profits or other income as described above.

Patent royalties paid by a company to individuals are paid net of 22% tax whilst interest paid to individuals is paid net of 20% tax. It is the gross amount which is deducted in the corporation tax computation, either from trading profits or from interest or other income as described above.

The way in which relief is given for the tax suffered at source is covered later in this Course Companion. Essentially, if tax suffered on income received net exceeds tax deducted from patent royalties and interest paid net, the difference is subtracted in calculating the mainstream corporation tax due.

Payments of royalties and interest by a company to a company are made gross and so there are no income tax implications.

121

computing profits chargeable to corporation tax

student notes

How it works

ST Ltd draws up accounts for the year ended 31 March 2007 which show the following results:

	£	£
Gross profit on trading		180,000
Dividends received from UK companies		7,900
Patent royalties received (actual amount received net)		222
Less: Trade expenses (all allowable)	82,400	
Bank interest payable (overdraft)	200	
Royalties paid (gross)	1,000	
Debenture interest payable (gross)	3,200	
Payment to charity under Gift Aid	100	
Depreciation	9,022	(95,922)
Profit before taxation		92,200

Notes

1. The capital allowances for the accounting period total £5,500.

2. The royalties received had been paid by a private individual on 31 March 2007 on rights acquired by the company as an investment on 1 October 2006. The royalties are payable six monthly in arrears.

3. The royalties paid were paid in arrears for a trading purposes to an unconnected UK company on 31 March 2007 and are equal to the amount accrued for the year.

4. The debentures were issued on 1 August 2006 to raise working capital. The £3,200 charged in the accounts represents six months interest (£2,400) paid and two months accrued;

5. A capital gain of £13,867 arose in the year. It is not included above.

You are required to compute the profits chargeable to corporation tax.

Solution

student notes

T LTD
CALCULATION OF PROFITS CHARGEABLE TO CORPORATION TAX
YEAR ENDED 31 MARCH 2007

	£	£
Net profit per accounts		92,200
Less: dividends received	7,900	
patent royalties received	222	
		(8,122)
		84,078
Add: gift aid payment	100	
depreciation	9,022	
		9,122
		93,200
Less: capital allowances		(5,500)
Trading profits		87,700
Other income (W)		285
Chargeable gain		13,867
		101,852
Less: charges paid:		
gift aid payment		(100)
PROFIT CHARGEABLE TO CORPORATION TAX		101,752

Working

Other income (Schedule D Case VI)

Patent royalties receivable

$(222 \times 100/78) = £285$

The royalties paid have been charged against trading profits on an accruals basis and are for a trading purpose so no adjustment is required.

Note. The dividends received from other UK companies are not included within PCTCT.

computing profits chargeable to corporation tax

student notes

> ## Activity 3
>
> A company had the following results in the year ended 31 March 2007.
>
> | | £ |
> |---|---|
> | Trading profits | 85,000 |
> | Bank deposit interest income | 6,000 |
> | Building society interest income | 1,500 |
> | UK dividends received | 3,200 |
> | Capital gains | 2,950 |
> | Gift Aid donation paid | 15,200 |
>
> What are the company's PCTCT?

LONG PERIODS OF ACCOUNT

A PERIOD OF ACCOUNT is the period for which a company prepares its accounts.

An ACCOUNTING PERIOD is the period for which corporation tax is charged.

A company's accounting period is often the same as its period of account. However, an accounting period cannot be longer than twelve months. This means that if a period of account exceeds 12 months, it must be divided into two accounting periods: the first will comprise the first 12 months and the second will comprise the balance. It is necessary to prepare separate computations of profits chargeable to corporation tax for each accounting period.

The following rules are applied in apportioning income, gains and gift aid donations between accounting periods:

a) Trading income (before deducting capital allowances) is apportioned on a time basis;

b) Capital allowances and balancing charges are calculated separately for each accounting period;

c) Rental income is apportioned on a time basis as applies for trading income;

d) Interest income on non trading loans is allocated to the period in which it accrues;

e) Other income is apportioned on a time basis;

f) Chargeable gains are allocated to the accounting period in which the disposal takes place;

g) Gift aid donations are allocated to the accounting period in which they are paid.

The apportionment rules are illustrated in the following example.

How it works

Beta Ltd makes up its accounts for a 15 month period ended 31 March 2007. Trading income is £150,000 for the 15 month period. No capital allowances were due for the period.

Bank deposit interest of £672 was credited on 31 March 2006 and £1,402 on 31 March 2007. The amounts accrued at 1 January 2006 and 1 January 2007 were £412 and £950 respectively.

The company made a payment of £3,630 under the gift aid scheme on 4 March 2006.

Disposals of chargeable assets realised a chargeable gain of £5,300 on 14 March 2006 and a chargeable gain of £807 on 14 March 2007.

Solution

BETA LTD – CORPORATION TAX COMPUTATION
PERIOD 1 JANUARY 2006 TO 31 MARCH 2007

	Note	AP 1.1.06 – 31.12.06 £	AP 1.1.07 – 31.3.07 £
Trading income (12/15:3/15)	1	120,000	30,000
Interest	W	1,210	452
Chargeable gains	2	5,300	807
Less: Gift Aid	3	(3,630)	–
PCTCT		122,880	31,259

Notes

1. Trading income is time apportioned.

2. Chargeable gains are allocated to the period in which the relevant disposal takes place.

3. Gift Aid donations are allocated to the period in which they are paid.

student notes

Working

Interest income is allocated to the period in which it accrued as follows:

	12m to 31.12.06 £	3m to 31.3.07 £
Bank interest credited	672	1,402
Less: opening accrual	(412)	(950)
Add: closing accrual	950	–
Amount accrued	1,210	452

Activity 4

X Ltd makes up an 15 month set of accounts to 30 June 2007 with the following results.

	£
Trading profits	300,000
Interest 15 months @ £500 accruing per month	7,500
Capital gain (1 May 2006 disposal)	250,000
Less: Gift aid donation (paid 31.12.06)	(50,000)
	507,500

What are the profits chargeable to corporation tax for each of the accounting periods based on the above accounts?

computing profits chargeable to corporation tax

CHAPTER OVERVIEW

- To compute PCTCT aggregate all sources of income and chargeable gains. Deduct gift aid donations

- Patent royalties are received/paid from individuals net of 22% tax. Interest paid to individuals is paid net of 20% tax. Include the gross amounts in the computation of PCTCT

- An accounting period cannot exceed 12 months in length

- A long period of account must be split into two accounting periods: a period of 12 months and then a period covering the balance of the period of account

- A company's chargeable gains are calculated in the same way as an individual's except that for companies:
    - there is no taper relief or annual exemption
    - indexation runs to the date of disposal of an asset
    - for shares the Finance Act 1985 pool continues beyond 6 April 1998

> **KEY WORDS**
>
> **Profits chargeable to corporation tax** The profits on which a company must pay corporation tax
>
> **Period of account** The period for which a company prepares its accounts
>
> **Accounting period** The period for which corporation tax is charged

computing profits chargeable to corporation tax

HOW MUCH HAVE YOU LEARNED?

1. In computing profits chargeable to corporation tax, how much would be included in respect of the following items (actual amount received in May 2006 in each case):

    a) building society interest : £6,000
    b) bank deposit interest : £3,900
    c) dividends from UK companies : £7,500
    d) patent royalties received from an individual : £5,850

    There were no amounts accrued at the beginning or end of the year.

2. A company shows the following accrual amounts (gross) for interest for the year ended 31 March 2007:

    Interest payable = £4,000

    The interest payable was paid on a loan taken out for trading purposes. How will this be treated in the corporation tax computation?

3. On 30 June 2006, Edelweiss Ltd makes a donation to Help the Aged of £385. The donation was made under the gift aid scheme.

    What deduction is available in respect of the charitable donation?

4. X Ltd had been making up accounts to 31 May for several years. Early in 2006 the directors decided to make accounts to 31 August 2006 (instead of 31 May 2006) and annually thereafter at 31 August. The two chargeable accounting periods for CT purposes will be:

    A   1 June 2005 – 31 March 2006   and   1 April 2006 – 31 August 2006
    B   1 June 2005 – 31 May 2006   and   1 June 2006 – 31 August 2006
    C   1 June 2005 – 31 December 2005   and   1 January 2006 – 31 August 2006
    D   1 June 2005 – 31 August 2005   and   1 September 2005 – 31 August 2006

5. C Ltd prepares accounts for the 16 months to 30 April 2007. The results are as follows:

	£
Business profits	320,000
Bank interest (accrued evenly over period)	1,600
Chargeable gain (realised 1.1.07)	20,000
Gift aid donation (paid 31.12.06)	15,000

    Calculate the PCTCT for the accounting periods based on the above results.

chapter 12:
COMPUTING CORPORATION TAX PAYABLE

chapter coverage

In this chapter we see how to compute the corporation tax that a company must pay on its PCTCT. We start by looking at single companies with 12 month accounting periods. We then consider the effect of short accounting periods and the effect of a company being associated with other companies. Finally, we look at the marginal rate of tax that applies when a company has profits between certain limits.

The topics that we shall cover are:

- determining the rate of corporation tax
- computing the corporation tax liability
- short accounting periods
- associated companies
- the marginal rate of tax

KNOWLEDGE AND UNDERSTANDING AND PERFORMANCE CRITERIA COVERAGE

knowledge and understanding

- Calculation of Corporation Tax payable by starting, small, large and marginal companies including those with associated companies (Element 18.4)

Performance criteria

- Calculate Corporation Tax due, taking account of marginal relief

computing corporation tax payable

student notes

DETERMINING THE RATE OF CORPORATION TAX

Corporation tax rates are fixed for financial years. A FINANCIAL YEAR runs from 1 April to the following 31 March and is identified by the calendar year in which it begins.

For example, the year ended 31 March 2007 is the Financial Year 2006 (FY 2006). This should not be confused with a tax year, which runs from 6 April to the following 5 April.

The corporation tax rate for any particular Financial Year depends on the level of a company's 'PROFITS'. 'Profits' are PCTCT plus the grossed-up amount of dividends received from other companies. The grossed-up amount of a dividend received is the dividend received grossed up by multiplying by 100/90.

How it works

A company had profits chargeable to corporation tax of £400,000 in the year ended 31 March 2007. In this year it received dividends of £9,000. What are the company's 'profits'?

Profits are:

	£
PCTCT	400,000
Dividend (£9,000 × 100/90)	10,000
'Profits'	410,000

Activity 1

A company had PCTCT of £60,000 and dividends received of £4,500 in the year to 31 December 2006. What were the company's 'profits' for the year?

COMPUTING THE CORPORATION TAX LIABILITY

In this section we look at how to compute corporation tax for a twelve month accounting period where the company does not have associated companies. We will look at other situations later in this chapter.

To work out the CT rate that applies 'profits' have to be compared with various limits. These limits will be given to you in the tax rates and allowances tables in the exam.

computing corporation tax payable

The full rate of corporation tax

The full rate of corporation tax (CT) for Financial Year 2006 is 30%.

If a company's 'profits' exceed the small companies upper limit for Financial Year 2006 the full rate of corporation tax is charged for the year. For the Financial Year 2006 the small companies' upper limit is £1,500,000.

How it works

J Ltd had the following results in the year to 31 March 2007:

PCTCT £1,450,000
Dividend received £90,000

Calculate the corporation tax due for the year.

'Profits' for the year are £1,450,000 + (£90,000 × 100/90) = £1,550,000

As 'profits' are above the small companies' upper limit, the full rate of corporation tax applies.

Corporation tax due is £1,450,000 × 30% = £435,000

Note that although 'profits' are used to determine the rate of CT, CT is only charged on PCTCT.

Activity 2

For the year to 31 March 2007, M Ltd had the following results:

	£
PCTCT	2,100,000
Dividend received	45,000

What is M Ltd's corporation tax liability for the year?

Small companies' marginal relief

Small companies' marginal relief (sometimes called taper relief) applies where the 'profits' of an accounting period are between the small companies' lower and upper limits. For Financial Year 2006 these limits are £300,000 and £1,500,000.

student notes

computing corporation tax payable

student notes

To calculate corporation tax first calculate the corporation tax at the full rate on PCTCT and then deduct:

(M − P) × 1/P × marginal relief fraction

where M = upper limit (currently £1,500,000)
P = 'profits'
I = PCTCT

The marginal relief fraction is 11/400 for FY 2006.

You will be given the marginal relief formula and the marginal relief fraction in the tax rates and allowances tables in the exam.

How it works

B Ltd has the following results for the year ended 31 March 2007:

	£
PCTCT	280,000
Dividend received 1 December 2006	45,000

Calculate the corporation tax liability.

Firstly, calculate 'profits' to determine the rate of corporation tax:

	£
PCTCT	280,000
Dividends received	50,000
'Profits'	330,000

As 'profits' are between the small companies' lower and upper limits, small companies' marginal relief applies:

	£
PCTCT @ 30%	84,000
Less: 11/400 £(1,500,000 − 330,000) × $\frac{280,000}{330,000}$	(27,300)
	56,700

Activity 3

For the year to 31 March 2007, M Ltd, has the following results:

	£
Trading profits	220,000
Dividend received from UK company	90,000

What is M Ltd's corporation tax liability for the year?

computing corporation tax payable

Small companies rate (SCR)

The SCR of corporation tax (19% for FY 2006) applies to the profits chargeable to corporation tax of companies whose 'profits' are below the small companies rate lower limit. For FY 2006 this limit is £300,000.

How it works

student notes

... Ltd had the following results for the year ended 31 March 2007:

	£
PCTCT	100,000
Dividend received	18,000

Compute the corporation tax liability.

Firstly calculate 'profits':

	£
PCTCT	100,000
Dividend received (× 100/90)	20,000
Profits	120,000

As profits are between £50,000 and £300,000, the small companies' rate of tax is applied to PCTCT.

CT payable 19% × £100,000 = £19,000

Activity 4

BD Ltd had the following results for the year to 31 March 2007:

PCTCT = £60,000

No dividends were received in the year.

Compute the corporation tax liability for the year.

The starting rate up to FY05

For FY05 a starting rate of corporation tax of 0% (i.e. there is no liability) applied to companies with 'profits' of up to the starting rate lower limit.

The starting rate lower limit for FY 2005 was £10,000.

computing corporation tax payable

student notes

How it works

D Limited has the following income for the year ended 31 March 2006.

a) PCTCT £5,000, and
b) Dividend received of £270.

Calculate the corporation tax liability for the year.

'Profits' are £5,000 + £270 × 100/90 = £5,300.

There is no corporation tax liability as 'profits' are below the starting rate lower limit.

Activity 5

H Ltd has PCTCT of £3,000 and dividends received of £900 in the year to 31 March 2006. What is the corporation tax liability.

Starting rate marginal relief up to FY05

Up to FY05, there was a starting rate marginal relief similar to that for small companies. You might need to calculate tax for FY05 so you need to know these rules, which are explained below.

For companies with 'profits' above the starting rate lower limit and up to the starting rate upper limit, the small companies' rate less a starting rate marginal relief applied, for FY 2005. These lower and upper limits were £10,000 and £50,000 respectively. The formula for calculating this marginal relief was the same as that given above except that 'M' was the upper limit for starting rate purposes. (£50,000 – FY 2005). The fraction used here was 19/400 for FY 2005.

How it works

A Ltd has the following income for its year ended 31 March 2006:

	£
PCTCT	40,000
Dividend received	4,500

Calculate the corporation tax liability.

'Profits' are £40,000 + £4,500 × 100/90 = £45,000.

computing corporation tax payable

This means starting rate marginal relief applied.

		£
£40,000 × 19%		7,600
Less: 19/400 £(50,000 – 45,000) × $\frac{40,000}{45,000}$		(211)
Corporation tax liability		7,389

Activity 6

D Ltd had PCTCT of £20,000 for the year to 31 March 2006. The company received dividends in the year of £900. Calculate the company's corporation tax liability for the year.

Changes in the rate – Accounting periods straddling 31 March

If there is a change in the corporation tax rate, and a company's accounting period does not fall entirely within one financial year, the profits of the accounting period are apportioned to the two financial years on a time basis. Note that the profits as a whole are apportioned. You do not look at components of the profits individually, unlike apportionment of profits of a long period of account to two accounting periods.

The 'profits' falling into each financial year determines the rate of corporation tax that applies to the PCTCT of that year. You will need to compare these profits to time apportioned upper and lower limits in the Financial Year you are considering.

How it works

Claude Ltd makes up accounts to 30 September each year. For the year ended 30 September 2006 it had PCTCT of £9,000. It received dividends of £270.

Calculate the corporation tax liability.

First divide the PCTCT and profits between the financial years.

	FY 2005 6 months to 31.3.06 £	FY 2006 6 months to 30.9.06 £
PCTCT (divided 6:6)	4,500	4,500
Dividends (× 100/90)(divided 6:6)	150	150
	4,650	4,650

computing corporation tax payable

student notes

Secondly time apportion the lower limit for starting rate (FY05 only)

£10,000 × 6/12 = 5,000

Starting rate applies

	£
Tax on PCTCT	
FY05	
£4,500 × 0%	0
FY06	
£4,500 × 19%	855
Corporation tax payable	855

Activity 7

Frances Ltd makes up accounts to 31 December each year. For the year ended 31 December 2006 its profit and loss account was as follows.

	£
PCTCT	40,000
Dividends plus tax credits	2,500
'Profits'	42,500

Calculate the corporation tax liability for the year.

Short accounting periods

We have seen above how to compute a corporation tax liability for a 12 month accounting period. If an accounting period lasts for less than 12 months the lower and upper 'profits' limits discussed above are reduced proportionately.

How it works

For the six months to 31 October 2006 L Ltd had PCTCT of £40,000 and no dividends received. Compute the corporation tax payable.

Firstly, work out 'profits' as usual:

	£
PCTCT	40,000
Dividends	0
'Profits'	40,000

Next compare this with the small companies marginal relief lower limit applicable in the short accounting period:

Small companies lower limit £300,000 × 6/12 = £150,000

computing corporation tax payable

student notes

s 'profits' are below the small companies' lower limit the small companies te of tax applies:

T liability £40,000 × 19% = £7,600

Activity 8

A Ltd had PCTCT of £200,000 in the nine month accounting period to 31 December 2006. The company received dividends of £45,000 in this period. Calculate A Ltd's corporation tax liability for the nine month period to 31 December 2006.

ASSOCIATED COMPANIES

he expression ASSOCIATED COMPANY in tax has no connection with nancial accounting.

or tax purposes a company is associated with another company if either ontrols the other or if both are under the control of the same person or ersons (individuals, partnerships or companies).

a company has one or more 'associated companies', then the 'profit' limits r starting rate and small companies rate purposes are divided by the umber of associated companies + 1 (for the company itself).

ompanies which have only been associated for part of an accounting period e deemed to have been associated for the whole period for the purpose of etermining the 'profit' limits.

n associated company is ignored for these purposes if it has not carried on ny trade or business at any time in the accounting period (or the part of the eriod during which it was associated). This means that you should ignore ormant companies. However, you should include non UK companies.

How it works

or the year to 31 March 2007, T Ltd, a company with one associated ompany, has the following results:

	£
PCTCT	330,000
Dividend received from UK company	45,000

alculate T Ltd's corporation tax liability for the year.

137

computing corporation tax payable

student notes

Firstly compute 'profits'

	£
PCTCT	330,000
Dividends £45,000 × 100/90	50,000
Profits	380,000

Next compare 'profits' to the lower and upper limits:

Small companies rate lower limit £300,000 × 1/2 = £150,000
Small companies rate upper limit £1,500,000 × 1/2 = £750,000

The limits are divided by two as there are two companies which are associated with each other.

As 'profits' are between these limits, small companies' rate marginal relief applies:

	£
£330,000 × 30%	99,000
Less: Small companies marginal relief	
$11/400 \; £(750{,}000 - 380{,}000) \times \dfrac{330{,}000}{380{,}000}$	(8,836)
	90,164

Activity 9

S Ltd, a company with two associated companies, had PCTCT of £360,000 in the year to 31 March 2007. Dividends of £22,500 were received in the year. Compute the company's corporation tax liability.

THE MARGINAL RATE OF TAX

In your exam you may need to be aware that there is a marginal rate of tax of 32.75% that applies to PCTCT between the small companies' limits.

This is calculated as follows:

	£		£
Upper limit	1,500,000	@ 30%	450,000
Lower limit	(300,000)	@ 19%	(57,000)
Difference	1,200,000		393,000

$$\dfrac{393{,}000}{1{,}200{,}000} = 32.75\%$$

Effectively any PCTCT (here £1,200,000) falling between the small companies upper and lower limits is taxed at a rate of 32.75%

computing corporation tax payable

How it works

student notes

A Ltd has PCTCT of £350,000 for the year ended 31 March 2007. Its corporation tax liability is:

	£
£350,000 × 30%	105,000
Less: Small companies' marginal relief	
11/400 £(1,500,000 − 350,000)	(31,625)
	73,375

This is the same as calculating tax at:

19% × £300,000 + 32.75% × £50,000 = £57,000 + £16,375 = £73,375

Consequently tax is charged at an effective rate of 32.75% on PCTCT that exceeds the small companies' lower limit.

Note that although there is an effective corporation tax charge of 32.75%, this rate of tax is never used in actually calculating corporation tax. The rate is just an effective marginal rate that you must be aware of.

The effective marginal rate of tax when PCTCT fell between the starting rate limits in FY05 was 23.75%. Again, this was an effective marginal rate of tax that you need to be aware of but it was a rate that was never actually used in working out the CT charge. It was calculated as:

£			£
50,000	@	19%	9,500
(10,000)	@	0%	Nil
40,000			9,500

$$\frac{9,500}{40,000} = 23.75\%$$

PCTCT falling into the band (here £40,000) suffers tax at an effective rate of 23.75%.

It may be important to consider the effective rate of tax suffered by a company when you are deciding how best to relieve losses. However, you do not need to remember how to perform the above computations calculating the marginal rate.

computing corporation tax payable

CHAPTER OVERVIEW

- The rate of corporation tax due in a Financial Year depends on the level of a company's 'profits'

- 'Profits' need to be compared with the upper and lower limits for starting rate (FY05) and small companies' rate purposes

- Reduce the limits proportionately in short accounting periods

- Divide the limits by the number of associated companies + 1 (for the company itself)

- Tax may be due at the full rate, the small companies' rate or (FY05) at the starting rate. Marginal relief applies when 'profits' are between certain limits

- If an accounting period straddles 31 March, PCTCT and 'Profits' need to be apportioned to the relevant FYs if the rates of tax are different in those FYs

KEY WORDS

A **Financial Year** runs from 1 April to the following 31 March and is identified by the calendar year in which it begins

'**Profits**' are PCTCT plus the grossed-up amount of dividends received from other companies

A company is **associated** with another company if either controls the other or if both are under the control of the same person or persons (individuals, partnerships or companies)

computing corporation tax payable

HOW MUCH HAVE YOU LEARNED?

1 S Ltd, a company with no associated companies, had profits chargeable to corporation tax of £255,000 for its six month accounting period to 31 March 2007. No dividends were paid or received in the period.

Its corporation tax liability for the period will be:

A £48,450
B £62,887
C £72,587
D £76,500

2 G Ltd, a company with no associated companies, made up accounts for the nine month period to 31 December 2006.

The total profits for this period were £55,000, including £5,000 of gross dividends. What will CT liability for the period will be?

3 J Ltd, a company with no associated companies, had profits chargeable to corporation tax of £9,000 in the year ended 31 December 2006. No dividends were received in the year.

Its corporation tax liability for the year will be:

A £Nil
B £810
C £1,282
D £1,710

4 S Ltd, a company with one associated company, had profits chargeable to corporation tax of £180,000 for the nine month period to 31 March 2007.

Its corporation tax liability for the year will be:

A £34,200
B £43,481
C £47,779
D £54,000

5 VAC Ltd, a company with no associated companies, has profits chargeable to corporation tax for the year to 31 March 2007 of £750,000.

What is the marginal rate of corporation tax paid by the company on its profits between £300,000 and £750,000?

A 19%
B 23.75%
C 30%
D 32.75%

6 When does Financial Year 2006 begin and end?

chapter 13:
CORPORATION TAX LOSSES

chapter coverage

In this chapter we look at the methods by which a company may obtain relief for any trading losses it incurs. We also look at how relief may be obtained for various non-trading losses.

The topics that we shall cover are:

- relieving trading losses
- relief against future trading profits
- relief against total profits
- relieving non-trading losses
- choosing loss relief

KNOWLEDGE AND UNDERSTANDING AND PERFORMANCE CRITERIA COVERAGE

knowledge and understanding

- Set-off of trading losses incurred by companies (Element 18.4)

Performance criteria

- Set-off and deduct loss reliefs and charges correctly

corporation tax losses

student notes

RELIEVING TRADING LOSSES

You need to be aware of the following three methods by which a company may obtain relief for its trading losses:

a) carry forward against future trading profits;
b) set-off against current profits;
c) carry back against earlier profits.

We will look at each of these three methods of obtaining loss relief below.

When doing questions involving corporation tax losses it is useful to have standardised layout. Your answer should be divided into two parts – the assessments and a loss memorandum. The examples in this session show the most convenient way of laying out your answer.

RELIEF AGAINST FUTURE TRADING PROFITS

A company can claim to set a trading loss against profits from the same trade in future accounting periods. Relief is given against the first available trading profits. This relief is often known as s393(1) RELIEF.

How it works

P Ltd has the following results for the three years to 31 March 2007:

	Year ended 31 March		
	2005	2006	2007
	£	£	£
Trading profit/(loss)	(8,000)	3,000	6,000
Bank interest	0	4,000	2,000

You are required to calculate the profits chargeable to corporation tax for all three years showing the extent of any losses available to carry forward as at 1 April 2007.

Solution

	Year ended 31 March		
	2005	2006	2007
	£	£	£
Trading profit	NIL	3,000	6,000
Less: s393(1) relief	–	(3,000) i)	(5,000) ii)
Bank interest	–	4,000	2,000
PCTCT	NIL	4,000	3,000

144

Loss memorandum

	£
Loss for year ended 31 March 2005	8,000
Loss carried forward at 1 April 2005	8,000
s393(1) relief year ended 31 March 2006	(3,000) i)
	5,000
Loss carried forward at 1 April 2006	5,000
s393(1) relief year ended 31 March 2007	(5,000) ii)
Loss carried forward under s393(1) at 1 April 2007	NIL

Note that the carried forward loss is set against the trading profits in future years. It cannot be set against other income such as the bank interest.

Activity 1

On 1 April 2006 M Ltd had the following amount brought forward:

Trading losses £50,000

M Ltd's results for the year to 31 March 2007 were:

	£
Trading profits	40,000
Rental income	25,000
Capital gain	2,000

Show the PCTCT for the year to 31 March 2007.

What amount, if any, of the trading losses remain to be carried forward at 1 April 2007?

RELIEF AGAINST TOTAL PROFITS

Continuing trades

A company may claim to offset a trading loss incurred in an accounting period against total profits (before deducting gift aid donations) of the same accounting period. This relief is known as s393A RELIEF. Note that gift aid donations may sometimes be referred to as non-trade charges on income.

A trading loss that cannot be fully relieved against profits of the same accounting period may be carried back and relieved against profits of the twelve months immediately preceding the loss making period. S393A relief must be set-off in the loss making period before carrying back the balance of the loss.

It is possible to set a loss against total profits in the current period but not to make a carry back claim.

corporation tax losses

student notes

Where the loss is being carried back it is set against profits before the deduction of gift aid donations. Any gift aid donations that become unrelieved, as a result of a carry back claim, are lost.

A s393A claim cannot specify how much of the loss is to apply and, once made, must relieve profits to the maximum possible extent.

Any loss remaining unrelieved after s393A claims must be carried forward under s393(1) against future profits of the same trade.

S393A relief is optional. Conversely, s393(1) relief must be taken against the first available profits of the trade.

How it works

Patagonia Ltd has the following results for the three accounting periods to 31 July 2006:

	Year ended 31 July		
	2004	2005	2006
	£	£	£
Trading profit (loss)	20,000	15,000	(50,000)
Building society interest	1,000	400	3,300
Charges on income:			
Gift aid		600	500	–

Show the profits chargeable to corporation tax for all years affected. Assume loss relief is claimed under s393A where possible.

Solution

	Year ended 31 July		
	2004	2005	2006
	£	£	£
Trading profit	20,000	15,000	–
Interest	1,000	400	3,300
	21,000	15,400	3,300
Less: s393A current period relief	–	–	(3,300)
	21,000	15,400	–
Less: s393A carry back	–	(15,400)	–
Less: gift aid	(600)	–	–
PCTCT	20,400	NIL	NIL
Unrelieved gift aid donations	–	500	–

Note. Trading losses can only be carried back to set against profits in the previous 12 months.

corporation tax losses

Loss memorandum

	£
Loss incurred in year ended 31 July 2006	50,000
Less: s393A – current period relief (year ended 31 July 2006)	(3,300)
	46,700
Less: s393A – carry back 12 months to 31 July 2005	(15,400)
Loss carried forward under s393(1)	31,300

If the accounting period immediately prior to the loss making period is for less than twelve months, two accounting periods will fall into the twelve month carry back period. The more recent accounting period is relieved in priority to the earlier accounting period. If only part of an accounting period falls in the twelve month carry back period, profits available for relief are apportioned on a time basis. You can see how this works in the following activity.

Activity 2

JB Ltd had the following results in the three accounting periods to 31 March 2007:

	Year ended 30 Sept 2005 £	Six months to 31 March 2006 £	Year ended 31 March 2007 £
Trading profits/(loss)	50,000	60,000	(100,000)
Gift Aid donation	(10,000)	(30,000)	(15,000)

What amount, if any, of the trading loss incurred in the year ended 31 March 2007 may be relieved under s393A in the year ended 30 September 2005?

student notes

corporation tax losses

student notes

RELIEVING NON-TRADING LOSSES

Capital losses

Capital losses can only be set against current or future capital gains, never against income.

The following activity includes an example of this.

Activity 3

Y Ltd had the following results for the three years to 31 March 2007:

	Year ended 31 March		
	2005 £	2006 £	2007 £
Trading profits/(loss)	50,000	40,000	(90,000)
Bank interest	10,000	5,000	5,000
Chargeable gain/(allowable loss)	(7,000)	–	12,000

Calculate PCTCT for each year assuming the company makes claims under s393A.

Losses arising from the rental of property

Rental losses are first set off against other income and gains of the company for the current period.

Any excess is then carried forward as a rental loss as if it had arisen in the later accounting period for offset against future income (of all descriptions).

CHOOSING LOSS RELIEF

Several alternative loss reliefs may be available. In making a choice consider:

a) The rate at which relief will be obtained:

   i) 30% at the full rate (FYs 2005 and 2006)

   ii) 19% at the small companies' rate (FYs 2005 and 2006)

   iii) 0% at the starting rate (FY 2005 only)

   iv) 23.75% if the starting rate marginal relief applies (FY 2005 only)

   v) 32.75% if the small companies' marginal relief applies (FYs 2005 and 2006)

   We previously outlined how the 23.75% and 32.75% marginal rates are calculated. Remember these are just marginal rates of tax; they are never actually used in computing a company's corporation tax.

b) If the carry back of a loss takes profits below the starting rate upper limit, consider whether the minimum rate of 19% needs to be applied in respect of any distribution to individual shareholders.

c) How quickly relief will be obtained: s393A relief is quicker than s393(1) relief.

d) The extent to which relief for gift aid donations might be lost.

corporation tax losses

CHAPTER OVERVIEW

- Trading losses may be set against future trading income

- S393A relief is given against total profits before deducting gift aid donations

- S393A relief is available in the loss making period and in the previous 12 months

- A claim for current period s393A relief can be made without a carry back claim

- A claim for current period relief must be made before a loss is carried back

- Capital losses can be set against capital gains of the same or future accounting periods

- Rental losses are first set-off against other income and gains of the current period and any excess is carried forward as a rental loss in the next period

- When selecting a loss relief, firstly consider the rate at which relief is obtained and, secondly, the timing of the relief

KEY WORDS

S393(1) relief allows a company to set a trading loss against profits from the same trade in future accounting periods

S393A relief allows a trading loss to be set against total profits, before deducting gift aid donations. The relief is available in the loss making period and in the previous 12 months (or, previous 36 months if the trade is ceasing)

corporation tax losses

HOW MUCH HAVE YOU LEARNED?

1   a)   CR Ltd has the following results for the two years to 31 March 2007:

	Year ended 31 March 2006 £	Year ended 31 March 2007 £
Trading profit (loss)	170,000	(320,000)
Interest	5,000	50,000
Capital gain (loss)	(20,000)	12,000
Gift aid payment	5,000	5,000

What amount of trading losses remain to be carried forward at 1 April 2007 assuming that all possible s393A claims are made?

A   £83,000
B   £95,000
C   £100,000
D   £105,000

b)   What amount of capital loss remains to be carried forward at 1 April 2007?

c)   What is the amount of unrelieved gift donations?

2   JB Ltd had the following results in the three accounting periods to 31 March 2007:

	Year ended 30 September 2005	Six months to 31 March 2006	Year ended 31 March 2007
Trading profit/(loss)	40,000	60,000	(100,000)
Gift Aid	(10,000)	(30,000)	(15,000)

What amount, if any, of the trading loss incurred in the year ended 31 March 2007 may be relieved under s393A in the year ended 30 September 2005?

A   £NIL
B   £20,000
C   £25,000
D   £40,000

151

chapter 14:
NATIONAL INSURANCE

chapter coverage

In this chapter we see that the self employed must pay two types of national insurance contribution (NIC). We will see how to calculate these contributions. We also see that employer's must pay two types of NIC and we will see how to calculate these contributions.

The topics that we shall cover are:

- NICs payable by the self employed
- NICs payable by employers

KNOWLEDGE AND UNDERSTANDING AND PERFORMANCE CRITERIA COVERAGE

knowledge and understanding

- Calculation of National Insurance Contributions payable by self employed persons and employers of not contracted out employees (Elements 18.2 & 18.4)

Performance criteria

- Identify the National Insurance Contributions payable by employers
- Identify the National Insurance Contributions payable by self-employed individuals

student notes

NICs PAYABLE BY THE SELF EMPLOYED

The self employed (ie sole traders and partners) must pay two types of NIC

a) CLASS 2 CONTRIBUTIONS, and
b) CLASS 4 CONTRIBUTIONS

Class 2 contributions are payable at a flat rate of £2.10 a week. It is possible to be excepted from Class 2 contributions if annual profits are less than £4,465.

Class 4 contributions are based on the level of the individual's business profits. Main rate contributions are calculated by applying a fixed percentage (8% for 2006/07) to the individual's profits between the lower limit (£5,035 for 2006/07) and the upper limit (£33,540 for 2006/07). Additional rate contributions are 1% (from 2005/06) on profits above the upper limit.

The rates of Class 2 and Class 4 NICs will be given to you in the exam.

How it works

If Jon had 'profits' of £40,000 for 2006/07 his Class 4 liability would be calculated in the following way:

	£
Profits (upper limit)	33,540
Less: lower limit	(5,035)
	28,505

	£
Class 4 NICs = 8% × £28,505	2,280.40
1% × (40,000 – 33,540)	64.60
Total	2,345.00

In addition Jon would pay Class 2 contributions of (52 × £2.10) £109.20.

Activity 1

Lawrence, who is a sole trader, had taxable profits of £34,850 for 2006/07. Calculate the NICs he must pay.

NICs PAYABLE BY EMPLOYERS

student notes

Employers pay two types of NIC:

a) Secondary Class 1 NICs, and
b) Class 1A NICs

SECONDARY CLASS 1 CONTRIBUTIONS must be paid at 12.8% on earnings in excess of the EARNINGS THRESHOLD. The earnings threshold is currently £5,035 per annum. This rate, which will be given to you in the tax tables in your exam, applies where the employee is not contracted out of the state second pension scheme. Rates where the employee is contracted out of this scheme are not examinable at Unit 18.

If the employee is paid monthly (or weekly) you should calculate the secondary NICs on a monthly (or weekly) basis. You may be given the monthly (or weekly) equivalent of the earnings threshold in your exam. If not, the monthly earnings threshold is the annual limit divided by 12. The limit is rounded to the nearest £1. Similarly, the weekly earnings limit is the annual limit divided by 52.

How it works

Mia works for A Ltd. She is paid £3,000 per month. Show the secondary class 1 contributions paid by A Ltd for 2006/07.

As Mia is paid monthly, the secondary contributions must be worked out on a monthly basis.

The monthly earnings threshold is £420 $\left(\frac{5,035}{12}\right)$

Class 1 NICs

£(3,000 − 420) × 12.8% = £330.24 per month

For 2006/07 secondary Class 1 contributions are £330.24 × 12 = £3,962.88

Activity 2

John is paid £450 weekly. Show the secondary Class 1 NICs payable by John's employer for 2006/07.

Broadly, earnings for Class 1 purposes comprise gross pay, excluding benefits. No deduction is made for pension contributions.

You will normally be told the earnings figure on which to base the NIC in the exam.

national insurance

student notes

Secondary class 1 NICs are an allowable expense in computing the employer's taxable trading profits.

Class 1A contributions

Employers must pay CLASS 1A NIC in respect of most taxable benefits provided to employees earning at the rate of £8,500 per annum or more. This applies, for example, where employers provide cars for the private use of their employees and where private use fuel is for use in an employer's car.

Class 1A contributions are paid at 12.8% of the taxable value of the benefit. There is no earnings threshold. You will be given the taxable value of any benefit in your exam.

How it works

Peter's employer provides him with private medical insurance throughout 2006/07. The taxable value of the benefit arising is £400.

Calculate the Class 1A national insurance contributions that will be payable by Peter's employer.

Class 1 A contributions are 12.8% × £400 = £51.20

> ### Activity 3
>
> Hugo's remuneration package for 2006/07 consisted of the following.
>
> | | |
> |---|---:|
> | Annual salary | £45,000 |
> | Company car – taxable benefit | £3,000 |
>
> **Task**
>
> Show the national insurance contributions payable by Hugo's employer for 2006/07.

CHAPTER OVERVIEW

- Self employed traders pay

  a) Class 2 contributions at £2.10 per week and

  b) Class 4 contributions based on the level of their profits

- Main rate Class 4 NICs are 8% of profits between the upper and lower limits

- Additional Class 4 NICs are 1% of profits above the upper limit

- Employers pay

  a) secondary Class 1 NICs, and
  b) Class 1A NICs

- 'Secondary contributions are 12.8% of earnings above the earnings threshold

- Class 1A contributions are payable at 12.8% on the taxable value of benefits

> **KEY WORDS**
>
> **Class 2 contributions** are flat rate contributions payable by the self employed
>
> **Class 4 contributions** are profit related contributions payable by the self employed
>
> **Secondary Class 1 contributions** must be paid by employers on employee earnings in excess of £5,035
>
> **Class 1A contributions** are NICs payable by an employer on the taxable value of any benefits
>
> The **Earnings Threshold** is the limit below which secondary Class 1 contributions are not due

national insurance

HOW MUCH HAVE YOU LEARNED?

1 Compute the following sole traders' liabilities to NICs for 2006/07.

    a) Acker
        Taxable trading profits   £4,450

    b) Bailey
        Taxable trading profits   £37,000

    c) Cartwright
        Taxable trading profit   £10,850

2 For the week ending Friday 27 January 2007 five employees of an engineering company earn gross pay as follows:

	£
Alan	73.00
Betty	100.00
Darren	240.00
Eleanor	690.00

Show the secondary Class 1 NICs payable for the week.

3 Shifty Sales Ltd provides three of its employees (all earning over £8,500 pa) with company car for 2006/07. Petrol is also provided. Taxable benefits are as follows:

Employee	Taxable car benefit £	Taxable fuel benefit £
Stuart	2,025	3,888
Terry	3,776	4,608
Una	5,850	3,600

Show the Class 1A NIC payable for 2006/07.

chapter 15:
ADMINISTRATION AND PAYMENT OF INCOME TAX, CGT AND CLASS 4 NICs

chapter coverage

In this chapter we look at when tax returns must be filed, for how long records must be kept and at the penalties chargeable for failure to comply with the requirements. You will be introduced to the two supplementary pages to the tax return that you may have to complete in the exam.

We then look at the due dates for payment of income tax, class 4 NICs and capital gains tax, and at the consequences of late payment.

Finally we consider the important topic of client confidentiality.

The topics that we shall cover are:

- tax returns and keeping records
- payment of tax, interest, surcharges and penalties
- client confidentiality
- Self employed tax pages

KNOWLEDGE AND UNDERSTANDING AND PERFORMANCE CRITERIA COVERAGE

knowledge and understanding

- Self assessment including payment of tax and filing of returns for unincorporated businesses (Element 18.2)

Performance criteria

- Identify the due dates of payment of Income Tax by unincorporated businesses, including payments on account
- Complete correctly the self employed and partnership supplementary pages for the tax return for individuals, together with relevant claims and elections and submit them within statutory time limits
- Ensure that computations and submissions are made in accordance with current tax law and take account of current HMRC practice
- Maintain client confidentiality at all times
- Give timely and constructive advice on the maintenance of accounts and the recording of information relevant to tax returns
- Consult with HMRC staff in an open and constructive manner

student notes

TAX RETURNS AND KEEPING RECORDS

An individual's tax return comprises a Tax Form, together with supplementary pages for particular sources of income. You may have to complete the supplementary self-employment pages in your exam and so we include a copy of them at the end of this chapter. Familiarise yourself with these pages now. You will be able to practise completing the pages when you try the activities later in this Course Companion.

Note that the examiner has said that you will not need to complete the partnership pages in your exam.

Individuals who are chargeable to tax for any tax year and who have not received a notice to file a return are, in general, required to give notice of chargeability within six months from the end of the year ie by 5 October 2007 for 2006/07. The maximum penalty where notice of chargeability is not given is 100% of the tax assessed that is not paid on or before 31 January following the tax year.

Filing tax returns

The FILING DUE DATE for filing a return is the later of:

- 31 January following the end of the tax year that the return covers eg for 2006/07 by 31 January 2008.
- three months after the notice to file the return was issued.

If an individual wishes HMRC to calculate tax and Class 4 NICs on their behalf, earlier deadlines may apply. The filing date is normally the later of:

- 30 September following the tax year; eg for 2006/07, by 30 September 2007.
- two months after notice to file the return was issued.

However, this earlier deadline does not apply to individuals issued with a four page short tax return. This form is used for taxpayers with simple tax affairs.

Penalties for late filing

The maximum penalties for filing a late tax return are:

a) Return up to 6 months late: £100
b) Return more than 6 months but not more than 12 months late: £200
c) Return more than 12 months late: £200 + 100% of the tax liability

In addition, a maximum penalty of £60 per day can be imposed where failure to deliver a tax return continues after notice has been given to the taxpayer. In this case the additional £100 penalty, imposed under b) if the return is more than six months late, is not charged.

The fixed penalties of £100/£200 can be set aside if the taxpayer had a reasonable excuse for not delivering the return. If the tax liability shown on the return is less than the fixed penalties, the fixed penalty is reduced to the amount of the tax liability. The tax geared penalty can be reduced.

Standard accounting information

'Three line' accounts (ie income less expenses equals profit) only need be included on the tax return of businesses with a turnover of less than £15,000 per annum. This is not as helpful as it might appear, as underlying records must still be kept for tax purposes (disallowable items etc) when producing three line accounts.

Large businesses with a turnover of at least £5 million that have used figures rounded to the nearest £1,000 in producing their published accounts can compute their profits to the nearest £1,000 for tax purposes.

The tax return requires trading results to be presented in a standard format. Although there is no requirement to submit accounts with the return, accounts may be filed.

Keeping of records

Taxpayers must keep and retain all records required to enable them to make and deliver a correct tax return.

Self employed individuals must retain records until the later of:

a) 5 years after the 31 January following the tax year concerned

b) provided notice to deliver a return is given before the date in a):

   i) the time after which enquiries by HMRC into the return can no longer be commenced

   ii) the date any such enquiries have been completed

Where a person receives a notice to deliver a tax return after the normal record keeping period has expired, he must keep all records in his possession at that time until no enquiries can be raised in respect of the return or until such enquiries have been completed.

The maximum penalty for each failure to keep and retain records is £3,000 per tax year.

administration and payment of income tax, CGT and Class 4 NICs

student notes

Activity 1

HMRC issued a tax return for 2006/07 to Myer on 3 September 2007. She filed this return on 31 March 2008. Myer calculates her own tax. State the date by which the return should have been filed and any penalties arising.

PAYMENT OF TAX, INTEREST, SURCHARGES AND PENALTIES

Payments of tax

A taxpayer must make three payments of income tax and Class 4 NICs:

Date	Payment
31 January in the tax year	1st payment on account
31 July after the tax year	2nd payment on account
31 January after the tax year	Final payment to settle the remaining liability

Each payment on account is equal to 50% of the income tax and class 4 NIC payable for the previous year.

Capital gains tax must all be paid on 31 January following the tax year. There are no payments on account of capital gains tax.

How it works

Jeremy paid tax for 2006/07 as follows:

	£
Income tax and Class 4 NICs payable	12,000
Capital gains tax payable	2,000

How much are the payments on account for 2007/08?

The income tax and Class 4 NICs payable for 2006/07 were £12,000.

Each payment on account is £12,000/2 = £6,000

Payments are made on account of income tax and Class 4 NICs but not on account of CGT.

administration and payment of income tax, CGT and Class 4 NICs

Activity 2

Karen paid tax for 2006/07 as follows.

	£
Income tax payable	14,000
Class 4 NICs	2,500
Class 2 NICs	109
Capital gains tax	8,000

What payments on account must Karen make for 2007/08?

student notes

Payments on account are not required if the income tax payable for the previous year is less than £500.

Payments on account are normally fixed by reference to the previous year's tax liability but if a taxpayer expects his liability to be lower than this he may claim to reduce his payments on account to:

a) a stated amount, or
b) nil.

If the taxpayer's eventual liability is higher than he estimated he will have reduced the payments on account too far. Although the payments on account will not be adjusted, the taxpayer will suffer an interest charge on late payment.

The balance of any income tax and class 4 NICs together with all CGT due for a year, is normally payable on or before the 31 January following the year.

How it works

Jameel made payments on account for 2006/07 of £7,500 each on 31 January 2007 and 31 July 2007, based on his 2005/06 liability. He later calculates his total income tax and Class 4 NICs payable for 2006/07 at £20,000. In addition he calculated that his CGT liability for disposals in 2006/07 is £4,900.

What is the final payment due for 2006/07?

The final payment is the remaining income tax and Class 4 NICs and all the CGT.

	£
Income tax and Class 4 NICs (£20,000 – £7,500 – £7,500)	5,000
Capital gains tax	4,900
Final payment	9,900

In one case the due date for the final payment is later than 31 January following the end of the year. If a taxpayer has notified chargeability by 5 October but the notice to file a tax return is not issued before 31 October,

163

then the due date for the payment is three months after the issue of the notice.

Surcharges

SURCHARGES are normally imposed in respect of balancing payments of income tax and Class 4 NICs and any CGT

	Paid	Surcharge
a)	within 28 days of due date:	none
b)	more than 28 days but not more than six months after the due date:	5%
c)	more than six months after the due date:	10%

Surcharges apply to balancing payments of income tax, Class 4 NICs and any CGT. The surcharges do not apply to late payments on account.

Interest

INTEREST is chargeable on late payment of both payments on account and balancing payments. In both cases interest runs from the due date until the day before the actual date of payment.

If a taxpayer claims to reduce his payments on account and there is still a final payment to be made, interest is normally charged on the payments on account as if each of those payments had been the lower of:

a) the reduced amount, plus 50% of the final income tax liability; and

b) the amount which would have been payable had no claim for reduction been made.

How it works

Harry made two payments on account of £2,500 each for 2006/07. The payments were made on 31 January 2007 and 31 July 2007. Harry had claimed to reduce these payments from the £4,000 that would have been due had they been based on his previous year's income tax liability.

Harry's 2006/07 tax return showed that his tax liabilities for 2006/07 (before deducting payments on account) were income tax: £10,000, capital gains tax: £3,000. Harry paid the balance of tax due of £8,000 on 30 September 2008.

For what periods and in respect of what amounts will Harry be charged interest?

The payments on account should have been £4,000 each. Interest will therefore be charged on the £1,500 not paid on 31 January 2007 until the date of payment 30 September 2008. Similarly interest will run on the other £1,500 that should have been paid on 31 July 2007 until 30 September 2008.

The final balancing payment should have been £13,000 – £8,000 = £5,000. Interest will run on £5,000 from the due date of 31 January 2008 until the date of payment 30 September 2008.

Note, there would also be a surcharge of 10% due on the balancing payment.

Repayment of tax and repayment supplement

Tax is repaid when claimed unless a greater payment of tax is due in the following 30 days, in which case it is set-off against that payment.

Interest is paid on overpayments of:

a) payments on account
b) final payments of income tax and CGT
c) penalties and surcharges

Interest runs from the original date of payment (even if this was prior to the due date), until the day before the date the repayment is made.

Enquiries

HMRC can enquire into a return if they give written notice of this by

a) the first anniversary of the due filing date (not the actual filing date); or
b) if the return is filed after the due filing date, the quarter day following the first anniversary of the actual filing date. The quarter days are 31 January, 30 April, 31 July and 31 October.

A reason for raising an enquiry does not have to be given. In particular the taxpayer will not be advised whether he has been selected at random for an audit. Enquiries may be full enquiries, or may be limited to 'aspect' enquiries.

In the course of the enquiries the taxpayer may be required to produce documents, accounts or other information. The taxpayer can appeal against this.

HMRC must issue a notice that enquiries are complete, and make any resulting amendments to the taxpayer's tax return. If the taxpayer is not satisfied with the HMRC's amendments he may, within 30 days, appeal against them.

Once an enquiry is complete, further enquiries cannot be made.

student notes

CLIENT CONFIDENTIALITY

Whenever you prepare accounts or returns on behalf of a client you should remember that you are bound by the ethical guideline of client confidentiality. This means that you should not discuss a client's affairs with third parties without the client's permission. You should also take care not to leave documents relating to a client's affairs in public places such as on trains or in restaurants.

CHAPTER OVERVIEW

- A tax return must be filed by the later of 31 January following a tax year and three months after HMRC issues a notice requiring a return. Earlier dates may apply if the taxpayer requires HMRC to calculate the tax

- Fixed penalties of £100/£200 apply if a return is filed up to/ more than six months late

- A tax geared penalty may apply if a return is filed more than 12 months late

- Self employed individuals must keep records until the later of:

> **KEY WORDS**
>
> The **filing due date** is the date by which a return must be filed
>
> **Payment on account** is an amount paid on account of income tax and Class 4 NICs
>
> **Surcharges** are normally imposed in respect of balancing payments of income tax, Class 4 NICs and any CGT paid late
>
> **Interest** is charged on late payments on account and on late balancing payments

   a) 5 years after the 31 January following the tax year concerned

   b) provided notice to deliver a return is given before the date in a):

      i) the time after which enquiries by HMRC into the return can no longer be commenced, and

      ii) the date any such enquiries have been completed

- Payments on account of income tax are required on 31 January in the tax year and on the 31 July following the tax year

- Balancing payments of income tax and Class 4 NICs and all CGT is due on 31 January following the tax year

- Surcharges apply to balancing payments of income tax, Class 4 NICs and any CGT. The surcharges do not apply to late payments on account

- Interest is chargeable on late payment of both payments on account and balancing payments

- HMRC can enquire into a return if they give written notice of this by

   a) the first anniversary of the due filing date (not the actual filing date); or

   b) if the return is filed after the due filing date, the quarter day following the first anniversary of the actual filing date. The quarter days are 31 January, 30 April, 31 July and 31 October

- The ethical guideline of confidentiality means that you should never discuss a client's tax affairs with third parties without the client's permission

administration and payment of income tax, CGT and Class 4 NICs

HOW MUCH HAVE YOU LEARNED?

1. What are the due filing dates for income tax returns for 2006/07? Assume the tax payer will calculate the tax due.

2. How will 2006/07 payments on account be calculated and when are they due?

3. A tax return for 2006/07 is issued in April 2007 and filed in May 2008. All income tax and Class 4 NICs were paid in May 2008. No payments on account were due. What charges will be made on the taxpayer?

4. Sase filed her 2006/07 tax return on 28 January 2008. By what date must HMRC give notice that they are going to enquire into the return?

5. Jamie, a sole trader, paid income tax and Class 4 NICs of £12,000 for 2005/06. In 2006/07, his tax liability was £16,000.

   State when payments must be made in respect of Jamie's 2006/07 income tax and Class 4 NIC liability.

6. Tim should have made two payments on account of his 2006/07 income tax liability of £5,000 each. He actually made both of these payments on 31 August 2007.

   State the amount of any surcharges due.

7. Zara has a CGT liability of £5,000 for 2006/07. State the date(s) by which this amount must be paid.

administration and payment of income tax, CGT and Class 4 NICs

Income for the year ended 5 April 2007

SELF-EMPLOYMENT

Name | **Tax reference**

Fill in these boxes first

If you want help, look up the box numbers in the Notes

Business details

Name of business — 3.1

Description of business — 3.2

Address of business — 3.3

Postcode

Accounting period - *read the Notes, page SEN3 before filling in these boxes*

Start — 3.4 / /   End — 3.5 / /

- Tick box 3.6 if details in boxes 3.1 or 3.3 have changed since your last Tax Return — 3.6

- Tick box 3.10 if you entered details for all relevant accounting periods on last year's Tax Return and boxes 3.14 to 3.73 and 3.99 to 3.115 will be blank *(read Step 3 on page SEN2)* — 3.10

- Date of commencement if after 5 April 2004 — 3.7 / /

- Tick box 3.11 if your accounts do not cover the period from the last accounting date (explain why in the 'Additional information' box, box 3.116) — 3.11

- Date of cessation if before 6 April 2007 — 3.8 / /

- Tick box 3.12 if your accounting date has changed (only if this is a permanent change and you want it to count for tax) — 3.12

- Tick box 3.9 if the special arrangements for particular trades apply - *read the Notes, page SEN11* — 3.9

- Tick box 3.13 if this is the second or further change (explain in box 3.116 on Page SE4 why you have not used the same date as last year) — 3.13

Capital allowances - summary

	Capital allowances	Balancing charges
Cars costing more than £12,000 (excluding cars with low CO_2 emissions) (A separate calculation must be made for each car.)	3.14 £	3.15 £
Other business plant and machinery (including cars with low CO_2 emissions and cars costing less than £12,000) *read the Notes, page SEN4*	3.16 £	3.17 £
Agricultural or Industrial Buildings Allowance (A separate calculation must be made for each block of expenditure.)	3.18 £	3.19 £
Other capital allowances claimed (separate calculations must be made). Claims to, and balancing charges arising on, Business Premises Renovation Allowance must also be included in boxes 23.7 and 23.8 respectively	3.20 £	3.21 £
	total of column above	total of column above
Total capital allowances/balancing charges	3.22 £	3.23 £

- Tick box 3.22A if box 3.22 includes enhanced capital allowances for designated environmentally beneficial plant and machinery — 3.22A

Income and expenses - annual turnover below £15,000

If your annual turnover is £15,000 or more, *ignore boxes 3.24 to 3.26. Instead fill in Page SE2*

If your annual turnover is below £15,000, *fill in boxes 3.24 to 3.26 instead of Page SE2. Read the Notes, page SEN4.*

- Turnover including other business receipts and goods etc. taken for personal use (and balancing charges from box 3.23) — 3.24 £

- Expenses allowable for tax (including capital allowances from box 3.22) — 3.25 £

box 3.24 minus box 3.25

- Net profit (put figure in brackets if a loss) — 3.26 £

You must now fill in Page SE3

SA103

169

administration and payment of income tax, CGT and Class 4 NICs

Income and expenses - annual turnover £15,000 or more

You must fill in this Page if your annual turnover is £15,000 or more - read the Notes, pages SEN2, SEN4 to SEN7

If you were registered for VAT, will the figures in boxes 3.29 to 3.64, include VAT? **3.27** [ ] or exclude VAT? **3.28** [ ]

Sales/business income (turnover) **3.29** £ _____

	Disallowable expenses included in boxes 3.46 to 3.63	Total expenses
• Cost of sales	3.30 £	3.46 £
• Construction industry subcontractor costs	3.31 £	3.47 £
• Other direct costs	3.32 £	3.48 £

box 3.29 minus (boxes 3.46 + 3.47 + 3.48)
Gross profit/(loss) **3.49** £ _____

Other income/profits **3.50** £ _____

• Employee costs	3.33 £	3.51 £
• Premises costs	3.34 £	3.52 £
• Repairs	3.35 £	3.53 £
• General administrative expenses	3.36 £	3.54 £
• Motor expenses	3.37 £	3.55 £
• Travel and subsistence	3.38 £	3.56 £
• Advertising, promotion and entertainment	3.39 £	3.57 £
• Legal and professional costs	3.40 £	3.58 £
• Bad debts	3.41 £	3.59 £
• Interest and alternative finance payments	3.42 £	3.60 £
• Other finance charges	3.43 £	3.61 £
• Depreciation and loss/(profit) on sale	3.44 £	3.62 £
• Other expenses	3.45 £	3.63 £

Put the total of boxes 3.30 to 3.45 in box 3.66 below

Total expenses **3.64** £ _____ (total of boxes 3.51 to 3.63)

Net profit/(loss) **3.65** £ _____ (boxes 3.49 + 3.50 minus 3.64)

Tax adjustments to net profit or loss

• Disallowable expenses — boxes 3.30 to 3.45 **3.66** £ _____

• Adjustments (apart from disallowable expenses) that increase profits. For instance; goods taken for personal use and amounts brought forward from an earlier year because of a claim under ESC B11 about compulsory slaughter of farm animals **3.67** £ _____

• Balancing charges (from box 3.23) **3.68** £ _____

Total additions to net profit (deduct from net loss) **3.69** £ _____ (boxes 3.66 + 3.67 + 3.68)

• Capital allowances (from box 3.22) **3.70** £ _____

• Deductions from net profit (add to net loss) **3.71** £ _____

3.72 £ _____ (boxes 3.70 + 3.71)

Net business profit for tax purposes (put figure in brackets if a loss) **3.73** £ _____ (boxes 3.65 + 3.69 minus 3.72)

HMRC 12/05 net   TAX RETURN ■ SELF-EMPLOYMENT: PAGE SE2   Now fill in Page SE3

chapter 16:
ADMINISTRATION AND PAYMENT OF CORPORATION TAX

chapter coverage

In this chapter we look at when corporation tax returns must be filed, for how long records must be kept and at the penalties chargeable for failure to comply with the requirements. You will also be introduced to the pages of the corporation tax return that you may have to complete in your exam.

We then look at the due dates for payment of corporation tax.

The topics that we shall cover are:

- notification of chargeability
- company tax returns and keeping records
- payment of tax and interest
- income tax suffered or withheld
- company return forms

KNOWLEDGE AND UNDERSTANDING AND PERFORMANCE CRITERIA COVERAGE

knowledge and understanding

- Self assessment including payment of tax and filing of returns for companies (Element 18.4)

Performance criteria

- Identify and set off income tax deductions and credits
- Identify the amount of Corporation Tax payable and the due dates of payment, including payments on account
- Complete corporation tax returns correctly and submit them, together with relevant claims and elections within statutory time limits
- Consult with HMRC staff in an open and constructive manner

NOTIFICATION OF CHARGEABILITY

A company must notify HMRC when it first comes within the scope of corporation tax. This will usually be when it starts trading. There is a list of information that needs to be included in the notice, which must be given in writing. The notice must be made within three months.

There is an initial penalty of £300 if the notice is not given within this time limit.

COMPANY TAX RETURNS AND KEEPING RECORDS

A company that does not receive a notice requiring a corporation tax return (Form CT 600) to be filed must, if it is chargeable to tax, notify HMRC within twelve months of the end of the accounting period concerned. Failure to do so results in a maximum penalty equal to the tax unpaid twelve months after the end of the accounting period. An obligation to file a return arises only when the company receives a notice requiring a return.

A return for each of the company's accounting periods is due on or before the FILING DATE. This is the normally the later of:

a) 12 months after the end of the period of account concerned, and

b) three months from the date on which the notice requiring the return was made.

A copy of two pages of the corporation tax return form (CT 600) are included at the end of this chapter. Familiarise yourself with them now. You will be able to practice completing these pages when you try the activities later in the Course Companion. The examiner has said that you will not need to complete any other pages of the corporation tax return form in your exam.

Activity 1

Size Ltd prepares accounts for the twelve months to 30 September 2006. A notice requiring a CT600 return for the year ended 30 September 2006 was issued on 1 June 2007. State the date by which Size Ltd must file its corporation tax return for the year to 30 September 2006.

You saw in chapter 11 of this Course Companion that if a period of account is more than twelve months long, there will be two accounting periods based on the period of account. The first accounting period is twelve months long, the second is for the remainder of the period of account.

A tax return must be filed for each accounting period. The tax returns for both accounting periods must be filed within twelve months of the end of the period of account.

administration and payment of corporation tax

Activity 2

Ocado Ltd prepares accounts for the eighteen months to 30 June 2006. State the date by which Ocado Ltd must file its corporation tax returns based on this period of account and the period(s) which these returns will cover. Assume a notice requiring the returns was issued shortly after the end of the period of account.

Penalties

There is a £100 penalty for a failure to submit a return on time, rising to £200 if the delay exceeds three months. These penalties become £500 and £1,000 respectively when a return was late (or never submitted) for each of the preceding two accounting periods.

An additional tax geared penalty is applied if a return is more than six months late. The penalty is 10% of the tax unpaid six months after the return was due if the total delay is up to 12 months, but 20% of that tax if the return is over 12 months late.

Activity 3

Box Ltd prepares accounts for the twelve months to 30 June 2006. Assume a notice requiring the return for the period was issued shortly after the end of the period of account. Box Ltd filed this return on 31 December 2007. State what penalties may be charged. Returns for all previous accounting periods had been filed on time.

Records

Companies must keep records until the latest of:

a) six years from the end of the accounting period
b) the date any enquiries are completed
c) the date after which enquiries may not be commenced

All business records and accounts, including contracts and receipts, must be kept.

If a return is demanded more than six years after the end of the accounting period, the company must keep any records that it still has until the later of the end of any enquiry and the expiry of the right to start an enquiry.

Failure to keep records can lead to a penalty of up to £3,000 for each accounting period affected.

student notes

student notes

Enquiries

HMRC may enquire into a return, provided that they give written notice that they are going to enquire by a year after the later of:

a) the due filing date

b) the 31 January, 30 April, 31 July or 31 October next following the actual date of delivery of the return

Only one enquiry may be made in respect of any one return.

If a notice of an enquiry has been given, HMRC may demand that the company produce documents. Documents relating to an appeal need not be produced and the company may appeal against a notice requiring documents to be produced.

If HMRC demand documents, but the company does not produce them, there is a penalty of £50. There is also a daily penalty, which applies for each day from the day after the imposition of the £50 penalty until the documents are produced.

An enquiry ends when HMRC give notice that it has been completed and notify what they believe to be the correct amount of tax payable. The company has 30 days from the end of an enquiry to amend its tax return in accordance with HMRC's conclusions. If HMRC are not satisfied with the company's amendments, they have a further 30 days to amend the return. The company then has another 30 days in which it may appeal against HMRC's amendments.

Activity 4

Green Ltd prepares accounts for the twelve months to 30 April 2006. The tax return for the year was filed on 30 September 2007. State the date by which HMRC may commence an enquiry into the return based on these accounts.

Activity 5

A company has been making up its accounts annually to 31 May for many years. For the year ended 31 May 2005, it did not submit its Corporation Tax Annual Return (CT600) until 1 November 2006. A notice requiring the return was issued on 31 August 2006.

What is the latest date by which HMRC can commence an enquiry into the company's Return?

administration and payment of corporation tax

PAYMENT OF TAX AND INTEREST

student notes

Large companies

LARGE COMPANIES must pay their corporation tax in instalments. Broadly, a large company is any company that pays corporation tax at the full rate (profits exceed £1,500,000 where there are no associated companies).

Instalments are based on the estimated corporation tax liability of the company for the current period (not the previous period). This means that it is extremely important for companies to forecast their tax liabilities accurately. Large companies whose directors are poor at estimating may find their company incurring significant interest charges. The company must estimate its corporation tax liability before the end of the accounting period, and must revise its estimate each quarter.

For a 12 month accounting period, quarterly instalments are due on the 14th day of months 7 and 10 in the accounting period and months 1 and 4 following the end of the period. You will not be expected to deal with periods other than 12 month periods in your exam.

A company which draws up accounts to 31 December 2006 will pay instalments as follows:

Instalment	Due date
1	14 July 2006
2	14 October 2006
3	14 January 2007
4	14 April 2007

Activity 6

S Ltd, a large company, has a corporation tax liability of £700,000 in respect of its accounting year 31 March 2007.

On which date will the company be required to pay its FINAL instalment of the liability?

A   14 October 2006
B   14 July 2007
C   31 July 2007
D   1 January 2008

Interest arises on late paid instalments (from the due date to the actual payment date (see below)). Interest is paid on over paid instalments, from the actual payment date to the date of repayment, except that interest does not run before the due date for the first instalment. The position is looked at cumulatively after the due date for each instalment.

175

administration and payment of corporation tax

student notes

How it works

J Ltd makes up accounts to 31 December 2006. At the end of June 2006 estimates that its total liability to corporation tax for the year will be £8m, a of which is due in instalments. The first instalment of £2m is paid on 14 Ju 2006.

In October 2006 the estimate of the corporation tax liability increases £10m. A payment of £3m is made on 14 October 2006.

In November 2006 a chargeable gain is realised and thus an additional ta payment of £3.5m is made on 1 December 2006.

A third instalment of £5m is paid on 14 January 2007 and a final instalme of £2.5m is paid on 14 April 2007. The CT return shows a corporation ta liability of £16m for the year.

Summary

Tax Paid	Instalment	Liability
14 July 2006	£2m	£4m
14 October 2006	£3m	£4m
1 December 2006	£3.5m	–
14 January 2007	£5m	£4m
14 April 2007	£2.5m	£4m

Interest will be charged as follows:

Amount on which interest is charged	Interest period	Note
£2m	14 July – 13 October 2006	
£3m	14 October – 30 November 2006	
£(0.5)m	1 December 2006 – 13 January 2007	(1)
£(1.5)m	14 January – 13 April 2007	(1)

(1) Interest paid to company on overpayment of corporation tax.

Exceptions

If a 'small' company is treated as large as a result of the associated companie rule, it will not have to pay corporation tax by instalments if its own liabili is less than £10,000.

If a company is a large company for an accounting period it will not have t pay corporation tax by instalments for that period if:

a) its PCTCT does not exceed £10m (reduced to reflect any associate companies); and

b) it was not a large company in the previous year.

administration and payment of corporation tax

Incorrect instalments

There are penalties if a company deliberately and flagrantly fails to pay instalments of sufficient size. After a company has filed its return or HMRC has determined its liability, HMRC may wish to establish the reason for inadequate instalment payments. It can do this by asking the company to produce relevant information or records The failure to supply these will lead to an initial fixed penalty which may also be followed by a daily penalty which may continue until the information/records are produced.

Small and medium sized companies

Corporation tax is due for payment by small and medium sized companies nine months and one day after the end of the accounting period.

How it works

A Ltd makes up accounts to 31 March 2007. It is not a large company. The corporation tax for the year to 31 March 2007 is £30,000.

The corporation tax is due on 1 January 2008.

INCOME TAX SUFFERED OR WITHHELD

A company must withhold income tax on payments made to individuals and partnerships, of:

a) annual interest
b) royalties
c) annuities
d) annual payments

20% tax is withheld on interest payments and 22% tax is withheld on the payment of patent royalties and other annual payments. The company pays the tax withheld to HMRC. The net amount is paid to the payee.

When the company pays interest or patent royalties it always deducts the gross amount in its corporation tax computation.

Companies may receive income from individuals or partnerships that has suffered 22% income tax at source. The cash income plus the income tax suffered, that is the gross figure, forms part of a company's income. The income tax suffered can be set against income tax due to be paid to HMRC. Any net income tax suffered is deductible from the corporation tax liability.

student notes

177

administration and payment of corporation tax

student notes

How it works

In the accounting period to 31 March 2007 B Ltd:

1. Paid patent royalties of £7,800 to an individual
2. Received patent royalties of £17,160 from an individual

The amounts shown are the amounts paid and received by the company. What is the net amount of income tax suffered that B Ltd may deduct in calculating its corporation tax payable for the period?

Solution

£2,200 (£7,800 × 22/78) of income tax was withheld by the company from the payment of the patent royalties.

Income tax of £4,840 (£17,160 × 22/78) was suffered on the receipt of the interest.

The income tax suffered can be set against the income tax due to HMRC of £2,200. The balance of income tax suffered, £2,640, is set against the corporation tax liability for the year.

CHAPTER OVERVIEW

- A company must usually file its CT600 return within twelve months of the end of the period of account concerned

- Fixed penalties arise if the return is up to six months late. If the return is over six months late there may be a tax geared penalty

- Companies must normally keep records until six years after the end of the accounting period concerned

- HMRC can enquire into a return. Notice of an enquiry must usually be given within twelve months of the filing date

- Large companies must pay their CT liability in instalments starting in the 7th month of the accounting period. The final instalment is due in the fourth month following the end of the accounting period

- Initial instalments of corporation tax are calculated as 3/N × CT liability. N is the number of months in the accounting period. The final instalment is the balance of any tax payable

- Small and medium sized companies must pay their corporation tax liability nine months after the end of an accounting period

- Income tax suffered is set against income tax payable to HMRC. Any excess income tax suffered can be set against the corporation tax liability for the year

> **KEY WORDS**
>
> The **filing date** is the date by which a tax return must be filed
>
> **Large companies** are companies that pay corporation tax at the full rate

administration and payment of corporation tax

HOW MUCH HAVE YOU LEARNED?

1. A company has been preparing accounts to 30 June for many years. It submitted its CT600 return for the year to 30 June 2005, on 1 June 2006. By what date must HMRC give notice that they are going to commence an enquiry into the return?

2. A company filed its CT600 return for the year to 31 December 2005 on 30 April 2007. The company's CT600 returns for both of the two preceding years were late in being filed. What fixed penalty arises in respect of the late filing of the return for the year to 31 December 2005?

3. Girton Ltd has no associated companies. When will the first instalment of corporation tax be payable on its taxable profits of £150,000 arising in the year ended 31 December 2006?

    A   14 July 2006
    B   1 October 2007
    C   1 December 2007
    D   1 January 2008

4. Eaton Ltd has profits chargeable to corporation tax of £2,400,000 for its year ended 31 December 2007. The first instalment of the corporation tax liability for this year will be due on

    A   14 April 2007
    B   14 April 2008
    C   14 July 2007
    D   1 October 2008

5. M Ltd, a large company, has an estimated corporation tax liability of £240,000 in respect of its accounting year 31 March 2007.

    What will be the amount of each of the company's quarterly instalments?

6. CCD Ltd, a company liable to pay its corporation tax (CT) by instalments, has an estimated CT liability of £800,000 for its eight-month chargeable accounting period ended 31 August 2007. Prior to this period, the company had made up accounts annually to 31 December.

    The amount of the company's FINAL instalment will be:

    A   £176,000
    B   £200,000
    C   £300,000
    D   £800,000

administration and payment of corporation tax

Company tax calculation

Turnover
1 Total turnover from trade or profession — 1 £

Income
3 Trading and professional profits — 3 £
4 Trading losses brought forward claimed against profits — 4 £
   box 3 minus box 4
5 Net trading and professional profits — 5 £
6 Bank, building society or other interest, and profits and gains from non-trading loan relationships — 6 £
11 Income from UK land and buildings — 11 £
14 Annual profits and gains not falling under any other heading — 14 £

Chargeable gains
16 Gross chargeable gains — 16 £
17 Allowable losses including losses brought forward — 17 £
   box 16 minus box 17
18 Net chargeable gains — 18 £

sum of boxes 5, 6, 11, 14 & 18
21 Profits before other deductions and reliefs — 21 £

Deductions and Reliefs
24 Management expenses under S75 ICTA 1988 — 24 £
30 Trading losses of this or a later accounting period under S393A ICTA 1988 — 30 £
31 Put an 'X' in box 31 if amounts carried back from later accounting periods are included in box 30 — 31
32 Non-trade capital allowances — 32 £
35 Charges paid — 35 £

box 21 minus boxes 24, 30, 32 and 35
37 Profits chargeable to corporation tax — 37 £

Tax calculation
38 Franked investment income — 38 £
39 Number of associated companies in this period — 39
or
40 Associated companies in the first financial year — 40
41 Associated companies in the second financial year — 41
42 Put an 'X' in box 42 if the company claims to be charged at the starting rate or the small companies' rate on any part of its profits, or is claiming marginal rate relief — 42

Enter how much profit has to be charged and at what rate of tax

Financial year (yyyy)	Amount of profit	Rate of tax	Tax
43	44 £	45	46 £ p
53	54 £	55	56 £ p

total of boxes 46 and 56
63 Corporation tax — 63 £   p
64 Marginal rate relief — 64 £   p
65 Corporation tax net of marginal rate relief — 65 £   p
66 Underlying rate of corporation tax — 66   •   %
67 Profits matched with non-corporate distributions — 67
68 Tax at non-corporate distributions rate — 68 £   p
69 Tax at underlying rate on remaining profits — 69 £   p

See note for box 70 in CT600 Guide
70 Corporation tax chargeable — 70 £   p

CT600 (Short) (2006) Version 2

administration and payment of corporation tax

79	Tax payable under S419 ICTA 1988	79 £	p
80	Put an 'X' in box 80 if you completed box A11 in the Supplementary Pages CT600A	80	
84	Income tax deducted from gross income included in profits	84 £	p
85	Income tax repayable to the company	85 £	p
86	**Tax payable** - this is your self-assessment of tax payable	86 £ *(total of boxes 70 and 79 minus box 84)*	p

Tax reconciliation

91	Tax already paid (and not already repaid)	91 £	p
92	Tax outstanding	92 £ *(box 86 minus box 91)*	p
93	Tax overpaid	93 £ *(box 91 minus box 86)*	p

Information about capital allowances and balancing charges

Charges and allowances included in calculation of trading profits or losses

Boxes	Description	Capital allowances	Balancing charges
105 - 106	Machinery and plant - long-life assets	105 £	106 £
107 - 108	Machinery and plant - other (general pool)	107 £	108 £
109 - 110	Cars outside general pool	109 £	110 £
111 - 112	Industrial buildings and structures	111 £	112 £
113 - 114	Other charges and allowances	113 £	114 £

Charges and allowances not included in calculation of trading profits or losses

Boxes	Description	Capital allowances	Balancing charges
115 - 116	Non-trading charges and allowances	115 £	116 £
117	Put an 'X' in box 117 if box 115 includes flat conversion allowances	117	

Expenditure

118	Expenditure on machinery and plant on which first year allowance is claimed	118 £
119	Put an 'X' in box 119 if claim includes enhanced capital allowances for designated energy-saving investments	119
120	Qualifying expenditure on machinery and plant on long-life assets	120 £
121	Qualifying expenditure on machinery and plant on other assets	121 £

Losses, deficits and excess amounts

Box	Description		Box	Description	
122	Trading losses Case I	*calculated under S393 ICTA 1988* 122 £	124	Trading losses Case V	*calculated under S393 ICTA 1988* 124 £
125	Non-trade deficits on loan relationships and derivative contracts	*calculated under S82 FA 1996* 125 £	127	Schedule A losses	*calculated under S392A ICTA 1988* 127 £
129	Overseas property business losses Case V	*calculated under S392B ICTA 1988* 129 £	130	Losses Case VI	*calculated under S396 ICTA 1988* 130 £
131	Capital losses	*calculated under S16 TCGA 1992* 131 £	136	Excess management expenses	*calculated under S75 ICTA 1988* 136 £

ANSWERS

ANSWERS TO CHAPTER ACTIVITIES

Chapter 1: Introduction

1

	Non-savings income £	Savings (excl dividend) income £	Dividend income £	Total £
Business profits	16,000	0	0	
Building society interest	0	6,000	0	
Dividends	0	0	8,750	
STI	16,000	6,000	8,750	30,750
Less: Personal allowance	(5,035)			
Taxable income	10,965	6,000	8,750	25,715

2

	£
£2,150 × 10%	215
£31,150 × 22%	6,853
£16,700 × 40%	6,680
£50,000	13,748

Chapter 2: Computing trading income

1

	£
Accounts profit	38,000
Add: entertaining expenses	2,000
depreciation	4,000
	44,000
Less: capital allowances	(3,500)
Taxable trading profit	40,500

2 As the cinema was usable on acquisition the repair expenditure is allowable. This point was decided in the case of Odean Associated Theatres v Jones. You do not need to remember case names for exam purposes.

3 40% × £600 = £240 must be added back in computing taxable profits.

4 £100 must be added back. HMRC allow the deduction of donations to small local charities.

answers to chapter activities

5 £7,000.

The expenses relating to the renewal of the employee service contracts are allowable as this is a revenue item.

The expenses relating to the purchase of new offices are disallowable as they relate to a capital item. Legal expenses relating to the renewal of a short lease are specifically allowable.

6 £18,000. The redundancy payments are allowable. The payment of a salary to the proprietor of a business is not deductible because it is just a method of extracting a profit from the business and that profit is taxable in the normal way.

7

	£
Heating (70%)	560

The private portion of the above bill must be added back in computing taxable trading profits

8

	£
Entertaining Customers	7,300
	7,300

9

	£	£
Profit per accounts		12,710
Add: Depreciation	1,500	
Provision against a fall in raw material prices	5,000	
Entertainment expenses	750	
Patent royalties (to treat as a charge)	1,200	
Legal expenses (relate to a capital item)	250	
		8,700
		21,410
Less rental income received (to tax as property income)		(860)
Adjusted trading profit		20,550

Chapter 3: Capital allowances

1

	£	Allowance £
B/f	10,000	
Addition	8,000	
Disposal	(6,000)	
	12,000	
WDA @ 25%	(3,000)	3,000
	9,000	

2

	£	Allowance £
B/f	47,000	
Less: disposal (restricted to cost)	(7,000)	
	40,000	
WDA @ 25%	(10,000)	10,000
C/f	30,000	

3

	Pool £	Allowance £
B/f	20,000	
Addition	4,000	
	24,000	
WDA @ 25% × 3/12	(1,500)	1,500
C/f	22,500	

4

	FYA @ 50% £	FYA @ 100% £	Pool £	Allowances £
WDA @ 25%			60,000	
Machine	5,000		(15,000)	15,000
FYA @ 50%	(2,500)			2,500
Transfer balance to pool			2,500	
Low emission car		2,000		
FYA @ 100%		(2,000)		2,000
C/f/allowances			47,500	19,500

5

	FYA @ 50% £	General pool £	Allowances £
B/f		36,000	
WDA @ 25% × 9/12		(6,750)	6,750
		29,250	
Additions	20,000		
FYA @ 50%	(10,000)		10,000
Transfer balance to pool		10,000	
C/f/allowances		39,250	16,750

WDAs are pro-rated in a short period, FYAs are not.

answers to chapter activities

6

	Expensive car £	Allowances £
10 months ended 31 March 2005		
Addition	15,000	
WDA £3,000 (max) × 10/12	(2,500)	2,500
	12,500	
Year ended 31 March 2006		
WDA £3,000 (max)	(3,000)	3,000
	9,500	
Year ended 31 March 2007		
WDA × 25%	(2,375)	2,375
	7,125	

7 *Year ended 30 June 2006*

	Private use asset £	Allowances 80% £
Computer	10,000	
FYA @ 50%	(5,000) × 80%	4,000
C/f	5,000	

8 Land does not qualify for IBAs.

The offices cost less than 25% of the total expenditure on the factory so all of the office expenditure qualifies for IBAs.

Total qualifying expenditure = £1,000,000

9 £1,200,000 × 4% = £48,000

10 £1,000,000 × 4% × 9/12 = £30,000. IBAs are apportioned because the period concerned is less than 12 months long.

11 Mr Khan

	£
Year ended 31 March 2005	
Cost	400,000
IBA @ 4%	(16,000)
	384,000
Year ended 31 March 2006	
IBA @ 4%	(16,000)
Year ended 31 March 2007	368,000
Disposal proceeds (restrict to cost)	(400,000)
Balancing charge	32,000

Mr Jones

IBAs are available on lower of:

a) original cost (£400,000)
b) purchase price (£500,000)

ie £400,000

Over the remaining tax life of the building (23.5 years), ie $\dfrac{400{,}000}{23.5} = £17{,}021$

12

	£
Cost	500,000
Years ended 30.9.04/30.9.05	
2 × 4% × £500,000	(40,000)
	460,000
Year ended 30.9.06	
Disposal proceeds	(400,000)
Balancing allowance	60,000

Chapter 4: Taxing unincorporated businesses

1 Year ended 30 September 2006. The period of account ending in the tax year.

2 2005/06 (1 June 2005 to 5 April 2006) £12,000 × 10/12 = £10,000
   2006/07 (year ended 31 May 2006) = £12,000
   2007/08 (year ended 31 May 2007) = £21,000

3 2005/06 (year ended 30 June 2005) = £12,000
   2006/07 (year ended 30 June 2006) = £8,000
   2007/08 (1 July 2006 to 31 January 2008) £6,000 + £5,000 = £11,000

4 2004/05 (1 March 2005 to 5 April 2005)
   £32,000 × 1/16 = £2,000

   2005/06 (6 April 2005 to 5 April 2006)
   £32,000 × 12/16 = £24,000

   2006/07 (year ended 30 June 2006)
   £32,000 × 12/16 = £24,000

   2007/08 (year ended 30 June 2007) = £36,800

   Overlap profits

   1 July 2005 to 6 April 2006 (£24,000 × 9/12) = £18,000

5

	£
2003/04 (1 May 2003 to 5 April 2004) (11/12 × £15,000)	13,750
2004/05 (year ended 30 April 2004)	15,000
2005/06 (year ended 30 April 2005)	9,000
2006/07 (year ended 30 April 2006)	10,500
2007/08 (1 May 2006 to 31 January 2008) (£16,000 + £950 − £13,750)	3,200
Total taxable profits	51,450

Overlap profits

1 May 2003 to 5 April 2004 (£15,000 × 11/12) = £13,750

The overlap profits are deducted in the final year of the trade.

answers to chapter activities

Chapter 5: Relieving trading losses

	£
STI	21,000
Less: loss	(21,000)
Taxable income	NIL

Loss c/f £30,000 – £21,000 = £9,000

The loss is set against STI before the deduction of the personal allowance, so the benefit of the personal allowance is wasted.

Chapter 6: Partnerships

1

	Total £	Roger £	Muggles £
Salaries	60,000	30,000	30,000
Profit (210,000 – 60,000)	150,000	120,000	30,000
Taxable trading profits	210,000	150,000	60,000

2

	Total £	James £	Kieran £	Jemmima £
Interest	3,000	1,000	1,000	1,000
Salary	70,000		35,000	35,000
Profits	197,000	118,200	39,400	39,400
Taxable trading profits	270,000	119,200	75,400	75,400

3

	£
1 July 2005 to 31 March 2006	60,000
1 April 2006 to 30 June 2006	20,000
Total profits	80,000

	Total £	Hansel £	Greta £
To 31 March 2006	60,000	30,000	30,000
1 April 2006 to 30 June 2006	20,000	16,000	4,000
	80,000	46,000	34,000

4

	Total £	New partner (30%)
Year ended 31 October 2005		
1 November 2004 to 31 May 2005 (7/12)	19,950	–
1 June 2005 to 31 October 2005 (5/12)	14,250	4,275
	34,200	
Year ended 31 October 2006	45,600	13,680

The new partner is taxed using the opening year rules from 2005/06:

2005/06 (1 June 2005 to 5 April 2006)
£4,275 + 5/12 × £13,680 = £9,975

Overlap profits are 5/12 × £13,680 = £5,700

2006/07 (year ended 31 October 2006) = £13,680

5

	Total	X	Y	Z
	£	£	£	£
Year ended 31 March 2005	24,000	8,000	8,000	8,000
Year ended 31 March 2006				
1 April 2005 to 30 June 2005 (3/12)	3,500	1,167	1,167	1,166
1 July 2005 to 31 March 2006 (9/12)	10,500	–	6,300	4,200
	14,000	1,167	7,467	5,366
Year ended 31 March 2007	48,000		28,800	19,200

Y and Z are taxed on a continuing basis of assessment throughout.

	Y	Z
2004/05 (year ended 31 March 2005)	8,000	8,000
2005/06 (year ended 31 March 2006)	7,467	5,336
2006/07 (year ended 31 March 2007)	28,800	19,200

X is treated as ceasing the business in 2005/06

2004/05 £8,000
2005/06 £1,167

Chapter 7: Capital gains tax for sole traders

1 The cost of the partitioning is not deductible as enhancement expenditure as it is not reflected in the state and nature of the office building at the date of disposal.

2

	£
Disposal proceeds	200,000
Less: cost	(100,000)
	100,000
Less: indexation allowance	
0.091 × £100,000	(9,100)
Chargeable gain	90,900

Note that for individuals indexation runs to April 1998 not the date of disposal of the asset.

3

	£
Disposal proceeds	20,000
Less: cost	(50,000)
Allowable loss	(30,000)

191

answers to chapter activities

Indexation cannot increase an allowable loss.

4

	£
Gains	50,000
Less: losses brought forward	(6,000)
Gain before taper relief	44,000

The asset has been held for at least two years for taper relief purposes from 6 April 1998, so the gain after taper relief is 25% × £44,000 = £11,000.

	£
Gain after taper relief	11,000
Annual exemption	(8,800)
Taxable gain	2,200

5 Taxable income £40,000 – £5,035 = £34,965

As this is above £33,300, all taxable gains are taxed at 40%.

	£
Net chargeable gains	28,800
Less: annual exemption	(8,800)
Taxable gain	20,000

CGT payable £20,000 × 40% = £8,000

Chapter 8: Chargeable gains: additional aspects

1

	£
Proceeds	300,000
Less: legal fees	(9,000)
	291,000
Less: cost	
£50,000 × $\dfrac{300,000}{300,000+500,000}$	(18,750)
Chargeable gain before taper relief	272,250

Note that it is the gross proceeds that are used in the above formula.

2 No gain/loss arises as wasting chattels are exempt from CGT.

3

	£
Proceeds	9,000
Less: commission	(900)
	8,100
Less: cost	(2,500)
Gain	5,600

Maximum 5/3 (£9,000 – £6,000) = £5,000

The gain before taper relief is £5,000

192

4

	£
Proceeds (deemed)	6,000
Less: commission £(3,825 × 15/85)	(675)
	5,325
Less: cost	(7,800)
Allowable loss	(2,475)

Chapter 9: Shares

1 *1 August 2006 (LIFO basis)*

	£
Proceeds $\left(\dfrac{1,500}{3,000} \times £8,000\right)$	4,000
Less: cost	(3,000)
Gain before taper relief	1,000

1 May 2005 (LIFO basis)

	£
Proceeds $\left(\dfrac{1,000}{3,000} \times £8,000\right)$	2,667
Less: cost	(2,000)
Gain before taper relief	667

1 June 2002 (sold 500 shares)

	£
Proceeds $\left(\dfrac{500}{3,000} \times £8,000\right)$	1,333
Less: cost $\left(\dfrac{500}{4,000} \times £6,000\right)$	(750)
Gain before taper relief	583

2

	No of shares	Cost £	Indexed cost £
February 1986: pool starts	4,000	5,000	5,000
Index to January 1995 £5,000 × 0.511			2,555
	4,000	5,000	7,555
Addition	2,000	5,000	5,000
	6,000	10,000	12,555
Index to April 1998 £12,555 × 0.114			1,431
Disposal			13,986
	6,000	10,000	13,986
	2,000	3,333	4,662
	4,000	6,667	9,324

answers to chapter activities

	£
Sale January 2007	9,000
Less: Cost	(3,333)
	5,667
Less: (4,662 – 3,333)	(1,329)
	4,338

Gain after taper relief:

25% × £4,338 = £1,085

3 Match 27 February 2002 shares first:

Number of shares	6,000
Bonus issue (1 for 4)	1,500
	7,500

	£
Sale proceeds $\left(\dfrac{7,500}{9,375} \times £20,000\right)$	16,000
Less: cost	(15,000)
Gain before taper relief	1,000

March with FA 1985 pool:

	No of shares	Cost £	Indexed cost £
19 August 1990 pool starts	4,000	8,000	8,000
Index to April 1998 (0.269 × £8,000)			2,152
	4,000	8,000	10,152
Bonus issue	1,000	–	–
	5,000	8,000	10,152
Disposal	1,875	3,000	3,807
	3,125	5,000	6,345

	£
Disposal proceeds $\left(\dfrac{1,875}{9,375} \times £20,000\right)$	4,000
Less: cost	(3,000)
	1,000
Less: indexation (3,807 – 3,000)	(807)
Gain before taper relief	193

4 *Match June 2004 shares*

	No of shares	Cost £
Bought	2,000	6,000
Rights issue (1 for 2)	1,000	2,000
	3,000	8,000

	£
Disposal proceeds $\left(\dfrac{3,000}{6,000} \times £18,000\right)$	9,000
Less: cost	(8,000)
Gain before taper relief	1,000

For taper relief purposes the shares have been held for two years.

Gain after taper relief

25% × £1,000 = £250

August 1997 shares (FA 1985 pool)

	No of shares	Cost £	Indexed cost £
August 1997	4,000	7,000	7,000
Index to April 1998 £7,000 × 0.026			182
Pool closes	4,000	7,000	7,182
Rights issue	2,000	4,000	4,000
	6,000	11,000	11,182
Disposal	3,000	5,500	5,591
	3,000	5,500	5,591

	£
Disposal proceeds	9,000
Less: cost	(5,500)
Less: indexation (5,591 − 5,500)	(91)
Gain before taper relief	3,409

For taper relief purposes the shares have been owned at least two years.

Gain after taper relief 25% × £3,409 = £852

The total gain after taper relief is £852 + £250 = £1,102.

Chapter 10: Deferring taxation of capital gains

1

	£
Sale proceeds	90,000
Less: cost	(35,000)
Gain before taper relief	55,000

Rolled over gain £55,000

Base cost of new factory = £65,000 (£120,000 – £55,000)

2 *Offices*

	£
Sale proceeds	100,000
Less: cost	(80,000)
Gain before taper relief	20,000

Rolled over again = £20,000

Factory

	£	£
Proceeds		375,000
Less: cost	350,000	
Less: rolled over gain	(20,000)	
		(330,000)
Gain before taper relief		45,000

Factory owed for one whole year.

Gain after taper relief £45,000 × 50% = £22,500

3 As a replacement factory is purchased in the period commencing one year before and ending three years after the sale of the first factory, rollover relief to defer the gain on the sale of the first factory can be claimed.

Rollover relief is restricted because the full proceeds of sale of the first factory are not reinvested. This means £20,000 of the gain on the first factory is immediately chargeable. The remaining gain of £100,000 is deducted from the base cost of the replacement factory. As a result any gain arising on the future sale of the replacement factory will be larger than it would have been had rollover relief not been claimed.

4 *Gift of premises*

	£
Deemed disposal proceeds	400,000
Less: cost	(80,000)
Gain before taper relief	320,000

Gift relief = £320,000

Sale of premises

	£	£
Disposal proceeds		675,000
Less: cost	400,000	
Gift relief	(320,000)	
		(80,000)
Gain before taper relief		595,000

Premises owed one whole year by Hugo.

Gain after taper relief 50% × £595,000 = £297,500

5 Assets qualifying for gift relief are the:

1 Unquoted trading company shares, and the
2 Freehold factory

6 a) If no gift relief claimed:

Gift of shares

	£
Deemed sale proceeds	85,000
Less: cost	(50,000)
Gain before taper relief	35,000

Shares held by Julie for at least two whole years.

Gain after taper relief 25% × £35,000 = £8,750

Sale of shares

	£
Proceeds	95,000
Less: cost	(85,000)
Gain before taper relief	10,000

Shares held by Jack for one whole year.

Gain after taper relief 50% × £10,000 = £5,000

b) If gift relief was claimed:

The gain before taper relief on the gift of shares is deferred by setting it against the base cost of the shares to be deducted on the future sale of the shares.

Sale of shares

	£	£
Proceeds		95,000
Less: cost	85,000	
Less: gift relief	(35,000)	
		(50,000)
Gain before taper relief		45,000

Gain after taper relief 50% × £45,000 = £22,500

Note that in this case, the gift relief is not worth claiming.

Chapter 11: Computing profits chargeable to corporation tax

1

	£
Trading profits (W1)	418,500
Other income (non-trade royalties)	4,000
PCTCT	422,500

Workings

1) Trading profits

	£
Net profit	429,000
Less: non-trade royalties	(4,000)
	425,000
Less: capital allowances (W2)	(6,500)
Trading profits	418,500

No adjustment needed for trade royalties paid/received.

2) Capital allowances

	Pool £	Allowances £
WDV b/f	15,000	
Addition (no FYA)	11,000	
	26,000	
Less: WDA @ 25%	(6,500)	6,500
WDV c/f	19,500	

No adjustment for private use in capital allowance company computation.

2

	£
Trading profits	200,000
Capital gains (W1, W2)	152,616
PCTCT	352,616

There is no annual exemption for companies.

Workings

1) Factory

	£
Proceeds	350,000
Less: cost	(225,000)
Unindexed gain	125,000
Less: indexation allowance	
0.141 × £225,000	(31,725)
Indexed gain	93,275

2) *FA 1985 pool*

	No of shares	Cost	Indexed cost
		£	£	£
April 1995 Acquisition	8,000	24,000	24,000
January 2003 Indexed rise 0.197 × £24,000			4,728
			28,728
Acquisition	2,000	8,000	8,000
	10,000	32,000	36,728
October 2006 Indexed rise (0.107 × £36,728)			3,930
			40,658
Sale	(10,000)	(32,000)	(40,658)
	NIL	NIL	NIL

	£
Proceeds	100,000
Less: cost	(32,000)
Unindexed gain	68,000
Less: indexation allowance £(40,658 – 32,000)	(8,658)
Indexed gain	59,342

Total gains £(93,275 + 59,342) = £152,616

3

	£
Trading profits	85,000
Interest income £(6,000 + 1,500)	7,500
Capital gains	2,950
Less: gift aid donation	(15,200)
PCTCT	80,250

Note. Dividends received do not form part of PCTCT.

4

	Year to 31 March 2007	3 months ended 30 June 2007
	£	£
Trading profits (12/15 : 3/15)	240,000	60,000
Interest accrued	6,000	1,500
Capital gain	250,000	–
Gift aid	(50,000)	–
PCTCT	446,000	61,500

Chapter 12: Computing corporation tax payable

1

	£
PCTCT	60,000
Dividends (× 100/90)	5,000
'Profits'	65,000

2

	£
PCTCT	2,100,000
Dividend (× 100/90)	50,000
'Profits'	2,150,000

The full rate of CT applies: £2,100,000 × 30% = £630,000

Note that although 'profits' are used to work out the rate of tax that applies, CT is only charged on PCTCT.

3

	£
PCTCT	220,000
Dividends (× 100/90)	100,000
'Profits'	320,000

Small companies' marginal relief applies.

	£
£220,000 × 30%	66,000
Less: 11/400 £(1,500,000 – 320,000) × $\frac{220,000}{320,000}$	(22,309)
CT liability	43,691

4

	£
PCTCT	60,000
Dividends	–
'Profits'	60,000

The small companies' rate applies.

CT liability £60,000 × 19% = £11,400

5

	£
PCTCT	3,000
Dividends (× 100/90)	1,000
'Profits'	4,000

Starting rate applied.

The corporation tax liability was £NIL.

answers to chapter activities

6

	£
PCTCT	20,000
Dividends (× 100/90)	1,000
'Profits'	21,000

Starting rate marginal relief applied.

	£
£20,000 × 19%	3,800
Less: $19/400 \, (50,000 - 21,000) \times \dfrac{20,000}{21,000}$	(1,312)
CT liability	2,488

7

	FY05 3 months to 31.3.06 £	FY06 9 months to 31.12.06 £
PCTCT (divided 3:9)	10,000	30,000
Dividends plus tax credits (divided 3:9)	625	1,875
	10,625	31,875
Lower limit for Starting rate (FY 2005 only)		
£10,000 × 3/12	2,500	
Upper limit for Starting rate (FY 2005 only)		
£50,000 × 3/12	12,500	
Tax on PCTCT		
FY05: £10,000 × 19%	1,900	
Less: Starting rate marginal relief		
£(12,500 − 10,625) × 10,000/10,625 × 19/400	(84)	
		1,816
FY06: £30,000 × 19%		5,700
Corporation tax payable		7,516

8

	£
PCTCT	200,000
Dividends (× 100/90)	50,000
'Profits'	250,000

Nine month period.

Small companies' lower limit

£300,000 × 9/12 = £225,000

Small companies' upper limit

£1,500,000 × 9/12 = £1,125,000

Small companies' marginal relief applies:

	£
£200,000 × 30%	60,000
11/400 £(1,125,000 – 250,000) × $\frac{200,000}{250,000}$	(19,250)
	40,750

9

	£
PCTCT	360,000
Dividends (× 100/90)	25,000
'Profits'	385,000

Small companies' rate lower limit

£300,000 × 1/3 = £100,000

Small companies' rate upper limit

£1,500,000 × 1/3 = £500,000

As there are three companies associated with each other, the lower and upper limits are divided by 3.

Small companies' marginal relief applies:

	£
£360,000 × 30%	108,000
Less: 11/400 £(500,000 – 385,000) × $\frac{360,000}{385,000}$	(2,957)
CT liability	105,043

Chapter 13: Corporation tax losses

1

	£
Trading profits	40,000
Less: s393(1) relief	(40,000)
	NIL
Rental income	25,000
Capital gain	2,000
PCTCT	27,000

Losses carried forward can be set only against the trading profits. They can not be set against other profits.

Trading losses of £10,000 (£50,000 – £40,000) remain to be carried forward on 1 April 2007.

2

	Year ended 30 September 2005 £	Six months to 31 March 2006 £	Year ended 31 March 2007 £
Trading profits	50,000	60,000	
Less: s393A carry back	(25,000)	(60,000)	
gift aid donation	(10,000)	–	
PCTCT	15,000	–	
Unrelieved gift aid donations		30,000	15,000

£25,000 of the loss may be relieved in the year ended 30 September 2005, ie £50,000 × 6/12

3

	Year ended 31 March		
	2005 £	2006 £	2007 £
Trading profits	50,000	40,000	–
Bank interest	10,000	5,000	5,000
Chargeable gain £(12,000 – 7,000)	–	–	5,000
	60,000	45,000	10,000
Less: s393A – current	–	–	(10,000)
– carry back	–	(45,000)	–
PCTCT	60,000	NIL	NIL

The capital loss has to be carried forward to set against the future chargeable gain. It cannot be set against other profits.

Loss memorandum

	£
Loss	90,000
s393A – current	(10,000)
	80,000
s393A – carry back	(45,000)
Loss c/f	35,000

Chapter 14: National insurance

1   Class 4 NICs

	£
8% × (£33,540 – £5,035)	2,280.40
1% × (£34,850 – £33,540)	13.10
	2,293.50

Class 2 NICs

52 × £2.10 = £109.20

answers to chapter activities

2 Weekly earnings threshold:

£5,035 ÷ 52 = £97

Secondary Class 1 NICs:

£(450 − 97) × 12.8% = £45.18 × 52 = £2,349.36

3 Class 1 NICs

(£45,000 − 5,035) × 12.8% = £5,115.52

Class 1A NICs

£3,000 × 12.8% = £384

Chapter 15: Administration and payment of income tax, CGT and Class NICs

1 Filing due date later of:

a) 31 January 2008
b) 2 December 2007

ie 31 January 2008.

A fixed penalty of £100 will be charged for the late filing, within six months of the due date.

2

	£
Income tax	14,000
Class 4 NICs	2,500
	16,500

Payments on account = £8,250

No payments on account are due in respect of Class 2 NICs or CGT.

Chapter 16: Administration and payment of corporation tax

1 The later of:

a) 30 September 2007, and
b) 1 September 2007.

ie 30 September 2007.

2 The two accounting periods are:

a) year ended 31 December 2005, and
b) Six months to 30 June 2006.

Tax returns are required for both of these accounting periods. The due date for filing both returns is 30 June 2007.

3 £200. The return is six months late but all previous returns have been filed on time.

4 The later of:

a) 30 April 2008, and
b) 31 October 2008

ie 31 October 2008.

5 The later of:

a) 30 November 2007, and
b) 31 January 2008

ie 31 January 2008.

6 B As S Ltd is a large company instalments is due as follows:

14 October 2006
14 January 2007
14 April 2007
14 July 2007

ie the final instalment is due on 14 July 2007.

HOW MUCH HAVE YOU LEARNED? - ANSWERS

Chapter 1 Introduction

1 A company may suffer

    a) Corporation tax
    b) NICs related to its employees' earnings

2 A sole trader may suffer

    a) Income tax
    b) Capital gains tax
    c) NICs on business profits/related to his employees' earnings

3 Statutory total income

4

	Non-savings income £	Savings (excl dividend) income £	Dividend income £	Total £
Non-savings income	20,000	0		
Savings (excl. dividend income)		12,000		
Dividend income			10,000	
STI	20,000	12,000	10,000	42,000
Less: Personal allowance	(5,035)			
Taxable income	14,965	12,000	10,000	36,965

Tax	£
£2,150 × 10%	215
£12,815 × 22%	2,819
£14,965	
£12,000 × 20%	2,400
£6,335 × 10%	633
£33,300	
£(10,000 − 6,335) = £3,665 × 32.5%	1,191
Income tax 2006/07	7,258

207

how much have you learned? – answers

Chapter 2: Computing trading income

1. Legal fees incurred on pursuing trade debtors are deductible. Legal fees on the acquisition of factory are capital expenditure and so not deductible.

2. £700. The cost of staff entertaining is allowable.

   Gifts of food are never allowable. The entertaining of customers is never allowable.

3.
   a) Disallowable
   b) Allowable
   c) Disallowable
   d) Allowable
   e) Allowable
   f) Disallowable

4. The normal selling price of £80 + 20% × £80 = £96 must be added to the accounts profit.

5. The movement on the general provision is disallowable. This means that the decrease in the general provision of £700 (£2,500 – £1,800) must be deducted from the accounts profit.

6. 80% × £450 = £360 is disallowable for tax purposes.

Chapter 3: Capital allowances

1. £2,000. A maximum of the original cost is deducted from the pool.

2. Year ended 30 June 2006

	FYA @ 40% £	Pool £	Allowances £
B/f		22,500	
Proceeds		(7,800)	
		14,700	
WDA @ 25%		(3,675)	3,675
		11,025	
Addition	2,300		
FYA @ 40%	(920)		920
		1,380	
Allowances c/f		12,405	4,595

208

3 Period ended 31 December 2006

	FYA @ 40% £	Pool £	Allowances £
Addition		8,000	
WDA @ 25% × 6/12		(1,000)	1,000
		7,000	
Addition	5,000		
FYA @ 40%	(2,000)		2,000
		3,000	
Allowances c/f		10,000	3,000

Note. WDAs are time apportioned in a short period. FYAs are not.

4

	£
B/f	12,500
Addition	20,000
Proceeds	(18,300)
	14,200
Balancing allowance	(14,200)

Note. There are no FYAs or WDAs in the final period.

5 Year ended 30 April 2006

	Private use asset @ 60% £		Allowances £
Addition	30,000		
WDA	(3,000)	× 60%	1,800
C/f	27,000		

6 £100,000 × 4% = £4,000

7
a) £320,000 × 4% = £12,800

b) 13 years of tax life has expired, so 12 years remain. IBAs are given on over the remaining 12 years. Beckwith is given allowances on the lower of his original cost and the purchase price.

$$\frac{128,000}{12} = £10,667$$

how much have you learned? – answers

Chapter 4: Taxing unincorporated businesses

1.
Tax year	Basis period
2006/07	1 May 2006 – 5 April 2007
2007/08	Year ended 31 December 2007
2008/09	Year ended 31 December 2008

    Overlap period   1 January 2007 – 5 April 2007

2. Overlap profits may be deducted from the final assessment on cessation of a business.

3.
   2004/05 (year ended 31 May 2004)   £18,000
   2005/06 (year ended 31 May 2005)   £32,000
   2006/07 (1 June 2005 – 31 December 2006)
         (£25,000 + £15,000 – £10,000)   £30,000

4. 2005/06 (1 February 2006 – 5 April 2006)
   £34,000 × 2/17 = £4,000

   2006/07 (6 April 2006 – 5 April 2007)
   £34,000 × 12/17 = £24,000

   2007/08 (12 months ended 30 June 2007)
   £34,000 × 12/17 = £24,000

   Overlap profits (1 July 2006 to 5 April 2007)
   9/12 × £24,000 = £18,000

5. 2005/06 (1 December 2005 – 5 April 2006)
   4/7 × £70,000 = £40,000

   2006/07 (1 December 2005 – 30 November 2006)
   £70,000 + 5/12 × £60,000 = £95,000

   2007/08 (year ended 30 June 2007) £60,000

   Overlap profits

	£
1 December 2005 – 5 April 2006	40,000
1 July 2006 – 30 November 2006	25,000
	65,000

Chapter 5: Relieving trading losses

1. 2006/07 and/or 2005/06

2. False. Trading losses can be carried forward indefinitely.

3. Taxable trading profits arising in the same trade.

how much have you learned? – answers

4   The loss is a loss of 2006/07.

It can be:

a) Set against statutory total income of £9,000 in 2006/07 and/or against STI of £19,000 2005/06.

b) Carried forward to set against taxable trading profits of £25,000 in 2007/08 and then in later years.

Chapter 6: Partnerships

1   The period of account concerned.

2

	Total £	Dave £	Joe £
1.1.06 – 30.9.06 (9/12)	13,500	6,750	6,750
1.9.06 – 31.12.06 (3/12)	4,500	2,700	1,800
	18,000	9,450	8,550

Dave has taxable profits of £9,450 for 2006/07 and Joe has taxable profits of £8,550 for 2006/07.

3

	Total £	Sunita £	Jasmine £
Salary	85,000	5,000	80,000
Profits (£200,000 – £85,000)	115,000	57,500	57,500
	200,000	62,500	137,500

4   2006/07 (year ended 31 March 2007)

Taxable profits of Barry and Steve for 2006/07 are £40,000 (1/2 × £80,000).

5   *Year ended 31 August 2007*

	Total £	Abdul £	Ghita £	Sase £
Profits (2:2:1)	120,000	48,000	48,000	24,000

The opening year rules apply to Sase.

2006/07 (1 September 2006 – 5 April 2007)

7/12 × £24,000 = £14,000

2007/08 (year ended 31 August 2007) = £24,000

Overlap profits are £14,000

how much have you learned? – answers

6   First divide the profits of the periods of account between the partners.

	Total £	William £	Ann £	John £
Y/e 31.10.05	21,000	7,000	7,000	7,000
Y/e 31.10.06	33,000	11,000	11,000	11,000
Year ended 31 October 2007				
1.11.06 – 31.12.06 (2/12)	6,000	2,000	2,000	2,000
1.1.07 – 31.10.08 (10/12)	30,000	–	15,000	15,000
	36,000	2,000	17,000	17,000

Ann and John will be taxed on the current year basis of assessment throughout:

	Ann £	John £
2005/06 (year ended 31 October 2005)	7,000	7,000
2006/07 (year ended 31 October 2006)	11,000	11,000
2007/08 (year ended 31 October 2007)	17,000	17,000

The cessation rules apply to William in 2006/07, the year he left the business:

2005/06 (year ended 31 October 2005) = £7,000
2006/07 (1 November 2005 – 31 December 2006) £11,000 + £2,000 – £5,000 = £8,000

Chapter 7: Capital gains tax for sole traders

1   Both disposals are chargeable disposals for CGT.

2
	£
Sale proceeds	160,000
Less: Cost	(125,000)
Gains before taper relief	35,000

The factory was owned for at least two complete years for taper relief purposes.

Therefore, gain after taper relief 25% × £35,000 = £8,750.

3
	£
Sale proceeds	60,000
Less: cost	(30,000)
Less: indexation £30,000 × 0.283	(8,490)
Gain before taper relief	21,510

The asset has been owned for at least two years (from 6 April 1998) for taper relief purposes so the gain arising after taper relief is:

£21,510 × 25% = £5,377

4

	£
Gains	12,000
Losses	(2,000)
	10,000
Less: loss b/f	(1,200)
	8,800
Less: annual exemption	(8,800)
Taxable gain	NIL

Losses c/f £5,800 (£7,000 − £1,200)

5

Basic rate band remaining £33,300 − £23,190 = £10,110

Taxable gains £(24,000 − 8,800) = £15,200

CGT:

	£
10,110 × 20%	2,022
5,090 × 40%	2,036
15,200	4,058

Chapter 8: Chargeable gains: additional aspects

1

	£
Proceeds	38,000
Less: costs of disposal	(3,000)
	35,000
Less: £41,500 × $\dfrac{38,000}{38,000+48,000}$	(18,337)
	16,663
Less: indexation £18,337 × 0.620	(11,369)
Gain before taper relief	5,294

2

a) As the chattel is sold for less than £6,000, the gain arising is exempt.

b)

	£
Proceeds	8,420
Less: expenses	(220)
	8,200
Less: cost	(5,500)
Gain before taper relief	2,700

Maximum gain 5/3 (8,420 − 6,000) = £4,033

Therefore, gain before taper relief = £2,700

3

No gain arises as a wasting chattel is an exempt asset.

how much have you learned? – answers

4

	£
Deemed proceeds	6,000
Less: cost	(7,000)
Allowable loss	(1,000)

5 False. Losses on disposals to a connected person can be set only against gains arising on disposals to the same connected person in the same or future years.

6 True.

Chapter 9: Shares

1 Match post April 1998 acquisitions on a LIFO basis:

	No
15 June 1998	3,000
Disposal	(3,000)

Next match with FA 1985 pool which contains:

	£
30 September 1987	2,000
10 July 1989	1,000
Pool	3,000
Disposal	(2,000)
Pool shares remaining	1,000

2 If the shareholder was a company all the shares would be put in the FA 1985 pool:

	No
15 June 1998	3,000
10 July 1989	1,000
30 September 1987	2,000
	6,000
Disposal	(5,000)
	1,000

5,000 of the pooled shares are sold, 1,000 remain.

3 An operative event is an acquisition or disposal of shares that needs to be reflected in the FA 1985 pool. It includes purchases, sales and rights issues. It does not include bonus issues.

4 False. Rights issue shares rank for indexation only from the day on which they were acquired.

5 In a rights issue shares are paid for. In a bonus issue shares are not paid for.

6 First match with the March 2006 acquisition:

	£
Disposal proceeds	12,000
Less: cost	(6,000)
Gain before taper relief	6,000

Next match with the FA 1985 pool shares:

	No of shares	Cost £	Indexed cost £
Purchase	2,000	1,700	1,700
Indexation 0.704 × £1,700			1,197
6 April 1998 pool closes	2,000	1,700	2,897

	£
Disposal proceeds	12,000
Less: cost	(1,700)
Less: indexation	(1,197)
Gain before taper relief	9,103

7 As this is a company, all shares are in the FA 1985 pool:

	No of shares	Cost £	Indexed cost £
1 September 1985	1,000	5,000	5,000
Index to July 2004			
0.957 × £5,000			4,785
	1,000	5,000	9,785
Addition	1,500	15,000	15,000
	2,500	20,000	24,785
Indexed to December 2006			
0.061 × £24,785			1,512
	2,500	20,000	26,297
Disposal	(2,500)	(20,000)	(26,297)

For a company indexation is available to the date of disposal of an asset.

	£
Disposal proceeds	34,000
Less: cost	(20,000)
Less: indexation £(26,297 – 20,000)	(6,297)
Chargeable gain	7,703

how much have you learned? – answers

Chapter 10: Deferring taxation of capital gains

1   B   The office block and the freehold warehouse were acquired outside the qualifying reinvestment period commencing one year before and ending three years after the disposal.

The fork lift truck is not fixed plant and machinery.

2   C   Land

	£
Sales proceeds	400,000
Less: cost	(100,000)
Gain	300,000

£20,000 of the proceeds are not reinvested, so £20,000 of the gain remains chargeable. £280,000 is rolled over.

Replacement land

	£	£
Sale proceeds		500,000
Less: cost	380,000	
Rolled over gain	(280,000)	
		(100,000)
Chargeable gain		400,000

Note. Companies are not entitled to taper relief.

3   True.

4   The replacement asset(s) must be bought in the qualifying period which is 16 January 2006 to 14 January 2010.

5   No jewellery is not a qualifying asset for gift relief purposes.

6   Gift

	£
Market value	200,000
Less: cost	(50,000)
Gain	150,000
Less: gift relief	(150,000)
Taxable gain	NIL

Sale

	£
Sale proceeds	350,000
Less: cost (£200,000 – £150,000)	(50,000)
Gain before taper relief	300,000

No taper relief due.

Chapter 11: Computing profits chargeable to corporation tax

1.
	£
Building society interest	6,000
Bank deposit interest	3,900
Dividends from UK companies	NIL
Patent royalties (× 100/78)	7,500

2. The gross interest payable is deducted in computing trading profits.

3. £385 may be deducted in computing PCTCT.

4. B The first accounting period is always 12 months in length in a long accounting period.

5.
	Year ended 31.12.06 £	4 months ended 30.4.07 £
Business profits (12/16 : 4/16)	240,000	80,000
Interest	1,200	400
Gain	–	20,000
Gift aid	(15,000)	–
PCTCT	226,200	100,400

Chapter 12: Computing corporation tax payable

1. B

	£
PCTCT	255,000
Dividend	–
'Profits'	255,000

Small companies' lower limit £300,000 × 6/12 = £150,000

Small companies' upper limit £1,500,000 × 6/12 = £750,000

As this is a six month period, the limits are multiplied by 6/12.

Small companies' marginal relief applies:

	£
£255,000 × 30%	76,500
Less: 11/400 £(750,000 – 255,000)	(13,613)
	62,887

2. 'Profits' = £55,000

Small companies' lower limit £300,000 × 9/12 = £225,000

Small companies' rate applies: £50,000 × 19% = £9,500

how much have you learned? – answers

3   C

	FY05 3 months to 31.3.06 £	FY06 9 months to 31.12.06 £
PCTCT/'Profits' (divided 3:9)	2,250	6,750
Lower limit for starting rate (FY05) £10,000 × 3/12	2,500	
Tax on PCTCT		
FY05 £2,250 × 0%		0
FY06 £6,750 × 19%		1,282
Corporation tax payable		1,282

4   B   PCTCT = £180,000

Small companies lower limit £300,000 × 9/12 × 1/2 = £112,500

Small companies upper limit £1,500,000 × 9/12 × 1/2 = £562,500

There are two associated companies, so the limits are divided by 2. The limits are also multiplied by 9/12 as this is a short accounting period.

Small companies marginal relief applies:

	£
£180,000 × 30%	54,000
Less: 11/400 £(562,500 – 180,000)	(10,519)
	43,481

5   B

6   1 April 2006 to 31 March 2007

Chapter 13: Corporation tax losses

1   a)   B

	Year ended 31 March	
	2006 £	2007 £
Trading profit	170,000	–
Interest	5,000	50,000
Capital gain £(12,000 – 20,000)	–	–
	175,000	50,000
Less s393A – current/carried back	(175,000)	(50,000)
	NIL	NIL

Trade losses of £95,000 (£320,000 – £175,000 – £50,000) remain to be carried forward at 1 April 2007.

b)   A capital loss of £8,000 (£20,000 – £12,000) remains to be carried forward at 1 April 2007.

c)   Gift Aid donations of £5,000 are unrelieved in each year.

2 B

	Year ended 30.9.05 £	Six months 31.3.06 £	Year ended 31.3.07 £
Trading profit	40,000	60,000	–
Less: s393A current	–	–	–
c/b	(20,000)	(60,000)	–
gift aid	(10,000)	–	–
PCTCT	10,000	–	–

The maximum relief is £40,000 × 6/12 = £20,000.

Chapter 14: National insurance

1 a) No Class 2 NICs as earnings below small profit exception

No Class 4 NICs due as profits below £5,035

b) Class 2 NICs 52 × £2.10 = £109.20

	£
Class 4 NICs (£33,540 – £5,035) × 8%	2,280.40
(£37,000 – £33,540) × 1%	34.60
	2,315.00

c) Class 2 NICs 52 × £2.10 = £109.20

Class 4 NICs (£10,850 – £5,035) × 8% = £465.20

2 Weekly earnings threshold $\frac{£5,035}{52}$ = £97

Alan = £NIL
Betty = (£100 – £97) × 12.8% = £0.38
Darren (£240 – £97) × 12.8% = £18.30
Eleanor (£690 – £97) × 12.8% = £75.90

3 Class 1A NICs

	£
Stuart (2,025 + 3,888) × 12.8%	756.86
Terry (3,776 + 4,608) × 12.8%	1,073.15
Uma (5,850 + 3,600) × 12.8%	1,209.60

Chapter 15: Administration and payment of income tax, CGT and Class 4 NICs

1. The due date is the later of:

    a) 31 January 2008
    b) 3 months after a notice requiring the return was issued.

2. Payments on account of income tax for 2006/07 are due on:

    31 January 2007; and
    31 July 2007

    Each payment on account due is equal to 50% of the prior years income tax and Class 4 NIC payable

3. £100 penalty (maximum) for failure to deliver return on time.

    5% surcharge on tax paid late. Interest on tax paid late.

4. 31 January 2009. A year after the due filing date

5.
    | £6,000 | 31 January 2007 |
    | £6,000 | 31 July 2007 |
    | £4,000 | 31 January 2008 |

6. No surcharges are due on late payments on account.

7. 31 January 2008.

Chapter 16: Administration and payment of corporation tax

1. By 30 June 2007 (12 months after the due filing date).

2. £1,000 (this is the third successive late filing and the return is over 3 months late).

3. B — 1 October 2007. Girton Ltd is a small or medium sized company, so all CT is due nine months after the end of the accounting period.

4. C — Eaton Ltd is a large company.

    The first instalment of CT is due in the seventh month of the accounting period concerned.

5. $\frac{1}{4} \times £240,000 = £60,000$

6. B — $£800,000 \times \frac{3}{8} = £300,000$

    14 July 2007 = £300,000
    14 October 2007 = £300,000
    14 December 2007 = £200,000

REVISION COMPANION UNIT 18

Chapter 1:
INTRODUCTION

John Smith has the following income and outgoings for the tax year 2006/07.

		£
i)	Taxable trading profits	45,000
ii)	Interest on a deposit account with the Scotia Bank	1,000
iii)	Dividends on UK shares	1,000

Tasks

a) Prepare a schedule of income for 2006/07, clearly showing the distinction between non-savings, savings and dividend income. John Smith's personal allowance should be deducted as appropriate.

b) Calculate the income tax liability for 2006/07.

Chapter 2: COMPUTING TRADING INCOME

When deciding whether or not a trade is being carried on, HM Revenue and Customs is often guided by the badges of trade.

Task

Write a memo to your manager explaining what you understand by the term badges of trade.

The profit and loss account of Mr Jelly for the year ended 31 December 2006 shows:

	£		£
Staff wages	2,500	Gross profit from trading account	10,000
Light and heat	300		
Motor car expenses	350		
Postage, stationery and telephone	100		
Repairs and renewals	450		
Bad debts	100		
Miscellaneous expenses	300		
Depreciation	600		
Net profit	5,300		
	10,000		10,000

The following information is also relevant:

1) One-seventh of the motor expenses relates to private motoring.

2) Repairs and renewals comprise:

	£
Painting shop internally	129
Plant repairs	220
Building extension to stockroom	101
	450

3) Bad debts account (all trade debts)

2006		£	2006		£
Dec 31	Bad debts written off	102	Jan 1	Balances b/f	
	Balances c/f			General	200
	General	400		Specific	360
	Specific	398			
			Dec 31	Bad debt recovered	240
				Profit & loss account	100
		900			900

4) Miscellaneous expenses include:

	£
Donations – Oxfam	10
Advertising	115
Customer Entertaining	90
Christmas gifts – ten bottles of gin and whisky	70
Legal expenses re debt collecting	15
	300

5) The staff wages include £260 paid to Mr Jelly.

Task

Compute Mr Jelly's taxable trading profit for the year ended 31 December 2006.

3 Brutus has been trading for many years as a retailer of the busts of Roman emperors.

His profit and loss account for the year ended 31 December 2006 was as follows:

	£	£
Gross profit		50,000
Wages and salaries	18,000	
Repairs	4,550	
Depreciation	4,000	
Bank interest	300	
Bad debts	700	
Legal expenses	400	
Rent and rates	2,450	
Entertaining	600	
		(31,000)
Net profit		19,000

The following items are relevant:

1) Brutus took two busts of the emperor Trajan to give to friends which were valued as follows

	£
Cost (each)	20
Market value (each)	25

No entry has been made in the accounts in respect of these busts.

2) The Provision for Bad and Doubtful Debts Account has been reconstructed as follows:

	£		£
		Provisions b/f	1,300
		Profit and loss account	700
Bad debts written off	600	Bad debts recovered	70
Provisions c/f	1,470		
	2,070		2,070

The provisions b/f and c/f can be analysed as follows:

			£
B/f	General		500
	Specific		800
C/f	General		470
	Specific		1,000

All the debts were trade debts.

3) Legal expenses were in connection with the proposed purchase of new freehold premises. It was eventually decided not to proceed with the purchase.

4) Entertaining has been analysed as follows:

	£
Staff party	325
Cocktail party held for UK customers	50
Dinner for Japanese trade delegation	150
Drinks given to coach party of German tourists	75
	600

Task

Compute Brutus' taxable profit for the year ended 31 December 2006.

Chapter 3:
CAPITAL ALLOWANCES

Bodie, a sole trader, makes up his accounts to 31 March each year.

The value of the general pool as at 1 April 2006 was £38,500.

A Jaguar car purchased in May 2005 had a tax written down value at 1 April 2006 of £15,000 (original cost £18,000)

His expenditure, all qualifying for capital allowances, has been as follows:

Date		£
14 July 2006	Microcomputer	3,800
30 March 2007	Mercedes car	18,000
31 March 2007	Rover car	8,000
31 March 2007	Computer printer	1,000

The Jaguar and Mercedes were for the proprietor's own use (20% private), whilst the other cars were for employees.

The Jaguar was sold for £16,500 on 20 March 2007 and a Volvo which had been acquired for £7,000 was sold for £3,000 on 19 March 2007.

Assume Bodie's business qualifies as a small business for capital allowance purposes.

Task

Calculate capital allowances for year ending 31 March 2007.

Mrs Frinton commenced trading on 1 January 2004 making up accounts to 31 August.

Expenditure on plant and equipment is as follows:

Date	Cost £
1 January 2004	10,500
1 December 2004	4,000
1 October 2005	6,000
1 June 2006	8,800

On 1 May 2005, plant which cost £2,700 was sold for £1,500.

Task

Calculate the capital allowances for the first three periods of account. The business is a small business for capital allowance purposes.

3 Jeremy Japer had been trading as a draper for many years producing accounts to 31 August each year. Unfortunately due to ill health he was forced to retire on 31 May 2006. Final accounts were prepared for the nine months to 31 May 2006. The business is a small sized business for capital allowance purposes.

The tax written down value of capital assets as at 1 September 2003 were as follows:

	£
General pool	19,200
Expensive car (business use by Jeremy 80%)	14,400

The following capital transactions took place:

		£
1 September 2004	Addition to plant	5,100
1 October 2005	Addition to plant	7,200
31 May 2006	Disposals (no item > cost)	
	plant	15,900
	expensive car	9,000

Task

Calculate the capital allowances for the last three periods of account.

4 Joe is a sole trader. His business is a medium-sized business for capital allowance purposes.

On 1 April 2006 the tax written down values of Joe's plant and machinery was as follows:

	£
General pool	84,600
Expensive motor car	15,400

The expensive motor car was sold on 31 August 2006 for £19,600.

In addition to any items of plant and machinery included in the cost of the industrial building (see below), the following assets were purchased during the year ended 31 March 2007.

		£
15 June 2006	Computer	3,400
15 August 2006	Motor car	17,200
12 October 2006	Lorry	32,000

The expensive motor cars were used 50% for private purposes. An election was made to depool the computer, as a short life asset.

Joe has a new factory constructed at a cost of £400,000 that was brought into use on 30 September 2006.

	£
Land	80,000
Levelling the land	19,200
Architects fees	30,800
Fixed machinery	20,000
General offices	62,500
Factory	187,500
	400,000

Task

Calculate the capital allowances available to Joe in the year ended 31 March 2007.

Dexter Ltd, makes accounts to 30 June. Despite substantial investment in new equipment, business has been indifferent and the company will cease trading on 31 December 2006. Its last accounts will be prepared for the six months to 31 December 2006.

The tax written down value of fixed assets at 1 July 2002 was as follows.

Pool	£
General	29,700

Fixed asset additions and disposals have been as follows.

		£
20.9.02	Digging machine cost	1,917
25.6.03	Computer cost	3,667
15.7.04	Car for managing director's use cost	13,400
14.7.05	Plant sold for	340
10.5.06	Computer sold for	2,000

An election to depool the computer was made when it was acquired in 2003. Private use of the managing director's car was 20% for all years.

At the end of 2006, the plant would be worth £24,000, the managing director's car £10,600.

Task

Calculate the capital allowances for the periods from 1 July 2002 to 31 December 2006. Dexter Ltd has always been a medium sized enterprise for First Year Allowance purposes.

6   On 1 April 2006 the tax written down values of plant and machinery in Green Ltd's tax computations were as follows.

	£
Pool	106,000
Expensive car	7,000
Short life asset (spring end grinding machine)	17,500

The short-life asset was purchased on 7 August 2001 and was sold on 19 November 2006 for £5,000

On 1 January 2007 the expensive car was traded in for £6,000 against a new car costing £14,000 (the full price before the trade-in allowance).

There were no other purchases or sales during the year. The company had always prepared accounts to 31 March.

Task

Calculate the maximum capital allowances available in the year ended 31 March 2007.

7   On 1 September 2006 Biswas Ltd purchased a second hand factory for £80,000. This had cost the original purchaser £100,000 on 1 September 1996 and had always been in industrial use. Biswas Ltd immediately used the factory as an industrial building.

Biswas Ltd had purchased its current factory (still in use) in August 2001 for a total cost £190,000. This cost had been made up as follows:

Land	£55,000
Tunnelling	£10,000
Showroom	£35,000
Factory	£85,000

Task

Calculate the maximum IBAs that can be claimed by Biswas Ltd for its accounting period ended 31 March 2007.

Chapter 4:
TAXING UNINCORPORATED BUSINESSES

Rachel commenced in business as a fashion designer on 1 July 2004, and made up her first accounts to 30 April 2006. Her profit for the period, adjusted for taxation, was £33,000.

Tasks

a) Calculate the taxable profit for the first three tax years.
b) Calculate the 'overlap profits'.

Mr Phone commenced trading on 1 July 2004 drawing up accounts to 31 May each year.

Profits are:

	£
1 July 2004 to 31 May 2005	22,000
Year ended 31 May 2006	18,000
Year ended 31 May 2007	30,000

Task

Calculate the taxable profits for the years 2004/05 to 2006/07. What are the overlap profits?

Mr Mug ceased trading on 31 December 2006. His overlap profits brought forward amount to £9,000. His profits for the last few periods of account were:

	£
Year ended 30 April 2004	36,000
Year ended 30 April 2005	48,000
Year ended 30 April 2006	16,000
8 months ended 31 December 2006	4,000

Task

Calculate taxable profits for the last three tax years of trade.

4 Jackie Smith started her picture framing business on 1 May 2002. Due to falling profits she ceased to trade on 28 February 2007.

Her profits for the whole period of trading were as follows.

	£
1 May 2002 – 31 July 2003	18,000
1 August 2003 – 31 July 2004	11,700
1 August 2004 – 31 July 2005	8,640
1 August 2005 – 31 July 2006	4,800
1 August 2006 – 28 February 2007	5,100

Task

Calculate the total assessable profits for each of the tax years concerned.

You are to assume that ALL possible claims are made.

5 Albert Limb started trading on 1 February 2006. He provides you with the following statement for his first period of account to 31 March 2007:

	£	£
Gross trading profit		87,314
Less: depreciation	9,000	
office desk (note 1)	1,800	
wages and salaries (note 2)	20,600	
workshop repairs and improvements (note 3)	3,150	
delivery van expenses	6,800	
heating and lighting	7,400	
general expenses (note 4)	5,800	
legal expenses re purchase of workshop	950	
motor car expenses (note 5)	1,800	
		(57,300)
Net profit for the period		30,014

Notes

1) The office desk was purchased on 10 April 2006 at an auction of second-hand office equipment.

2) Wages and salaries is made up of:

	£
Employee wages	14,600
Salary to Albert Limb	5,000
Salary to Mrs Limb	1,000
	20,600

Mrs Limb carries out secretarial duties in the business and the amount paid is reasonable for the duties performed.

3) Workshop repairs and improvements related to the repair of a leaking roof. It was possible to use the workshop prior to making these repairs.

4) Included in general expenses is £450 for ten gifts of leather bound diaries embossed with the business name which Albert gave to this best customers at Christmas. The other general expenses are all allowable.

5) The private use of the motor car is 20%.

6) The following items were not included in the above statement:

6 May 2006	Purchased plant and machinery for £28,000.
10 July 2006	Purchased motor car for £13,000.
1 August 2006	Purchased delivery van for £8,400.

Assume the business is a small business for capital allowance purposes.

Task

Calculate taxable trading profits for the first two tax years of trading, showing clearly any overlap profits.

Tutor's hint

In order to complete this task you will need to do the following:

1) Compute the capital allowances for the period 1 February 2006 to 31 March 2007
2) Compute taxable trading profits for the period 1 February 2006 to 31 March 2007
3) Work out the basis periods for the first two years of account
4) Assign the taxable trading profits in 2) to the basis periods and calculate any overlap profits.

Miss Farrington started to trade as a baker on 1 January 2004 and made up her first accounts to 30 April 2005. Adjusted profits before capital allowances are as follows.

	£
Period to 30 April 2005	20,710
Year to 30 April 2006	15,125

Miss Farrington incurred the following expenditure on plant and machinery.

Date	Item	£
4.1.04	General plant	3,835
1.3.04	Secondhand oven acquired from Miss Farrington's father	1,200
25.3.04	Delivery van	1,800
25.3.04	Typewriter	425
15.5.04	Car for Miss Farrington	6,600
15.4.06	General plant	1,000
30.4.06	General plant	1,556

In addition Miss Farrington brought into the business on 1 January 2004 a desk and other office furniture. The agreed value was £940.

The agreed private use of the car is 35%. Miss Farrington's business is a small enterprise for capital allowance purposes.

Task

(a) Calculate Miss Farrington's capital allowances for her first two periods of account.

(b) Compute Miss Farrington's trading profits for her first two periods of account.

(c) Calculate the taxable trading profits for the first four tax years and the overlap profits carried forward.

Chapter 5:
RELIEVING TRADING LOSSES

Pipchin has traded for many years, making up accounts to 30 September each year. His recent results have been:

Year ended	£
30 September 2004	12,000
30 September 2005	(45,000)
30 September 2006	8,000
30 September 2007	14,000

He has received rental income as follows:

	£
2004/05	10,400
2005/06	11,000
2006/07	11,000
2007/08	11,000

Task

Compute Pipchin's STI for 2004/05 to 2007/08, assuming maximum claims for s380 relief are made and using any other loss relief available.

The following information relates to Mr N who has run a shop for many years. Mr N's taxable trading profits and losses have been, or are expected to be, as follows:

		£
Year ended 30 June 2005	Profit	4,000
Year ended 30 June 2006	Loss	(11,000)
Year ended 30 June 2007	Profit (projected)	14,000

Mr N's other income (Rental income) is as follows.

	£
2005/06	0
2006/07	19,000
2007/08	12,000

Tasks

a) State the ways in which Mr N may obtain relief for the loss of £11,000.

b) Calculate Mr N's taxable income for 2005/06 to 2007/08 assuming that loss relief is claimed in the most efficient way.

237

Assume that the personal allowance and rates of tax applicable to 2006/07 apply to all the years involved.

Tutor's hint

1. You must first work out the year in which the loss arose and Mr N's options for relieving the loss. These should be listed, briefly stating the income against which the loss would be relieved.

2. You must then choose the best form of loss relief. You should find that there is only one option which both gives relief quickly and does not set the loss against income which would otherwise be covered by the personal allowance.

3. Having made your choice, you should set out a working with a column for each year covered and a line for each source of income, a line for loss relief and a line for the personal allowance. Also allow space for sub-totals.

4. You can now insert the figures from the question into your working, and get the taxable income for each year.

Chapter 6:
PARTNERSHIPS

Fimbo and Florrie commenced in partnership on 1 January 2005. They produce accounts to 31 December each year and their profits have been as follows:

	Taxable profit £
Year ended 31 December 2005	10,000
Year ended 31 December 2006	20,000
Year ended 31 December 2007	25,000

Until 31 December 2006 Fimbo took 60% of the profits after receiving a £5,000 salary. Florrie took the remaining 40% of profits.

On 1 January 2007, Fimbo and Florrie invite Pom to join the partnership. It is agreed that Fimbo's salary will increase to £6,500 and the profits will then be split equally between the three partners.

Task

Calculate the taxable trading profit for each partner for 2004/05 to 2007/08 and show the overlap profits that arise for Pom.

John, Paul and George began to trade as partners on 1 January 2004. The profits of the partnership are shared in the ratio 4:3:3. The accounts for recent periods have shown the following results:

	£
Period to 31 July 2004	24,300
Year to 31 July 2005	16,200
Year to 31 July 2006	14,900

Task

Calculate the taxable trading profits of John, Paul and George for all tax years. Identify all overlap periods and overlap profits.

3. Strange and his partners Pavin and Lehman had traded for many years. Strange had contributed £20,000 to the business and Pavin £10,000.

Profits were shared in the ratio of 3:2:1 after providing Strange and Pavin with salaries of £15,000 and £5,000 and interest on capital of 5%.

On 1 August 2005 the profit sharing arrangements were amended to 2:2:1 after providing Strange with a salary of £20,000.

Recent results have been as follows:

	£
Year ended 31 December 2004	47,500
Year ended 31 December 2005	48,000
Year ended 31 December 2006	60,000

Task

Calculate the taxable trading profit for each partner for all relevant tax years.

4. Bob, Annie and John started their partnership on 1 June 2001 and make accounts up to 31 May each year. The accounts have always shown taxable profits.

For the period up to 31 January 2006 each partner received a salary of £15,000 per annum and the remaining profits were shared 50% to Bob and 25% each to Annie and John. There was no interest on capital or drawings.

Bob left the partnership on 1 February 2006. The profit sharing ratio, after the same salaries, changed to 50% each to Annie and John.

Profits for the years ending 31 May 2006 and 31 May 2007 were £90,000 and £120,000 respectively.

Task

Calculate each partner's share of the profits for the periods to 31 May 2006 and 31 May 2007 respectively.

Chapter 7:
CAPITAL GAINS TAX FOR SOLE TRADERS

Ambrose made the following chargeable disposals of business assets in 2006/07:

	Asset A	Asset B	Asset C
Purchase date	1.1.87	1.4.92	31.12.05
Purchase price	£7,500	£4,400	£7,500
Enhancement date	1.5.98	–	–
Enhancement cost	£500	–	–
Proceeds	£40,000	£18,000	£16,000
Disposal date	1.7.06	1.11.06	1.1.07

Task

Calculate the capital gains tax payable by Ambrose for 2006/07 assuming he has taxable income of £30,700.

Assume indexation factors: January 1987 to April 1998 = 0.626
April 1992 to April 1998 = 0.171

Mattheus made gains of £17,200 (all on business assets owned for many years) and losses of £7,000 in 2006/07. He has losses brought forward of £5,000.

Task

Calculate the losses to carry forward to 2007/08.

3 Charles, a sole trader, sold the following business assets in 2006/07:

	Office block £	Factory £	Shop £
Date of sale	1.12.06	31.12.06	12.2.07
Cost	100,000	700,000	120,000
Enhancement expenditure	–	–	20,000
Sale proceeds	300,000	400,000	500,000
Date of purchase	10.4.82	6.7.99	31.1.06

The enhancement expenditure on the shop was spent on installing shop fittings that had been removed by the date of sale.

Charles had taxable income of £34,000 in 2006/07.

Task

Calculate the CGT payable by Charles for 2006/07.

Indexation factor:

April 1982 to April 1998 = 1.006

4 John carried out the following disposals of assets during 2006/07.

a) On 6 June 2006 he sold land used in his business for £23,000. John had purchased the land in December 2000 for £26,000.

b) On 2 October 2006 he sold his 1956 motor car to a friend for £2,000. He had purchased the car in December 2004 for £300 and had spent many hours restoring it as a hobby.

c) On 30 January 2007 he sold for £80,000 his business premises, which had been acquired in July 1985 for £20,000.

John had unused capital losses carried forward at 5 April 2006 of £2,500 and transactions in the following two years gave rise to gains and losses as follows.

Task

Compute John's taxable gains for 2006/07 after taking into account all available exemptions, reliefs and losses. Assume an annual exemption of £8,800 for all years.

Assume indexation factors:

July 1985 – April 1998 = 0.708

Chapter 8:
CHARGEABLE GAINS:
ADDITIONAL ASPECTS

Kidson purchased a plot of land on 1 January 1983 for £8,000. On 31 August 2006, he sold part of the land for £45,000 but declined an offer of £50,000 for the rest. The land is a business asset for taper relief.

Task

Calculate the taxable gain arising on the sale assuming this is the only capital transaction Kidson has in 2006/07.

Assume an indexation factor:

January 1983 to April 1998 = 0.968

In 2006/07 Ian, a sole trader, made the following capital disposals:

1) An antique office desk which had been left to him when his father died in January 1987. The desk was worth £1,500 on his Father's death. Ian sold the desk in September 2006 at auction for £10,000. Auctioneer's fees of 5% were incurred on the sale. The desk is a business asset for taper relief purposes.

2) 2 acres of land from an 8 acre plot. The land had been bought in March 1982 for £10,000. Ian's neighbour paid £12,000 for the 2 acres in November 2006. Ian rejected a subsequent offer of £40,000 for the rest of the land. The land had always been used in Ian's business.

3) A freehold factory, to his wife, Susie. The factory had cost £50,000 in 2000 and he sold it for £80,000 (its market value) to Susie in June 2006. The factory had always been used in Ian's business.

4) A racehorse used to advertise Ian's business. A dealer paid Ian £1,000 for the racehorse in March 2007. Ian had bought it for £8,000 in July 2004.

Task

Calculate Ian's chargeable gains after taper relief but before the annual exemption for 2006/07. There were no capital losses brought forward on 6 April 2006.

Assume an indexation factor   January 1987 to April 1988 = 0.626
                                March 1982 to April 1998 = 1.047

3   Hilary Spencer disposed of the following capital items during the tax year 2006/07.

- A building which she had used for business purposes. The building was purchased for £28,000 in July 1991 and was sold for £106,000 in August 2006.

- A chattel, used for business purposes, was sold for £7,000 on 14 February 2007. It had originally cost £5,000 on 18 October 1999.

- A chattel, used for business purposes, was sold for £5,000 in 14 March 2007. This had cost £7,000 on 14 March 2002.

Task

Calculate Hilary's total amount chargeable to capital gains tax (CGT) for the year 2006/07.

Assume indexation

July 1991 to April 1998   0.215
July 1991 to August 2005   0.422

Chapter 9:
SHARES

Mr Jones carried out the following transactions in the shares of XYZ Ltd.

Date	Number of shares bought/(sold) £	Cost (proceeds) £
September 1982	2,000	3,000
November 1985	5,000	9,500
October 1987	(3,000)	(6,500)
May 2001	1,000	3,000
July 2006	(5,000)	(90,000)

His taxable income for 2006/07 was £19,800.

He made no other disposals of chargeable assets in 2006/07. The shares are business assets for the purposes of taper relief.

Task

Calculate the capital gains tax liability of Mr Jones for 2004/05.

Indexation factors: September 1982 to April 1985 = 0.158
April 1985 to November 1985 = 0.012
November 1985 to October 1987 = 0.073
October 1987 to April 1998 = 0.580

Mark Snow's dealings in Quack plc were as follows:

	Shares	Cost £
10 February 1986	12,000	18,000
10 April 1999	8,000	29,000
20 September 1999	Bonus issue of 1 for 4	NIL
15 March 2007	(12,000)	(48,000)

Tasks

a) Compute the chargeable capital gains assessable on the above disposal assuming the shares are business assets for taper relief purposes.

b) Recalculate the chargeable gain assuming that on 20 September 1999 there was a rights issue of 1:4 at £3.00 per share instead of the bonus issue.

Assume an indexation factor February 1986 to April 1998 = 0.683

Revision Companion – shares – chapter activities

3   Eric James sold 4,000 shares in JB Ltd on 4 November 2006 for £26,180. The shares had been acquired as follows:

	No.	£
9 December 1986	3,600	10,900
12 October 1998 (rights issue 1:3 at £5)		
10 November 2006	200	1,150

The shares are business assets for taper relief purposes.

Task

Calculate the chargeable gains arising from the sale.

Indexation factor December 1986 to April 1998 = 0.632

4   Jeff Brown is experiencing short-term cash flow difficulties and, in order to raise funds, made the following disposals during 2006/07:

6 October 2006

His entire holding of 50,000 ordinary shares in Faltskog Ltd were sold for £160,000.

These shares had been acquired, in a single batch on 1 January 1983 at a cost of £75,000. (The indexed cost at 6 April 1985 was £86,025.)

30 December 2006

25,000 ordinary shares in Anderson Ltd, were sold for £40,000.

These shares had been acquired in two batches as follows:

1 January 1986: 15,000 at a cost of £14,500
1 January 2001: 10,000 at a cost of £9,000

All shares were business assets for taper relief purposes.

Task

Calculate the chargeable gains on disposal of the shares after taper relief.

Indexation factors:

April 1985 to April 1998 = 0.716
January 1986 to April 1998 = 0.689

5   Brooklyn sold 11,000 ordinary shares in Biggs Ltd a trading company on 17 May 2006 for £66,000. She had bought ordinary shares in the company, for which she worked full time, on the following dates.

	No of shares	Cost £
19 September 1982	2,000	1,700
17 January 1985	2,000	6,000
12 December 1985	2,000	5,500
29 June 2004	3,000	11,500
3 November 2005	2,000	12,800

Task

Calculate, after taper relief but before the annual exemption, the capital gain for 2006/07. The shares are a business asset for taper relief purposes.

Assume indexation factors

September 1982 – April 1985	0.158
January 1985 – April 1985	0.039
April 1985 –December 1985	0.013
December 1985 – April 1998	0.694

Tutor's hints

1   Disposals should initially be matched with post 6.4.98 acquisitions. There will be no indexation allowance on these disposals but there may be taper relief.

2   Next build up the FA 1985 pool (including all the first three acquisitions). Indexation is first given up to April 1985, and then up to each later purchase or sale. Remember that the FA 1985 pool closes on 5 April 1998 so the final indexation allowance calculation will be to that date.

3   Gains and losses arising in a year must be set against each other even if this means wasting the annual exemption. Losses are set off in the most beneficial way before taper relief.

Standring Ltd owned 20,000 shares in Smart plc acquired as follows:

5,000 shares acquired September 1990 for £10,000
1 for 5 rights acquired October 2000 at £5 per share
14,000 shares acquired August 2001 for £84,000

Standring Ltd sold 18,000 shares in January 2007 for £135,000.

Task

Calculate the gain arising on the sale in January 2007.

Indexation factors:

September 1990 to October 2000 = 0.327
October 2000 to August 2001 = 0.014
August 2001 to January 2007 = 0.141

247

Question 7 – Box plc

Disposal: 26 May 2006 – 22,000 shares sold for £136,400

Matching rules (company)
1. Same day – none
2. Previous 9 days – 22 May 2006 acquisition (11,000 shares)
3. FA 1985 pool – balance (11,000 shares)

(1) Match with 22 May 2006 acquisition (11,000 shares)

	£
Proceeds (11,000/22,000 × £136,400)	68,200
Less: cost	(67,800)
Chargeable gain	**400**

(2) FA 1985 pool

	No. of shares	Cost £	Indexed cost £
26 May 1992 Purchase	4,000	24,000	24,000
30 June 1993 Bonus 1 for 2	2,000	–	–
	6,000	24,000	24,000
Indexation to Oct 2000: 24,000 × 0.232			5,568
24 Oct 2000 Purchase	5,000	27,500	27,500
	11,000	51,500	57,068
Indexation to May 2006: 57,068 × 0.139			7,932
	11,000	51,500	65,000
Disposal 26 May 2006	(11,000)	(51,500)	(65,000)
	nil	nil	nil

	£
Proceeds (11,000/22,000 × £136,400)	68,200
Less: cost	(51,500)
Unindexed gain	16,700
Less: indexation allowance (65,000 – 51,500)	(13,500)
Chargeable gain	**3,200**

Total chargeable gain

	£
Previous 9 days match	400
FA 1985 pool	3,200
Total chargeable gain included in PCTCT	**3,600**

Chapter 10:
DEFERRING TAXATION OF CAPITAL GAINS

You have received the following memorandum from a client of your firm:

To: Accountancy Trainee
From: Simon Evans
Date: 3 December 2006
Subject: Deferral of gains

I have just disposed of my 30% holding in Blue Ltd, an unquoted company.

You may like to know that I acquired the Blue Ltd shares in September 1988 as a gift from my father. He had originally acquired them as an investment in 1983 and we elected to defer the gain arising. You will find the details in my personal tax affairs file. I sold the Blue shares for £200,000 on 30 November 2006. I have no other assets for CGT purposes and made no other disposals in 2006/07.

Task

Calculate the taxable gain arising on the sale of the Blue Ltd shares. The shares are a business asset for taper relief purposes.

Additional information

You ascertain that the held over gain on the Blue shares was £15,000 and that they were worth £65,000 in September 1988.

Indexation factor:

September 1988 to April 1998 = 0.500

Fran gave a factory worth £500,000 to her friend Anna on 1 June 2006. Fran had bought the factory on 1 January 1993 for £75,000. On 1 July 2008 Anna sold the factory for £520,000.

Both Fran and Anna have elected for gift relief to apply and have used the factory for the purposes of their respective trades.

Task

Calculate the chargeable gains for Fran and Anna. Assume that tax rates and legislation remain the same in 2008/09 as in 2006/07.

Indexation factor:

January 1993 to April 1998 = 0.179

3   On 23 May 2003 Del Ltd sold a freehold property for £125,000 which had cost originally £50,000 on 9 May 1982. On 15 April 2006 Del Ltd completed a contract to acquire the freehold of another property for £120,000. The old and the new property are both used in the business of Del Ltd.

Task

Calculate the chargeable gain, and show any reliefs available. Show the base cost of the new factory.

Indexation factors:

May 1982 to May 2003 = 1.159

4   On 6 April 1985 Edward acquired for £60,000 a small workshop where he carried on his trade as a furniture maker. On 6 August 2006 he sold the workshop for £125,000 having moved on 1 April 2006 to smaller premises which cost £123,500.

Task

Calculate Edward's capital gain for 2006/07 (before annual exemption), assuming that Edward makes any necessary claim to reduce his capital gain.

Indexation factor:

April 1985 to April 1998 = 0.716

5   Explain the rules governing rollover relief on the replacement of business assets and state how the relief is granted.

6   Reeve sold his factory on 5 August 2006 for £120,000. It had cost him £25,000 in April 1982. On 14 April 2006 he had bought a larger factory for £180,000. The old and new factory were wholly used in Reeve's trade.

Tasks

a)   Calculate Reeve's chargeable gain on the factory he has sold and the base cost of the new factory.

b)   As above, but the new factory cost only £85,000.

Indexation factor:

April 1982 to April 1998 = 1.006

The directors of Priscilla Ltd decided to make a number of asset disposals during the accounting period of 12 months to 30 April 2007.

The assets were as follows:

1) 1 October 2006

   An office block was sold for £500,000. Its costs were built up as follows:

		£
November 1984	Original cost	120,000
December 1985	Extension built	25,000
October 1986	Lift installed (to replace existing broken lift)	80,000
August 1990	New roof fitted	30,000

2) 30 October 2006

   A plot of land was sold for £140,000. This had been acquired in August 1990 at a cost of £60,000. The 1990 purchase had been partly funded from the sale of a plot of land sold in June 1990 for £38,000, realising a gain of £32,000 which has been rolled over against the replacement land.

3) 30 November 2006

   An office building, which had been used for business purposes, was sold for £210,000. This had been bought in November 1983 for £120,000, using all of the proceeds of the sale, during November 1983, of a previously owned building. This latter building had been purchased in May 1982 for £50,000 and, on its sale, full rollover relief had been claimed against the new building for the gain arising in November 1983.

Task

Compute the capital gains arising from each of the above disposals.

Indexation factors:

November 1984 to October 2006 = 1.170
December 1985 to October 2006 = 1.055
October 1986 to October 2006 = 1.005
August 1990 to October 2006 = 0.541
May 1982 to November 1983 = 0.062
November 1983 to November 2006 = 1.282

Chapter 11:
COMPUTING PROFITS CHARGEABLE TO CORPORATION TAX

Geronimo Ltd's summarised profit and loss account for the year ended 31 March 2007 is as follows:

	£	£
Gross profit		925,940
Operating expenses		
Depreciation	83,420	
Gifts (note 1)	2,850	
Professional fees (note 2)	14,900	
Patent royalties accrued (note 3)	7,200	
Repairs and renewals (note 4)	42,310	
Other expenses (all allowable)	158,780	
		(309,460)
Operating profit		616,480
Income from investments		
Debenture interest (note 5)	24,700	
Bank interest (note 5)	4,800	
Dividends (note 6)	56,000	
		85,500
		701,980
Interest payable		(45,000)
Profit before taxation		656,980

Note 1 – Gifts

Gifts are as follows:

	£
Donation to national charity (made under the Gift Aid scheme)	1,900
Donation to local charity (Geronimo Ltd received free advertising in the charity's magazine)	50
Gifts to customers (food hampers costing £30 each)	900
	2,850

Note 2 – Professional fees

Professional fees are as follows:

	£
Accountancy and audit fee	4,100
Legal fees in connection with the renewal of a 20-year property lease	2,400
Legal fees in connection with the issue of a debenture loan	8,400
	14,900

Note 3 – Patent royalties

The patent royalties were paid for trade purposes to other corporate bodies. The amounts shown in the accounts is the gross amount accrued in the year.

Note 4 – Repairs and renewals

The figure of £42,310 for repairs includes £6,200 for replacing part of a wall that was knocked down by a lorry, and £12,200 for initial repairs to an office building that was acquired during the year ended 31 March 2007. The office building was not usable until the repairs were carried out and this fact was represented by a reduced purchase price.

Note. The bank interest and the debenture interest were both received on non-trade investments.

Note 6 – Dividends received

The dividends were received from other UK companies. The figure of £56,000 is the actual amount received.

Note 7 – Capital allowances

Capital allowances for the year have been calculated as £13,200.

Task

Calculate Geronimo Ltd's taxable trading profit (Schedule D Case I profit) for the year ended 31 March 2007.

The detailed profit and loss account for Goat Ltd for the year ended 31 December 2006 is as follows:

	£	£
Turnover		2,500,000
Cost of sales		(1,000,000)
Gross profit		1,500,000
Add: dividends received (net)	1,460	
profit on sale of shares	780	
bank interest	1,500	
		3,740
Less: debenture interest	6,750	
directors' salaries	90,000	
depreciation	150,000	
wages and salaries	220,000	
office overheads (all allowable)	400,000	
bank overdraft interest (gross)	7,000	
gift aid donation	1,500	
staff party	400	
customer entertainment	750	
		(876,400)
Net profit		627,340

Notes

1) A chargeable gain of £1,000 arose on the sale of shares.

2) Capital allowances for the year amount to £123,000.

Tasks

a) Compute taxable trading profits (Schedule D Case I profits) for the year to 31 December 2006.

b) Compute profits chargeable to corporation tax for the year to 31 December 2006.

Traders Ltd profit and loss account for the year to 31 March 2007 was as follows:

	£		£
General expenses	73,641	Gross profit b/d	245,000
Repairs and renewals	15,000	Impairment losses recovered	
Legal and accountancy	1,170	(previously written off)	373
Subscriptions	2,000	Profit on sale of investment	
Impairment losses (trade)	500	(purchased in 1996 and	
Directors' remuneration	15,000	sold in May 2006)	5,770
Salaries and wages	18,000	Dividends from UK companies	750
Debenture interest (gross)	5,000	Bank interest receivable	1,875
Depreciation	20,000		
Rent and rates	1,500		
Net profit	101,957		
	253,768		253,768

Notes

1) General expenses include the following:

	£
Travelling expenses of staff, including directors	1,000
Entertaining expenses: suppliers	630

2) Repairs and renewals include:

	£
Redecorating existing premises	3,000

3) Legal and accounting charges are made up as follows:

	£
Debt collection service	200
Staff service agreements	50
Lease on new premises	100
Audit and accountancy	820
	1,170

4) Subscriptions and donations include the following:

	£
Payments to charities under Gift Aid	200
Donation to political party	500
Sports facilities for staff	500

5) The chargeable gain on the investment is £2,356.

The written down value of the general pool at 1 April 2006 was £15,000. No new assets were bought during the year to 31 March 2007.

Tasks

a) Calculate the capital allowances due in the year to 31 March 2007.

b) Calculate taxable trading profits (Schedule D Case I profits) for the year to 31 March 2007.

c) Calculate profits chargeable to corporation tax for the year to 31 March 2007.

Righteous plc used to make its accounts up to 31 December. However, the directors decided to change the accounting date to 31 May and make up accounts for a 7 month period to 31 May 2007. The following information relates to the period of account from 1 January 2006 to 31 May 2007:

	£
Trading profit (Schedule D Case I)	500,000
Rental income (Schedule A) (£900 per month received 6 monthly in arrears on 31 March and 30 Sept)	
31 March 2006	5,400
30 September 2006	5,400
31 March 2007	5,400
Capital gain on property sold on	
1 May 2007	3,000
Gift aid donations paid	
28 February 2006	15,000
31 August 2006	15,000
28 February 2007	40,000

No capital allowances are claimed.

Task

Compute profits chargeable to corporation tax for the accounting periods based on the above accounts.

5   Dove plc made the following disposals of assets during its 12 month accounting period ending December 2006.

- 14 April 2006 – A factory for £230,000. This had originally been purchased April 1986 for £140,000.

- 18 July 2006 – A warehouse for £80,000. This had been purchased in May 1999 for £100,000.

- 17 September 2006 – Another factory for £280,000. This had been purchased in June 1991 for £85,000.

- 14 November 2006 – Two offices for £140,000. These had been part of a large office block from which Dove plc has traded. The whole block had cost £250,000 in August 1995 and in November 2006 the remaining offices had a market value of £320,000.

Tasks

(a) Calculate the chargeable gain arising on the disposal of the factory sold on 14.4.06.

(b) Calculate the allowable loss on disposal of the warehouse.

(c) Calculate the chargeable gain arising on disposal of the factory sold on 17.9.06.

(d) Calculate the chargeable gain arising on disposal of the offices.

(e) Calculate the net chargeable gains that Dove plc will include in its computation of PCTCT for the year ended 31 December 2006.

Indexation factors

April 1986 – April 2006	1.099
May 1999 – July 2006	0.185
June 1991 – September 2006	0.469
August 1995 – November 2006	0.320

Chapter 12:
COMPUTING CORPORATION TAX PAYABLE

Teletubbies Ltd has four associated companies. Results for the 8 months to 31 August 2006 show the following:

	£
Taxable trading profit (Schedule D Case I)	35,000
Capital gains	6,000
Dividends received March 2006	6,750
Gift Aid donation	3,000

Task

Calculate Teletubbies Ltd's corporation tax liability for the accounting period.

Basil Ltd, a company with no associated companies, has had the following results:

	Year to 31 December 2006 £
Taxable trading profit (Schedule D Case I)	10,000
Interest (Schedule D Case III)	5,000
Chargeable gains	6,000
Gift aid donation	3,000
Dividend received (net)	5,400

Task

Calculate Basil Ltd's corporation tax liability for its above accounting period.

Rosemary Ltd has the following results for the 10 month period ended 31 March 2007:

	£
Taxable trading profits (Schedule D Case I)	600,000
Rental income (Schedule A)	300,000
Dividends received	162,000

Task

Calculate Rosemary Ltd's corporation tax liability for the period.

4   Island Limited has two associated companies. In order to align its accounts date with its associate Island draws up accounts for the 8 months to 31 December 2006, showing the following results

	£
Trading profits (Schedule D Case I)	2,000,000
Chargeable gain	600,000

Task

Calculate the corporation tax liability.

5   Dorothy Limited started trading on 1 November 2005, and draws up its first set of accounts 31 December 2006, for which it has the following results:

	£
Trading profits (Schedule D Case I)	5,000,000
Interest (Schedule D Case III)	140,000
Chargeable gain (July 2006)	300,000

Task

Calculate the corporation tax liabilities arising in the accounting periods based on the above peric of account.

Chapter 13:
CORPORATION TAX LOSSES

Pennington Ltd produced the following results:

	Year ended 30 June			
	2003	2004	2005	2006
	£	£	£	£
Trading profit/(loss)	6,000	12,000	2,000	(13,000)
Interest	1,200	1,200	600	1,200
Gift Aid donation	100	100	50	100

Task

Compute Pennington Ltd's PCTCT for the above accounting periods, assuming the loss relief is claimed as soon as possible.

Arlene Ltd produced the following results having started trading on 1 January 2004:

	Year ended 31 December		
	2004	2005	2006
	£	£	£
Trading profit/(loss)	10,000	(25,000)	11,000
Interest	5,000	5,000	5,000
Gift Aid (gross)	1,000	1,000	1,000

Task

Compute Arlene Ltd's PCTCT for the above accounting periods, assuming the loss relief is claimed as soon as possible.

Revision Companion – corporation tax losses – chapter activities

3 Daley plc has had the following results since it started to trade.

	Year ended 31 December 2004 £	Nine months ended 30 September 2005 £	Year ended 30 September 2006 £
Trading profit/(loss)	45,000	85,000	(200,000)
Interest	8,000	12,000	14,000
Chargeable gains/(allowable losses)	10,000	2,000	(2,000)
Gift Aid donations (gross)	1,000	1,000	1,000

Task

Compute the profits chargeable to corporation tax for all the above periods, and show all amounts to be carried forward at 30 September 2006. (Assume Daley plc wishes to claim any loss relief early as possible.)

4 P Ltd is a UK resident company, it has no associated companies.

The following details relate to the 12 month accounting period ending 31 March 2007.

	£
Income	
Taxable trading profit	360,000
Rental income	18,000
Bank deposit interest	6,000
Capital gain	14,000
Dividend (cash amount received)	10,800
Payments	
Gift aid payment (gross amount)	6,000

A capital loss of £15,000 and a trading loss of £10,000 were brought forward as at 1 April 2006.

Task

Calculate the corporation tax payable for the year ending 31 March 2007.

Chapter 14:
NATIONAL INSURANCE

a) Abraham has profits of £12,830 for 2006/07.

   Task

   Calculate his liability to pay Class 4 and Class 2 NICs.

b) John has profits of £35,000 for 2006/07.

   Task

   Calculate his liability to Class 4 and Class 2 NICs.

c) Raj has profits of £4,000 for 2006/07.

   Task

   Calculate his liability to Class 4 and Class 2 NICs for 2006/07.

Employers

Write a memorandum to one of your office colleagues explaining what NICs must be paid by an employer.

Josephine receives a weekly salary of £405. Josephine is provided with a company car by her employer. The taxable benefit arising in respect of this car was £6,850 in 2006/07.

Task

Calculate the national insurance contributions payable by Josephine's employer for the year 2006/07.

Zoë is a self employed author. In the year to 31 December 2006 she had taxable trading profits of £80,000.

Tasks

a) Calculate the NICs payable by Zoë for 2006/07.

b) State the date by which a self employed person must notify that he or she is liable to Class 2 NICs.

263

5   Wendy and Jayne have been in partnership as interior designers for many years, trading Dramatic Decors.

On 1 January 2007, Wendy and Jayne admitted Paula to the partnership. From that date partnership profits were shared 40% to each of Wendy and Jayne and 20% to Paula. The partnership continued to make up its accounts to 31 December and the trading profit for the year to 31 December 2007 was £120,000.

Paula had not worked for many years prior to becoming a partner in Dramatic Decors.

Tasks

(a) Compute the share of profits taxable on Paula for 2006/07 and 2007/08 and identify the overlap profits to carry forward.

(b) Calculate the Class 4 National Insurance Contributions payable by Paula for 2006/07.

Chapter 15:
ADMINISTRATION AND PAYMENT OF INCOME TAX, CGT AND CLASS 4 NICs

Simon received an income tax return for 2006/07 on 16 June 2006. Simon, a self employed plumber, intends to calculate his own tax.

Task

Write a memo to your office assistant advising him:

a) By what date Simon must submit his tax return for 2006/07 to the HMRC.

b) What penalties may be imposed by HMRC if Simon:

   i) Misses the deadline for submitting his tax return.
   ii) Fails to pay any associated tax liability by the due date.

Savannah commenced trading on 1 October 2006. Her income tax and Class 4 NIC liabilities for 2006/07 and 2007/08 have been calculated as £12,000 and £14,000 respectively. Prior to 2006/07 Savannah was a student with no taxable income.

Tasks

a) State the due date of payment of the above liabilities.
b) State what consequences will arise if Savannah is late in paying her income tax and NIC.

3 Martin has been trading as a greengrocer for many years, under the name of Martin's Th Greengrocer. He makes up accounts to 31 March each year.

In the year to 31 March 2007, Martin had the following results:

	£	£
Turnover	100,000	
Less: cost of sales	(40,000)	
Gross profit		60,000
Less: wages (N1)	35,000	
rent and rates	7,000	
administration expenses	1,000	
depreciation	3,000	
motor expenses (N2)	2,500	
entertaining (N3)	1,000	
bank interest	500	
legal costs (N4)	1,250	
other allowable expenses	3,750	
		(55,000)
Net profit		5,000

Notes

1 The figure for wages includes Martin's wages of £15,000.

2 20% of motor expenses relate to Martin's private use.

3 Entertaining suppliers £750; entertaining staff £250.

4 Legal expenses include £450 for the costs for the grant of a lease for 20 years.

5 There are capital allowances of £1,600 for the year to 31 March 2007. These arose on various shop fittings purchased for the business.

Tasks

a) Compute Martin's taxable trading profits for 2006/07.

b) Calculate the National Insurance contributions payable by Martin as a self-employed individual for 2006/07.

c) State the entries that should be made on the self-employment pages for Martin for 2006/0

Tutor's hint

The self employment pages are at the end of Chapter 15. Make a note of the box numbers tha need to need to be filled and then the entries that need to be made in those boxes. Alternativel you might find it helpful to fill in the specimen pages at the end of Chapter 15, but we recommen that you do so in pencil so that you can erase the entries.

Chapter 16:
ADMINISTRATION AND PAYMENT OF CORPORATION TAX

Sims Ltd has four associated companies. PCTCT for the 8 months to 30 November 2006 is £48,000. Dividends of £1,800 were received in the period.

Task

Calculate the corporation tax liability for the accounting period, and state the due date of payment and the filing date for the return covering this accounting period.

Port Ltd has two associated companies. Port Ltd's PCTCT for the 8 months to 31 December 2005 is £3,000,000.

Task

Calculate the corporation tax liability and state the due dates for payment of tax.

D Ltd had been trading for several years, preparing accounts to 31 August and paying corporation tax at the full rate. In 2006 it changed its accounting date and draw up accounts for the 16 months to 31 December 2006, for which it has the following results:

Trading profits = £3,200,000

No dividends were received in the period. A notice requiring a corporation tax to be filed for the period to 31 December 2006 was issued on 1 February 2007.

Tasks

a) Calculate the corporation tax liabilities arising in the accounting periods based on the above period of account.

b) State the due date(s) for the payment of tax and the date by which any returns must be filed.

Write a memo to your office colleague explaining the dates by which corporation tax returns must be filed and the penalties that arise for late filing. Also state the date by which HMRC must commence an enquiry into a tax return.

5   Cranmore Ltd is a trading company manufacturing specialist engineering tools. It makes up accounts to 31 March each year. It is a small enterprise for capital allowance purposes with associated companies.

For the year to 31 March 2007, the company had the following results:

	£
Turnover	525,000
Trading profit before capital allowances	405,000
Interest received from building society deposit	3,000
Rental income from letting out part of factory	10,000
Gross patent royalty received (non-trade) from Mr Wilkes	6,000
	424,000

The tax written down value of the general pool at 1 April 2006 was £12,000. The company ma[de] the following purchases during the year:

	£
Car for salesman	10,000
Car for managing director	25,000
Computer for office	5,000
	40,000

Tasks

a) Compute the capital allowances for Cranmore Ltd for the year to 31 March 2007.

b) Compute the corporation tax payable for the year to 31 March 2007.

c) State the entries that need to be made on the form CT600.

Tutor's hint

The relevant corporation-tax return (Form CT600) is at the end of Chapter 16. Make a note of t[he] box numbers and then the entries that need to be made in those boxes. Alternatively, you mi[ght] find it helpful to fill in the specimen pages at the end of Chapter 16, but we recommend that y[ou] do so in pencil so that you can erase the entries.

PRACTICE EXAM 1
(DECEMBER 2003 PAPER)

UNIT 18

Time allowed: 3 hours plus 15 minutes' reading time

practice exam 1 (December 2003 paper)

This exam is in TWO sections.

You must show competence in BOTH sections. You should therefore attempt and aim to complete EVERY task in EACH section.

You are advised to spend approximately 100 minutes on Section 1 and 80 minutes on Section 2.

All essential workings should be included within your answers, where appropriate.

SECTION 1 (Suggested time allowance: 100 minutes)

DATA

You work in the tax department of a firm of Chartered Accountants.

James Reed and Linda Cann are new clients who commenced trading as JL Traders on 1 January 200 You have been asked to do the tax work for the business from the date of commencement to the year of 2006/07.

The accounting department supplies you with the following information.

1   Adjusted trading profits, before deducting capital allowances:

	£
Period ended 30 September 2005	14,363
Year ended 30 September 2006	38,114

2   Fixed asset additions and disposals:

Additions

		£
May 2005	Plant and machinery	12,750
March 2005	Car, 25% private use	13,800
December 2005	Plant and machinery	8,050
May 2006	Plant and machinery	16,902
August 2006	Car, no private use	10,000

Disposals

January 2006	Plant and machinery (Original cost	5,050 £6,890)

Neither of the cars bought has low emissions.

3   In April 2005, a new industrial building was bought for the business, costing £95,000. The building was in industrial use throughout the period of ownership.

4   The partnership agreement states that the profit share ratio is 2/3 for James and 1/3 for Linda.

5   The business is a small enterprise for capital allowance purposes.

practice exam 1 (December 2003 paper)

Task 1.1

Calculate the capital allowances on the plant and machinery for each accounting period.

Task 1.1 (continued)

b) Calculate the Industrial Buildings Allowance for each accounting period.

Task 1.2

Calculate the taxable trading profit for each accounting period.

practice exam 1 (December 2003 paper)

Task 1.3

Calculate the taxable profits for all tax years, from commencement of trade to 2006/07, clearly showing all relevant dates and the amount of overlap profit.

Task 1.4

Calculate the amount of taxable profit assessable individually on James and Linda for 2006/07.

practice exam 1 (December 2003 paper)

Task 1.5

Explain which National Insurance Contributions James and Linda are required to pay, and calculate the NIC payable by each for 2006/07.

Task 1.6

James Reed informs you that nine months after buying the car in March 2004, £300 was paid for new tyres. He wants to know how this expenditure will be treated for taxation purposes.

Explain how such expenditure would be treated in a taxation computation, providing reasons for the treatment.

practice exam 1 (December 2003 paper)

DATA

You received the following e-mail from James Reed.

From: Jreed@boxmail.net
To: AATStudent@boxmail.net
Sent: 27 November 2006 11:37
Subject: Buildings

During October 2006, we sold the industrial building that we bought in April 2005. We immediately replaced it with another new industrial building. However, we are concerned that the sale will give rise to a Capital Gains Tax liability.

We would be grateful if you could explain to us the Capital Gains Tax implications of these transactions.

Many thanks.

James Reed

Task 1.7

Reply to James's e-mail, explaining to him how rollover relief for Capital Gains Tax purposes works.

From: AATStudent@boxmail.net
To: Jreed@boxmail.net
Sent: 5 December 2006 15:45
Subject: Buildings

practice exam 1 (December 2003 paper)

This page is for the continuation of the email. You may not need all of it.

practice exam 1 (December 2003 paper)

SECTION 2 (Suggested time allowance: 80 minutes)

DATA

You work for a company, Quinten Ltd, preparing its tax information prior to being entered in the CT600 tax form.

The Chief Accountant for Quinten Ltd has supplied you with the accounts for the twelve month period ended 31 December 2006.

The profit and loss account shows:

	£	£
Gross profit		935,750
Profit on the sale of shares (Note 1)		32,800
General expenses (Note 2)	386,740	
Impairment losses (Note 3)	4,890	
Administrative expenses	65,900	
Salaries and wages	250,660	
Depreciation	98,320	
		(806,510)
Net profit		162,040

Notes

1. Profit on the sale of shares:

In August 2006, Quinten Ltd sold all of its shares in Hart Ltd for £72,300. These shares had been acquired as follows:

	No of shares	£
February 1994	5,000	16,900
November 1997 – rights issue	1 for 10	£2 per share
May 1999	5,000	21,600

2. General expenses includes:

	£
Entertaining customers	1,640
Gifts to customers (1,000 calendars with Quinten Ltd clearly visible)	2,000
Staff Christmas party (45 people)	750

3. Impairment losses are made up of:

	£
Debts written off – trade	6,830
Bad debt recovered – non-trade	(1,500)
Bad debts recovered – trade	(440)
	4,890

277

practice exam 1 (December 2003 paper)

Additional information

1. The capital allowances for the year ended 31 December 2006 are £23,700
2. Quinten Ltd has capital losses brought forward from 2005 of £2,353.
3. Quinten Ltd has no associated companies.

Task 2.1

Calculate the capital gain arising from the disposal of the shares in Hart Ltd.

Task 2.2

Calculate the adjusted trading profit, after capital allowances, for the year ended 31 December 2006.

Task 2.3

Show the PCTCT (profit chargeable to corporation tax) for the year ended 31 December 2006.

Task 2.4

Calculate the corporation tax payable for the year ended 31 December 2006, stating the due date for payment.

practice exam 1 (December 2003 paper)

DATA

The Chief Accountant for Quinten Ltd informs you that the company is considering acquiring an associated company during 2007. He asks for your advice regarding the taxation implications of such a purchase.

Task 2.5

Using the headed paper below, write a memo to the Chief Accountant explaining how the purchase of an associated company will affect the taxation computation of Quinten Ltd.

	MEMO		
To:	Chief Accountant	Subject:	Associated Companies
From:	Accounting Technician	Date:	December 2006

TAXATION TABLES

Capital allowances

	%
Writing down allowance	
Plant and machinery	25
Industrial buildings	4
First year allowance	
Plant and machinery, after 02 July 1998 – all businesses	40
Plant and machinery (6 April 2004 to 5 April 2005 and 6 April 2006 to 5 April 2007) – small enterprises	50

National Insurance contributions

Class 2	
Weekly contribution	£2.10
Small earnings exemption limit	£4,465
Class 4	
Rate	8%
Lower profits limit	£5,035
Upper profits limit	£33,540

Capital gains indexation factors

February 1994 to November 1997	0.123
November 1997 to May 1999	0.038
May 1999 to August 2006	0.187

Corporation tax

	Full rate	Small Co rate	Taper relief fraction	Upper limit	Lower limit
FY 2005	30%	19%	11/400	1,500,000	300,000
FY 2006	30%	19%	11/400	1,500,000	300,000

Formula: Fraction $\times (M - P) \times 1/P$

PRACTICE EXAM 2
(JUNE 2004 PAPER)

UNIT 18

Time allowed: 3 hours plus 15 minutes' reading time

practice exam 2 (June 2004 paper)

This exam is in TWO sections.

You must show competence in BOTH sections. You should therefore attempt and aim to complete EVERY task in EACH section.

You are advised to spend approximately 100 minutes on Section 1 and 80 minutes on Section 2.

All essential workings should be included within your answers, where appropriate.

SECTION 1 (Suggested time allowance: 100 minutes)

DATA

You work for George and Carol Checkers, a partnership that makes and sells pottery. You prepare the tax information before completing the tax returns for the partners.

The profit and loss account for the year ended 31 January 2007 shows:

	£	£
Gross profit		256,550
General expenses (note 1)	85,480	
Bad and doubtful debts (note 2)	585	
Motor expenses (note 3)	7,880	
Wages and salaries	54,455	
Depreciation	21,080	
		169,480
Net profit		87,070

Notes

1 General expenses include:

	£
Gifts to customers – Christmas cakes costing £4.50 each	1,350
Cost of installing new machinery bought in August 2006	2,200

2 Bad and doubtful debts are made up of:

	£
Trade debts written off	350
Increase in general provision	400
Trade debts recovered	(165)
	585

Motor expenses

	Private usage %	Annual expenses £
George	25	4,680
Carol	15	3,200

Additional information

For capital allowances purposes, the balances brought forward from the year ended 31 January 2006 showed:

	Pool £	George's car £	Carol's car £
Balance	18,444	15,630	8,780

New machinery was bought in August 2006 for £15,400.

On 1 August 2006, the business bought a new industrial building for £88,000. The building was in industrial use throughout the period.

The partnership agreement states that George and Carol share profits equally.

Task 1.1

Calculate the adjusted trading profit, before capital allowances, for the year ended 31 January 2007.

Task 1.2

a) Calculate the capital allowances on the plant and machinery and motor vehicles for the year ended 31 January 2007.

b) Calculate the industrial buildings allowance for the year ended 31 January 2007.

Task 1.3

Calculate the net trading profit for the year ended 31 January 2007.

practice exam 2 (June 2004 paper)

Task 1.4

State the due dates of payment of the tax liability arising from the above profit, including any payments on account.

Task 1.5

Calculate the total National Insurance Contributions payable by Carol for the tax year 2006/07.

DATA

In March 2007 you receive a telephone call from George saying that he is thinking of giving his half of the business to his son, Elliot. He has heard of something called 'gift relief' but doesn't know anything about it. He asks for information on gift relief.

Task 1.6

State what information you would give to George.

practice exam 2 (June 2004 paper)

DATA

You have received the following e-mail from George.

From:	george007@boxmail.net
To:	AATStudent@boxmail.net
Sent:	27 May 2007 16:22
Subject:	Important news

I asked you a while ago about the implications of giving away my half of the business to my son.

However, Carol and I have now decided that we want to sell the business completely. We will therefore cease to trade on 31 May 2007.

As it is only four months since the last year end, I was wondering how the business income will be assessed in the closing years. We hope that we will make a profit in the four months from 1 February 2007 to 31 May 2007.

Thank you for your advice.

George

Task 1.7

Reply to George's e-mail, explaining which profit periods will be assessed for the past two tax years. Your answer must include the impact of overlap relief.

Note. Assume all tax rules are the same in 2007/08 as for 2006/07.

From:	AATStudent@boxmail.net
To:	george007@boxmail.net
Sent:	15 June 2007
Subject:	Re: Important news

This page is for the continuation of the e-mail. You may not need all of it.

practice exam 2 (June 2004 paper)

SECTION 2 (Suggested time allowance: 80 minutes)

DATA

You work in the tax department of a firm of Chartered Accountants. Abbey Ltd is a client of the firm and has one associated company. You have been asked to do the tax work for the company for the year ended 31 March 2007.

Abbey Ltd has the following information for the year ended 31 March 2007.

1. The adjusted trading profit, after deducting capital allowances, was £623,024.

2. In May 2006, Abbey Ltd sold 4,000 of the shares it held in Blue Ltd for £120,000. These shares had been acquired as follows:

	No of shares	£
April 1986	2,000	25,000
June 1991	2,000	35,000
July 1994 – bonus issue	1 for 10	
September 1999 – rights issue	1 for 5	£10 per share

3. In November 2006, Abbey Ltd sold its factory for £260,000. It bought the factory in December 2000 for £150,000. In March 2007, it bought a replacement factory for £230,000. The industrial buildings allowances adjustment has already been made in calculating taxable trading profits.

Task 2.1

Calculate the capital gain arising from the disposal of the shares in Blue Ltd.

Task 2.2

Calculate the capital gain arising from the disposal of the factory, and show the amount of rollover re[lief]
to be carried forward.

Task 2.3

Calculate the corporation tax payable for the year ended 31 March 2007, stating the due date [for]
payment.

Task 2.4

Complete the following extract from the tax return for Abbey Ltd for the year ended 31 March 2007, using all the relevant information from above.

practice exam 2 (June 2004 paper)

Page 2
Company tax calculation

Turnover
1. Total turnover from trade or profession — 1 £

Income
3. Trading and professional profits — 3 £
4. Trading losses brought forward claimed against profits — 4 £
   box 3 minus box 4
5. Net trading and professional profits — 5 £
6. Bank, building society or other interest, and profits and gains from non-trading loan relationships — 6 £
11. Income from UK land and buildings — 11 £
14. Annual profits and gains not falling under any other heading — 14 £

Chargeable gains
16. Gross chargeable gains — 16 £
17. Allowable losses including losses brought forward — 17 £
    box 16 minus box 17
18. Net chargeable gains — 18 £

sum of boxes 5, 6, 11, 14 & 18
21. **Profits before other deductions and reliefs** — 21 £

Deductions and Reliefs
24. Management expenses under S75 ICTA 1988 — 24 £
30. Trading losses of this or a later accounting period under S393A ICTA 1988 — 30 £
31. Put an 'X' in box 31 if amounts carried back from later accounting periods are included in box 30 — 31
32. Non-trade capital allowances — 32 £
35. Charges paid — 35 £

box 21 minus boxes 24, 30, 32 and 35
37. **Profits chargeable to corporation tax** — 37 £

Tax calculation
38. Franked investment income — 38 £
39. Number of associated companies in this period — 39
   or
40. Associated companies in the first financial year — 40
41. Associated companies in the second financial year — 41
42. Put an 'X' in box 42 if the company claims to be charged at the starting rate or the small companies' rate on any part of its profits, or is claiming marginal rate relief — 42

Enter how much profit has to be charged and at what rate of tax

Financial year (yyyy)	Amount of profit	Rate of tax	Tax
43	44 £	45	46 £ p
53	54 £	55	56 £ p

total of boxes 46 and 56
63. Corporation tax — 63 £ p
64. Marginal rate relief — 64 £ p
65. Corporation tax net of marginal rate relief — 65 £ p
66. Underlying rate of corporation tax — 66 . %
67. Profits matched with non-corporate distributions — 67
68. Tax at non-corporate distributions rate — 68 £ p
69. Tax at underlying rate on remaining profits — 69 £ p
   enter value of box 63 or 65 or the total of boxes 68 and 69 if greater
70. **Corporation tax chargeable** — 70 £ p

CT600 (Short) (2005) Version 2

practice exam 2 (June 2004 paper)

Page 3

79	Tax payable under S419 ICTA 1988	79 £	p
80	Put an 'X' in box 80 if you completed box A11 in the Supplementary Pages CT600A	80	
84	Income tax deducted from gross income included in profits	84 £	p
85	Income tax repayable to the company	85 £	p
86	Tax payable - this is your self-assessment of tax payable	*total of boxes 70 and 79 minus box 84* 86 £	p

Tax reconciliation

91	Tax already paid (and not already repaid)	91 £	p
92	Tax outstanding	*box 86 minus box 91* 92 £	p
93	Tax overpaid	*box 91 minus box 86* 93 £	p

Information about capital allowances and balancing charges

Charges and allowances included in calculation of trading profits or losses

		Capital allowances	Balancing charges
105 - 106	Machinery and plant - long-life assets	105 £	106 £
107 - 108	Machinery and plant - other (general pool)	107 £	108 £
109 - 110	Cars outside general pool	109 £	110 £
111 - 112	Industrial buildings and structures	111 £	112 £
113 - 114	Other charges and allowances	113 £	114 £

Charges and allowances not included in calculation of trading profits or losses

		Capital allowances	Balancing charges
115 - 116	Non-trading charges and allowances	115 £	116 £
117	Put an 'X' in box 117 if box 115 includes flat conversion allowances	117	

Expenditure

118	Expenditure on machinery and plant on which first year allowance is claimed	118 £
119	Put an 'X' in box 119 if claim includes enhanced capital allowances for designated energy-saving investments	119
120	Qualifying expenditure on machinery and plant on long-life assets	120 £
121	Qualifying expenditure on machinery and plant on other assets	121 £

Losses, deficits and excess amounts

122	Trading losses Case I	*calculated under S393 ICTA 1988* 122 £	124	Trading losses Case V	*calculated under S393 ICTA 1988* 124 £
125	Non-trade deficits on loan relationships and derivative contracts	*calculated under S82 FA 1996* 125 £	127	Schedule A losses	*calculated under S392A ICTA 1988* 127 £
129	Overseas property business losses Case V	*calculated under S392B ICTA 1988* 129 £	130	Losses Case VI	*calculated under S396 ICTA 1988* 130 £
131	Capital losses	*calculated under S16 TCGA 1992* 131 £	136	Excess management expenses	*calculated under S75 ICTA 1988* 136 £

CT600 (Short) (2005) Version 2

practice exam 2 (June 2004 paper)

DATA

One of your friends works for Abbey Ltd. He knows that you have prepared the accounts for the company for the year ended 31 March 2007 and he has contacted you to find out if the company making a profit.

Task 2.5

State how you should respond to this query from your friend.

TAXATION TABLES

Capital allowances

	%
Writing down allowance	
Plant and machinery	25
Industrial buildings	4
First year allowance	
Plant and machinery, after 02 July 1998 – all businesses	40
Year commencing 6 April 2004 and year commencing 6 April 2006 – small enterprises	50

National Insurance contributions

Class 2
Weekly contribution	£2.10
Small earnings exemption limit	£4,465

Class 4
Lower profits limit	£5,035
Upper profits limit	£33,540
Rate on profits between upper and lower limits	8%
Rate on profits over upper limit	1%

Capital gains indexation factors

April 1986 to June 1991	0.373
June 1991 to July 1994	0.074
June 1991 to September 1999	0.239
July 1994 to September 1999	0.154
September 1999 to May 2006	0.176
December 1999 to November 2006	0.182

Corporation tax

	Full rate	Small Co rate	Taper relief fraction	Upper limit	Lower limit
FY 2006	30%	19%	11/400	1,500,000	300,000

Formula: Fraction × (M − P) × I/P

practice exam 2 (June 2004 paper)

PRACTICE EXAM 3
(DECEMBER 2004 PAPER)

UNIT 18

Time allowed: 3 hours plus 15 minutes' reading time

practice exam 3 (December 2004 paper)

This exam based assessment is in TWO sections.

You must show competence in BOTH sections, so you should attempt and aim to complete EVERY ta in EACH SECTION.

You should spend about 80 minutes on Section 1 and 100 minutes on Section 2.

SECTION 1 (Suggested time allowance: 80 minutes)

DATA

You work in the tax department of a small firm of Chartered Accountants. One of the firm's clien Angela Graham, has just given you the information you need to complete her 2006/07 tax return.

Trading profits

Angela ceased trading on 30 September 2006. Her summarised profit and loss account for the nir month period showed:

	£
Sales	257,200
Cost of sales	79,400
Gross profit	177,800
Expenses	124,800
Net profit	53,000

All expenses were allowable for taxation purposes.

On 31 December 2005, the balances for capital allowances purposes were:

	£
General pool	7,330
Car, private usage 30%	9,570

The plant and machinery in the general pool was sold on 30 September 2006 for £8,200. Ange decided to keep the car after the business ceased trading. The market value of the car on 30 Septemb 2006 was £6,000. It had originally cost £15,570.

The overlap profit brought forward from commencement of trade was £21,050.

Capital Transactions

On 31 January 2007, Angela disposed of an asset that has been classified as a business asset for capi gains tax purposes. The proceeds were £225,000. She bought the asset in July 1995 for £82,500. S spent £17,000 on improving the asset in February 2004.

Payments on account

Angela paid £5,000 on both 31 January 2007 and 31 July 2007 as income tax payments on account f 2006/07.

Task 1.1

Calculate the capital allowances to the date of cessation.

Task 1.2

Calculate the net taxable trading profits for the final tax year of the business.

practice exam 3 (December 2004 paper)

Task 1.3

Calculate the net gain chargeable to capital gains tax, before the annual exemption.

DATA

In the paper work received from Angela was a note saying that she wants to start another business with her sister. She wants to know:

- if the way in which a partnership is taxed is different to how she was taxed as a sole trader
- how tax payable by each partner is determined
- which National Insurance Contributions she and her sister will need to pay
- the records that should be kept to maintain the accounts to an acceptable level.

Task 1.4

Using the memo below, answer Angela's queries.

	MEMO		
To:	Angela Graham	**Subject:**	Various queries
From:	Accounting Technician	**Date:**	30 November 2006

This page is for the continuation of your memo. You may not need all of it.

Task 1.5

Assuming that Angela's final total tax liability for 2006/07 exceeds the £10,000 payments on account that she has already paid, explain how and when the remaining tax will be paid to HMRC.

practice exam 3 (December 2004 paper)

Task 1.6

As far as is possible given the available information, complete the attached tax return

Income for the year ended 5 April 2007

HM Revenue & Customs

SELF-EMPLOYMENT

Fill in these boxes first

Name

Tax reference

If you want help, look up the box numbers in the Notes

Business details

Name of business 3.1

Description of business 3.2

Address of business 3.3

Postcode

Accounting period - *read the Notes, page SEN3 before filling in these boxes*

Start 3.4 / /   End 3.5 / /

- Tick box 3.6 if details in boxes 3.1 or 3.3 have changed since your last Tax Return 3.6

- Tick box 3.10 if you entered details for all relevant accounting periods on last year's Tax Return and boxes 3.14 to 3.73 and 3.99 to 3.115 will be blank *(read Step 3 on page SEN2)* 3.10

- Date of commencement if after 5 April 2004 3.7 / /

- Tick box 3.11 if your accounts do not cover the period from the last accounting date (explain why in the 'Additional information' box, box 3.116) 3.11

- Date of cessation if before 6 April 2007 3.8 / /

- Tick box 3.12 if your accounting date has changed (only if this is a permanent change and you want it to count for tax) 3.12

- Tick box 3.13 if this is the second or further change (explain in box 3.116 on Page SE4 why you have not used the same date as last year) 3.13

- Tick box 3.9 if the special arrangements for particular trades apply - *read the Notes, page SEN11* 3.9

Capital allowances - summary

	Capital allowances	Balancing charges
• Cars costing more than £12,000 (excluding cars with low CO_2 emissions) (A separate calculation must be made for each car.)	3.14 £	3.15 £
• Other business plant and machinery (including cars with low CO_2 emissions and cars costing less than £12,000) *read the Notes, page SEN4*	3.16 £	3.17 £
• Agricultural or Industrial Buildings Allowance (A separate calculation must be made for each block of expenditure.)	3.18 £	3.19 £
• Other capital allowances claimed (separate calculations must be made). Claims to, and balancing charges arising on, Business Premises Renovation Allowance must also be included in boxes 23.7 and 23.8 respectively	3.20 £	3.21 £
Total capital allowances/balancing charges	total of column above 3.22 £	total of column above 3.23 £

- Tick box 3.22A if box 3.22 includes enhanced capital allowances for designated environmentally beneficial plant and machinery 3.22A

Income and expenses - annual turnover below £15,000

If your annual turnover is £15,000 or more, **ignore** boxes 3.24 to 3.26. Instead fill in Page SE2

If your annual turnover is below £15,000, **fill in** boxes 3.24 to 3.26 instead of Page SE2. Read the Notes, page SEN4.

- Turnover including other business receipts and goods etc. taken for personal use (and balancing charges from box 3.23) 3.24 £

- Expenses allowable for tax (including capital allowances from box 3.22) 3.25 £

Net profit (put figure in brackets if a loss)   box 3.24 minus box 3.25 3.26 £

You must now fill in Page SE3

SA103

HMRC 12/05 net   TAX RETURN ■ SELF-EMPLOYMENT: PAGE SE1

practice exam 3 (December 2004 paper)

Income and expenses - annual turnover £15,000 or more

You must fill in this Page if your annual turnover is £15,000 or more - read the Notes, pages SEN2, SEN4 to SEN7

If you were registered for VAT, will the figures in boxes 3.29 to 3.64, include VAT? **3.27** [ ] or exclude VAT? **3.28** [ ]

Sales/business income (turnover) **3.29** £ _____

	Disallowable expenses included in boxes 3.46 to 3.63	Total expenses
• Cost of sales	3.30 £	3.46 £
• Construction industry subcontractor costs	3.31 £	3.47 £
• Other direct costs	3.32 £	3.48 £

box 3.29 minus (boxes 3.46 + 3.47 + 3.48)
Gross profit/(loss) **3.49** £ _____

Other income/profits **3.50** £ _____

• Employee costs	3.33 £	3.51 £
• Premises costs	3.34 £	3.52 £
• Repairs	3.35 £	3.53 £
• General administrative expenses	3.36 £	3.54 £
• Motor expenses	3.37 £	3.55 £
• Travel and subsistence	3.38 £	3.56 £
• Advertising, promotion and entertainment	3.39 £	3.57 £
• Legal and professional costs	3.40 £	3.58 £
• Bad debts	3.41 £	3.59 £
• Interest and alternative finance payments	3.42 £	3.60 £
• Other finance charges	3.43 £	3.61 £
• Depreciation and loss/(profit) on sale	3.44 £	3.62 £
• Other expenses	3.45 £	3.63 £

Put the total of boxes 3.30 to 3.45 in box 3.66 below

total of boxes 3.51 to 3.63
Total expenses **3.64** £ _____

boxes 3.49 + 3.50 minus 3.64
Net profit/(loss) **3.65** £ _____

Tax adjustments to net profit or loss

- Disallowable expenses

boxes 3.30 to 3.45
3.66 £ _____

- Adjustments (apart from disallowable expenses) that increase profits. For instance; goods taken for personal use and amounts brought forward from an earlier year because of a claim under ESC B11 about compulsory slaughter of farm animals

3.67 £ _____

- Balancing charges (from box 3.23)

3.68 £ _____

Total additions to net profit (deduct from net loss)

boxes 3.66 + 3.67 + 3.68
3.69 £ _____

- Capital allowances (from box 3.22)

3.70 £ _____

- Deductions from net profit (add to net loss)

3.71 £ _____

boxes 3.70 + 3.71
3.72 £ _____

Net business profit for tax purposes (put figure in brackets if a loss)

boxes 3.65 + 3.69 minus 3.72
3.73 £ _____

HMRC 12/05 net　　　TAX RETURN ■ SELF-EMPLOYMENT: PAGE SE2　　　Now fill in Page SE3

practice exam 3 (December 2004 paper)

SECTION 2 (Suggested time allowance: 100 minutes)

DATA

You are employed by Horatio Ltd, and work in the accounts department. The Company Accountant has asked you to prepare the tax information before it is entered in the CT600 tax form.

The accounts department has supplied you with the accounts for the 15-month period ended 31 March 2007.

The profit and loss account shows:

	£	£
Gross profit		487,500
Profit on sale of shares (Note 1)		12,850
UK dividends received (Note 2)		4,500
Rental income (Note 3)		7,500
		512,350
General expenses (Note 4)	240,780	
Wages and salaries	120,650	
Administrative expenses	87,230	
Depreciation	14,600	
		463,260
Net profit		49,090

Notes

1 **Profit on sale of shares**

Horatio Ltd sold all its shares in Yellow Ltd for £24,500 in March 2007. 2,000 shares had been bought in November 2001 for £11,650. In January 2003, Horatio Ltd received a bonus issue of for 2 shares.

2 **UK dividends received**

The dividends were received on 15 October 2006. The company that paid the dividends is not associated with Horatio Ltd.

3 **Rental income**

Horatio Ltd received £500 per month in rental income.

4 **General expenses**

These include:

	£
Gift aid donation (paid July 2006)	3,500
Entertaining customers	8,450

ADDITIONAL DATA

- The capital allowances for the year ended 31 December 2006 are £8,750, and £2,600 for the period ended 31 March 2007.

- Horatio Ltd has Schedule A losses of £1,000 brought forward from the year ended 31 December 2005.

Task 2.1

Calculate the chargeable gain, or allowable loss, arising from the sale of the shares in Yellow Ltd.

Task 2.2

Calculate the adjusted trading profit, before capital allowances, for the 15-month period ended 31 March 2007.

Task 2.3

Calculate the PCTCT (profit chargeable to corporation tax) for the:

a) 12 months ended 31 December 2006

b) Period ended 31 March 2007

Task 2.4

Calculate the corporation tax payable for the:

(a) 12 months ended 31 December 2006

(b) Period ended 31 March 2007

DATA

You have received the following e-mail from the Managing Director of Horatio Ltd.

From:	MD@horatio.co.uk
To:	AAT@horatio.co.uk
Sent:	26 May 2007 13.25
Subject:	Tax return

I know that you have recently joined the company, but we have a problem that I would like you to sort out.

For the year ended 31 December 2005, we calculated our corporation tax liability at £15,000. We paid this bill on time on 1 October 2006. We received the tax return in January 2004, but the Company Accountant didn't submit it until 30 September 2007.

We have recently had a demand from HM Revenue and Customs stating that the corporation tax liability for the year was finally assessed at £19,600.

We have never done anything like this before, so hopefully HM Revenue and Customs will be sympathetic to us, but we are really worried now that we will incur heavy penalties.

Please let us know what we need to do, and what penalties and interest HM Revenue and Customs will impose.

Many thanks.

Managing Director

Reply to the Managing Director's e-mail.

From:	AAT@horatio.co.uk
To:	MD@horatio.co.uk
Sent:	30 May 2007 15.55
Subject:	Tax return

practice exam 3 (December 2004 paper)

TAXATION TABLES

Capital allowances

	%
Writing down allowance	
Plant and machinery	25
First year allowance	
Plant and machinery, after 2 July 1998 – all businesses	40
Year commencing 6 April 2004 and year commencing 6 April 2006	
– small enterprises	50

National Insurance contributions

Class 2	
Weekly contribution	£2.10
Small earnings exemption limit	£4,465
Class 4	
Lower profits limit	£5,035
Upper profits limit	£33,540
Rate on profits between upper and lower limits	8%
Rate on profits over upper limit	1%

Capital gains indexation factors

July 1995 to April 1998	0.091
November 2001 to March 2007	0.149

Tapering relief for business assets

No of years held after 5 April 1998	% of gain chargeable
0	100
1	50
2 or more	25

Corporation tax

	FY 2006	FY 2005
Starting rate	0%	0%
Lower limit	n/a	£10,000
Upper limit	n/a	£50,000
Marginal relief fraction	n/a	19/400
Small companies rate	19%	19%
Lower limit	£300,000	£300,000
Upper limit	£1,500,000	£1,500,000
Marginal relief fraction	11/400	11/400
Full rate	30%	30%

PRACTICE EXAM 4
(JUNE 2005 PAPER)
UNIT 18

Time allowed: 3 hours plus 15 minutes' reading time

PP Note. This exam has been amended in order to remove tasks that are no longer examinable.

practice exam 4 (June 2005 paper)

TAXATION TABLES FOR BUSINESS TAX

Capital allowances:

	%
Writing down allowance –	
Plant and machinery	25
Industrial buildings	4
First year allowance –	
Plant and machinery	40
On expenditure incurred by 'small' businesses between 6.5.06-5.4.07 and 6.4.04-5.4.05, or 'small' companies between 1.4.06-31.3.07 and 1.4.04-31.3.05	50

National insurance contributions:

Class 2 –	
Weekly contribution	£2.10
Small earnings exemption limit	£4,465
Class 4 –	
Lower profits limit	£5,035
Upper profits limit	£33,540
Rate on profits between lower and upper limits	8%
Rate on profits over upper limits	1%

Capital gains indexation factors:

April 2001 to December 2003	0.060
April 2001 to June 2006	0.131
December 2003 to June 2006	0.067

Corporation tax:

Financial Year	2005	2006
Starting rate	0%	-
Lower limit	10,000	-
Marginal relief fraction	19/400	-
Small companies rate	19%	19%
Lower limit	300,000	300,000
Upper limit	1,500,000	1,500,000
Marginal relief fraction	11/400	11/400
Full rate	30%	30%

Formula: Fraction x (M – P) x I/P

318

practice exam 4 (June 2005 paper)

This examination paper is in TWO sections. You must show competence in BOTH sections. You should therefore attempt and aim to complete EVERY task in EACH section.

You should spend about 100 minutes on Section 1 and 80 minutes on Section 2.

Blank space for workings is included, but all essential calculations should be included within your answers, where appropriate.

SECTION 1 (Suggested time allowance: 100 minutes)

DATA

You work in the tax department of a firm of Chartered Accountants.

Philip Andrews is a client of the firm, and works as a heating engineer. He commenced trading on 1 February 2005, and made his first accounts to 31 January 2006. The adjusted trading profit, before capital allowances, for this twelve month period is £14,556.

The accounts department of the firm has completed his accounts for the year ended 31 January 2007. The profit and loss account shows:

	£	£
Gross profit		63,846
Profit on sale of equipment		310
		64,156
Staff wages	13,220	
Salary – Philip	22,500	
wife (works as a secretary)	6,000	
Depreciation	8,780	
Bad and doubtful debts (Note 1)	1,020	
Advertising	2,000	
Motor Expenses (Note 2)	7,630	
Sundry Expenses (Note 3)	680	
		(61,830)
Net profit		2,326

practice exam 4 (June 2005 paper)

Note 1: Bad and doubtful debts

	£
Trade debts written off	500
Increase in specific provision	300
Increase in general provision	220
	1,020

Note 2: Motor expenses

	£
Relating to motor van	2,000
Relating to motor car	5,630
	7,630

It was agreed with HMRC that 30% of the mileage for the motor car related to private usage.

Note 3: Sundry expenses

	£
Parking fine incurred by employee	80
Entertaining customers	250
Cost of calendars at £3 each, with company details clearly displayed	350
	680

ADDITIONAL INFORMATION

Although the adjusted trading profit was calculated for the first accounting period, capital allowance have not been included in these calculations. Philip's capital transactions from the date of commencement are:

ADDITIONS

		£
February 2005	Plant and machinery	8,040
March 2005	Motor van	10,020
December 2005	Plant and machinery	2,130
August 2006	Motor car, 30% private usage	10,000
November 2006	Plant and machinery	3,300

DISPOSALS

April 2006	Plant and machinery	2,800
	Original cost £4,000	

The business is classified as a 'small' business for capital allowances purposes.

The car does not have low emissions.

Task 1.1

Calculate the adjusted trading profits before capital allowances, for the year ended 31 January 2007.

practice exam 4 (June 2005 paper)

Task 1.2

Calculate the capital allowances on the plant and machinery for:

(a) the year ended 31 January 2006

(b) the year ended 31 January 2007

Task 1.3

Calculate the taxable trading profit for each accounting period.

Task 1.4

Calculate the assessable profits for all tax years, from commencement of trade to 2006/07, clearly showing ALL relevant dates and the amount of overlap profit.

Task 1.5

Calculate the TOTAL amount of National Insurance Contributions payable by Philip Andrews in 2006/07.

Task 1.6

DATA

When looking through Philip Andrew's file, you notice a letter from Philip addressed to the tax department that says that his uncle uses the same accounting firm. As his uncle is planning to be out of the country for the next few months, Philip wonders if he could be told approximately what the tax bill for his uncle will be and he will forward this information on.

Note under what circumstances you would agree to give Philip this information about his uncle.

practice exam 4 (June 2005 paper)

Task 1.7

DATA

You received the following email from Philip Andrews:

From: Philip.Andrews@boxmail.net
To: AATStudent@boxmail.net
Sent: 25 May 2007 13.17
Subject: Cars

I have now received the tax computations that your department has kindly done.

I was wondering if you could clarify something for me, though. My car cost £10,000 and a friend told me that this would get capital allowances at 50% in the year of purchase. Is that right?

Also, my profit and loss account shows motor car expenses of £5,630. Have I received the full tax relief on this amount?

With cars being so expensive, I want to get the most tax relief that I can, so thanks for your help in this matter,

Philip

Reply to Philip's email, explaining to him how cars are treated for tax purposes.

From: AATStudent@boxmail.net
To: Philip.Andrews@boxmail.net
Sent: 15 May 2007 09.37
Subject: Cars

practice exam 4 (June 2005 paper)

practice exam 4 (June 2005 paper)

SECTION 2 (Suggested time allowance: 80 minutes)

DATA

You work for a company, Woodpecker Ltd, preparing its tax information. A summary of this informat for the twelve-month period ended 31 October 2006 is as follows:

1. The adjusted trading profit, before capital allowances, was £470,200.

2. The capital allowances on plant and machinery for the year were calculated at £37,110.

3. On 1 April 2006, the company bought an industrial building for £120,000. It was bought fr Blackbird Ltd, who bought the building new on 1 April 1997 for £80,000, and brought it i immediate use. The building has been used for industrial purposes throughout.

4. In June 2006, Woodpecker sold 4,000 shares in Dove Ltd for £58,000. It had bought 10,000 sha in April 2001 for £9.50 per share. In December 2003, there was a rights issue of 1 for 4 share £5 a share. These are not exempt assets.

5. Woodpecker Ltd has one associate company, Nuthatch Ltd.

practice exam 4 (June 2005 paper)

Task 2.1

Calculate the industrial building allowance for the year ended 31 October 2006.

Task 2.2

Calculate the adjusted taxable trading profit for the year ended 31 October 2006.

Task 2.3

Calculate the capital gain arising from the disposal of the shares in Dove Ltd. Clearly show the number of shares, and their value, to carry forward.

Task 2.4

(a) Calculate the PCTCT (profit chargeable to corporation tax) for the year ended 31 October 2006.

(b) Calculate the Corporation Tax payable for the year ended 31 October 2006, stating the due date for payment.

practice exam 4 (June 2005 paper)

Task 2.5

DATA

Woodpecker Ltd has filed its corporation tax return late for the last two years. The Managing Director Woodpecker Ltd is determined that the return will be filed on time this year and he has written to a you for the due date.

Using the memo below, reply to the query from the Managing Director, explaining when the compa must file its corporation tax return for the year to 31 October 2006 and the penalties that will apply this return is filed late.

MEMO

To: Managing Director **Subject:** Filing Corporation Tax Return

From: Accounting Technician **Date:** June 2007

practice exam 4 (June 2005 paper)

Task 2.6

DATA

The associated company of Woodpecker Ltd, Nuthatch Ltd, has asked if you could also help with its tax computations. All the tax figures have been calculated, but Nuthatch Ltd has made some losses.

The following information is available for the four years ended 31 December 2006:

	31.12.03 £	31.12.04 £	31.12.05 £	31.12.06 £
Adjusted trading profit	320,000	175,000	(95,000)	48,000
Rental income/loss	5,000	(4,000)	3,000	(1,500)
Capital gains/losses	14,500	(12,000)	6,000	17,000

Using the proforma below, show the PCTCT for each year, assuming losses are relieved by Nuthatch Ltd as soon as possible.

	31.12.03 £	31.12.04 £	31.12.05 £	31.12.06 £
Trading profit				
Rental income				
Capital gains/losses				

PRACTICE EXAM 5
(DECEMBER 2005 PAPER)
UNIT 18

Time allowed: 3 hours plus 15 minutes' reading time

TAXATION TABLE FOR BUSINESS TAX

Capital allowances:

	%
Writing down allowance –	
Plant and machinery	25
Industrial buildings	4
First year allowance –	
Plant and machinery	40
On expenditure incurred by 'small' businesses between 6.5.06-5.4.07 and 6.4.04 – 5.4.05, or 'small' companies between 1.4.06-31.3.07 and 1.4.04-31.3.05	50

National insurance contribution:

Class 2	
Weekly contribution	£2.10
Small earnings exemption limit	£4,465
Class 4	
Lower profits limit	£5,035
Upper profits limit	£33,540
Rate on profits between lower and upper limits	8%
Rate on profits over upper limits	1%

Capital gains indexation factors

January 2006 to September 2006	0.019

Taper relief for business assets: Numbers of years held After 5 April 1998	% of gain chargeable
0	100
1	50
2 or more	25

Corporation tax

	2005	2006
Financial year	2005	2006
Starting rate	0%	-
Lower limit	10,000	-
Upper limit	50,000	-
Marginal relief fraction	19/400	-
Small companies rate	19%	19%
Lower limit	300,000	300,000
Upper limit	1,500,000	1,500,000
Marginal relief fraction	11/400	11/400
Full rate	30%	30%

Formula: Fraction x (M – P) x I/P

practice exam 5 (December 2005 paper)

This examination paper is in TWO sections. You must show competence in BOTH sections.

You should therefore attempt and aim to complete EVERY task in EACH section.

You should spend about 100 minutes on Section 1 and 80 minutes on Section 2.

All essential calculations should be included within your answers, where appropriate.

SECTION 1 (Suggested time allowance: 100 minutes)

DATA

You work in the tax department of a firm of Chartered Accountants.

The firm has a new client, Andrena Milburn, who has traded for many years as a sole trader manufacturing footwear. Her previous accountant has calculated the tax relevant figures for the year ended 30 November 2005, but has not completed the tax return. These figures are:

	Total £	Disallowable £
Turnover	87,435	n/a
Gross profit	62,100	n/a
Rental of premises	2,500	n/a
Depreciation	1,200	1,200
Motor expenses (Note 1)	4,400	1,760
Capital allowances	3,560	n/a

Andrena also supplies you with her accounts for the year ended 30 November 2006. These show:

	£	£
Gross profit		54,000
Rental of premises	2,500	
Trade association subscription	300	
Depreciation of equipment	1,200	
Motor expenses (Note 1)	3,600	7,600
Net profit		46,400

Note 1: Motor expenses

H M Revenue & Customs (HMRC) has agreed that 40% of the car mileage relates to business usage.

Note 2: Capital allowances

You have already calculated the capital allowances for the year ended 30 November 2006, to be £2,840, after adjusting for private usage.

Andrena informs you that a partner, Abdul Mohamed, joined the business on 1 March 2006. Profits are to be shared equally.

Assume that the date is December 2007, and you should be able to complete the tax return for 2005/06 by the end of the month.

Task 1.1

Give the date by which the 2005/06 tax return was due to be filed, and state the penalty that the late submission will attract.

practice exam 5 (December 2005 paper)

Task 1.2

As far as possible, given the information provided, complete the following tax return for Andrena for 2005/06.

HM Revenue & Customs

Income for the year ended 5 April 2007

SELF-EMPLOYMENT

Fill in these boxes first

Name	Tax reference

If you want help, look up the box numbers in the Notes

Business details

Name of business
3.1

Description of business
3.2

Address of business
3.3

Postcode

Accounting period - *read the Notes, page SEN3 before filling in these boxes*

Start 3.4 / /
End 3.5 / /

- Tick box 3.6 if details in boxes 3.1 or 3.3 have changed since your last Tax Return **3.6**

- Tick box 3.10 if you entered details for all relevant accounting periods on last year's Tax Return and boxes 3.14 to 3.73 and 3.99 to 3.115 will be blank *(read Step 3 on page SEN2)* **3.10**

- Date of commencement if after 5 April 2004 **3.7** / /

- Tick box 3.11 if your accounts do not cover the period from the last accounting date (explain why in the 'Additional information' box, box 3.116) **3.11**

- Date of cessation if before 6 April 2007 **3.8** / /

- Tick box 3.12 if your accounting date has changed (only if this is a permanent change and you want it to count for tax) **3.12**

- Tick box 3.9 if the special arrangements for particular trades apply - *read the Notes, page SEN11* **3.9**

- Tick box 3.13 if this is the second or further change (explain in box 3.116 on Page SE4 why you have not used the same date as last year) **3.13**

Capital allowances - summary

	Capital allowances	Balancing charges
• Cars costing more than £12,000 (excluding cars with low CO_2 emissions) (A separate calculation must be made for each car.)	3.14 £	3.15 £
• Other business plant and machinery (including cars with low CO_2 emissions and cars costing less than £12,000) *read the Notes, page SEN4*	3.16 £	3.17 £
• Agricultural or Industrial Buildings Allowance (A separate calculation must be made for each block of expenditure.)	3.18 £	3.19 £
• Other capital allowances claimed (separate calculations must be made). Claims to, and balancing charges arising on, Business Premises Renovation Allowance must also be included in boxes 23.7 and 23.8 respectively	3.20 £	3.21 £
Total capital allowances/balancing charges	total of column above 3.22 £	total of column above 3.23 £

- Tick box 3.22A if box 3.22 includes enhanced capital allowances for designated environmentally beneficial plant and machinery **3.22A**

Income and expenses - annual turnover below £15,000

If your annual turnover is £15,000 or more, **ignore** boxes 3.24 to 3.26. Instead fill in Page SE2
If your annual turnover is below £15,000, **fill in** boxes 3.24 to 3.26 instead of Page SE2. Read the Notes, page SEN4.

- Turnover including other business receipts and goods etc. taken for personal use (and balancing charges from box 3.23) **3.24** £

- Expenses allowable for tax (including capital allowances from box 3.22) **3.25** £

box 3.24 minus box 3.25
Net profit (put figure in brackets if a loss) **3.26** £

You must now fill in Page SE3

SA103

HMRC 12/05 net   TAX RETURN ■ SELF-EMPLOYMENT: PAGE SE1

341

practice exam 5 (December 2005 paper)

Income and expenses - annual turnover £15,000 or more

You must fill in this Page if your annual turnover is £15,000 or more - read the Notes, pages SEN2, SEN4 to SEN7

If you were registered for VAT, will the figures in boxes 3.29 to 3.64, include VAT? **3.27** ☐ or exclude VAT? **3.28** ☐

Sales/business income (turnover) **3.29** £ _____

	Disallowable expenses included in boxes 3.46 to 3.63	Total expenses	
• Cost of sales	3.30 £	3.46 £	
• Construction industry subcontractor costs	3.31 £	3.47 £	
• Other direct costs	3.32 £	3.48 £	box 3.29 minus (boxes 3.46 + 3.47 + 3.48)
		Gross profit/(loss)	3.49 £
		Other income/profits	3.50 £
• Employee costs	3.33 £	3.51 £	
• Premises costs	3.34 £	3.52 £	
• Repairs	3.35 £	3.53 £	
• General administrative expenses	3.36 £	3.54 £	
• Motor expenses	3.37 £	3.55 £	
• Travel and subsistence	3.38 £	3.56 £	
• Advertising, promotion and entertainment	3.39 £	3.57 £	
• Legal and professional costs	3.40 £	3.58 £	
• Bad debts	3.41 £	3.59 £	
• Interest and alternative finance payments	3.42 £	3.60 £	
• Other finance charges	3.43 £	3.61 £	
• Depreciation and loss/(profit) on sale	3.44 £	3.62 £	
• Other expenses	3.45 £	3.63 £	
	Put the total of boxes 3.30 to 3.45 in box 3.66 below	Total expenses	3.64 £ (total of boxes 3.51 to 3.63)
		Net profit/(loss)	3.65 £ (boxes 3.49 + 3.50 minus 3.64)

Tax adjustments to net profit or loss

		boxes 3.30 to 3.45	
• Disallowable expenses		3.66 £	
• Adjustments (apart from disallowable expenses) that increase profits. For instance; goods taken for personal use and amounts brought forward from an earlier year because of a claim under ESC B11 about compulsory slaughter of farm animals		3.67 £	
• Balancing charges (from box 3.23)		3.68 £	
Total additions to net profit (deduct from net loss)			3.69 £ (boxes 3.66 + 3.67 + 3.68)
• Capital allowances (from box 3.22)		3.70 £	
• Deductions from net profit (add to net loss)		3.71 £	3.72 £ (boxes 3.70 + 3.71)
Net business profit for tax purposes (put figure in brackets if a loss)			3.73 £ (boxes 3.65 + 3.69 minus 3.72)

HMRC 12/05 net   TAX RETURN ■ SELF-EMPLOYMENT: PAGE SE2   Now fill in Page SE3

Task 1.3

Calculate the taxable trading profits, AFTER capital allowances, for the year ended 30 November 2006.

Task 1.4

Calculate how the profit for the year ended 30 November 2006 would be divided between:

a) Andrena as a sole trader from 1 December 2005 to 28 February 2006

b) the partnership from 1 March 2006 to 30 November 2006.

practice exam 5 (December 2005 paper)

Task 1.5

Show the taxable trading profits for Andrena for 2006/07.

Task 1.6

Calculate the TOTAL amount of National Insurance Contributions payable for 2006/07, by Andrena.

practice exam 5 (December 2005 paper)

DATA

You have received the following email from Andrena Milburn.

From: Amilburn@boxmail.net
To: AATStudent@boxmail.net
Sent: 4 December 2006 10.58
Subject: Buildings

We have been renting premises for the past few years, and Abdul and I feel that it is time to buy premises from which to work. However, we have no idea what the tax implications of this purchase would be.

We have seen two buildings. One is new and would cost £50,000. The other is a used building that would cost £50,000, but the current owner says he paid £40,000 for it nine years ago when he bought it new.

We don't know which building to buy and thought we would find out the tax implications of both buildings before deciding which one to choose.

We are asking your advice and would be grateful for any information that would help us to make decisions.

Regards

Andrena

Task 1.7

Using the next two pages, reply to Andrena's email, explaining to her how industrial building allowances (IBAs) apply to:

- new buildings, and
- used buildings.

You need to consider only those buildings that have been in continuous industrial use.

Note 1: You can assume that all expenditure incurred is eligible for IBAs.

From: AATStudent@boxmail.net
To: Amilburn@boxmail.net
Sent: 6 December 2006 15.41
Subject: Buildings

This page is for the continuation of your email. You may not need all of it.

SECTION 2 (Suggested time allowance: 80 minutes)

DATA

One of your firm's clients, Harrison Ltd, commenced trading on 1 January 2006. The tax information for this company is as follows.

- The adjusted trading profit, before capital allowances, has been calculated for the nine-month period ended 30 September 2006 at £25,000.

- Harrison Ltd had the following capital transactions during the nine months:

Purchases:		£
May 2006	Plant and machinery	7,500
May 2006	Managing director's car, used 80% privately	25,000
November 2006	Plant and machinery	10,000

- Harrison Ltd is classified as a 'small' company for capital allowances purposes.

- In January 2006, Harrison Ltd bought an asset for £10,000. In September 2006, it sold the asset for £25,000. This asset is treated as a business asset for capital gains purposes.

- Harrison Ltd has rental income of £500 per month.

- Harrison Ltd has no associated companies.

practice exam 5 (December 2005 paper)

Task 2.1

a) Calculate the capital allowances for the period ended in September 2006.

b) Calculate the taxable trading profit for the period ended 30 September 2006.

practice exam 5 (December 2005 paper)

Task 2.2

Calculate the capital gain, if any, arising from the disposal of the business asset in September 2006.

Task 2.3

Calculate the PCTCT (profit chargeable to corporation tax) for the period ended 30 September 2006.

Task 2.4

Calculate the corporation tax payable for the period ended 30 September 2006 stating the due date for payment.

practice exam 5 (December 2005 paper)

DATA

The Managing Director of Harrison Ltd informs you that the company is considering acquiring an associated company during 2007. He asks for your advice regarding the taxation implications of such purchase. He expects the profits chargeable to corporation tax for the year ended 31 December 200 for Harrison Ltd to be about £200,000.

Task 2.5

Write a memo to the Managing Director explaining how the purchase of an associated company w affect the taxation computation of Harrison Ltd. You do not need to give detailed calculations

MEMO

To: Managing Director	Subject: Associated Companies
From: Accounting Technician	Date: 6 December 2006

practice exam 5 (December 2005 paper)

This space is for the continuation of your memo. You may not need all of it.

DATA

After you have completed all the above information, you realise that Harrison Ltd has failed to tell HMRC that they have started trading.

Task 2.6

State the penalties that can be imposed for failing to notify HMRC that the company has commenced trading.

REVISION COMPANION UNIT 18

answers

Answers to chapter 1: INTRODUCTION

(a) Income tax computation

	Non-savings £	Savings (excl dividend) £	Dividend £	Total £
Taxable trading profits	45,000			
Dividend			1,000	
Bank deposit interest		1,000		
	45,000	1,000	1,000	47,000
Less personal allowance	(5,035)			
Taxable income	39,965	1,000	1,000	41,965

(b)

	£
Tax on non – savings income	
£2,150 × 10%	215
£31,150 × 22%	6,853
£6,665 × 40%	2,666
Tax on savings (excl dividend) income £1,000 × 40%	400
Tax on dividend income £1,000 × 32.5%	325
Tax liability	10,459

Answers to chapter 2: COMPUTING TRADING INCOME

To: Tax Manager
From: AN Accountant
Subject: Badges of Trade

In order to decide whether a trade is being carried on the following 'badges of trade' need to be considered:

a) *Subject matter*. When people engage in trade, they frequently do so by purchasing and re-selling objects with a view to making a profit. Objects bought for this purpose are often not the type of objects that would be bought for investment or enjoyment. This means that the subject of a transaction will very often indicate whether a trade is being carried on or not.

b) *Length of ownership*. A short period of ownership is an indication of an intention to trade in a commodity.

c) *Frequency of transactions*. Where the same type of article is repeatedly bought and sold, it will normally suggest that there is trading in that article.

d) *Supplementary work* on or in connection with the property sold, e.g. modification, processing, packaging, or renovating the item sold suggests the carrying on of a trade.

e) *Acquisition of asset*. If goods are acquired deliberately, trading may be indicated. If goods are acquired by gift or inheritance, their later sale is unlikely to constitute trading.

f) *Profit motive*. This is usually the most important consideration though its absence does not prevent a trade being carried on if, in fact, the operation is run on commercial lines and a profit does result.

These *badges of trade* are only general indications and, in each case, all the facts must be considered before any decision can be made.

2

	£	£
Profits per accounts		5,300
Add: salary paid to Mr Jelly (N1)	260	
motor expenses (N2) (£350 × ½)	50	
stockroom extension (N3)	101	
increase in general provision (N1)	200	
donations (N2)	10	
entertaining (N4)	90	
gifts (N5)	70	
depreciation (N3)	600	
		1,381
Taxable trading profit		6,681

Notes

1) Appropriation of profit.
2) Not expenditure incurred wholly and exclusively for the purpose of trade.
3) Capital items.
4) Entertaining expenses specifically disallowed.
5) Gifts of alcohol specifically disallowed.

3

	£	£
Net profit per accounts		19,000
Add: market value of goods taken for own use	50	
depreciation	4,000	
legal expenses (N1)	400	
entertaining £(50 + 150 + 75) (N2)	275	
		4,725
Less: decrease in general bad debt provision		(30)
Adjusted trading profits		23,695

Notes

1) Legal expenses are disallowed as they relate to a capital item.

2) Staff entertaining is allowable. Other types of entertaining is specifically disallowable.

Answers to chapter 3: CAPITAL ALLOWANCES

	FYA @ 50% £	General pool £	Private use asset (1) £	Private use asset (2) £	Allowances £
Y/e 31 March 2007					
TWDV b/f		38,500	15,000		
Additions		8,000		18,000	
Disposals		(3,000)	(16,500)		
		43,500	(1,500)	18,000	
Balancing charge			1,500 × 80%		(1,200)
WDA @ 25%		(10,875)			10,875
WDA @ £3,000				(3,000) × 80%	2,400
Additions	4,800				
FYA @ 50%	(2,400)				2,400
		2,400			
TWDV c/f		35,025		15,000	14,475

Capital allowances for periods of account:

	FYA @ 40% £	FYA @ 50%	General pool £	Allowances £
1.1.04 – 31.8.04				
Addition (1.1.04)	10,500			
FYA @ 40%	(4,200)			4,200
			6,300	
1.9.04 – 31.8.05				
Disposals			(1,500)	
			4,800	
WDA @ 25%			(1,200)	1,200
Addition (1.12.04)		4,000		
FYA @ 50%		(2,000)		2,000
			2,000	
			5,600	3,200
1.9.05 – 31.8.06				
WDA @ 25%			(1,400)	1,400
Addition (1.10.05)	6,000			
FYA @ 40%	(2,400)		3,600	2,400
Addition (1.6.06)		8,800		
FYA @ 50%		(4,400)	4,400	4,400
				8,200
			12,200	

FYAs are not pro-rated in the first short period of account.

Revision Companion – capital allowances: answers

3 Capital allowances for periods of account:

	FYAs £	General pool £	Expensive Prop's asset (80%) £	£
1.9.03 – 31.8.04				
TWDV b/f		19,200	14,400	
WDA @ 25%		(4,800)		4,800
WDA – restricted			(3,000) × 80%	2,400
		14,400	11,400	7,200
1.9.04 – 31.8.05				
WDA @ 25%		(3,600)	(2,850) × 80%	5,880
Additions	5,100			
FYA @ 50%	(2,550)			2,550
				8,430
		2,550		
		13,350	8,550	
1.9.05 – 31.5.06				
Addition		7,200		
Disposals		(15,900)	(9,000)	
		(4,650)	450	
Balancing (allowance)/Charge		(4,650)	450 × 80%	4,290

No FYAs or WDAs are given in the final period of account.

4 Plant and machinery

	FYAs £	General pool £	Expensive car (1) £	Expensive car (2) £	Short life asset £	Allowance
TWDV b/f		84,600	15,400			
Addition				17,200		
Disposal			(19,600)			
Balancing charge			4,200 × 50%			(2,100)
WDA @ 25%/£3,000		(21,150)		(3,000) × 50%		22,650
		63,450		14,200		
Additions						
Fixed machinery	20,000					
Computer					3,400	
Lorry	32,000					
	52,000					
Less: FYA @ 40%	(20,800)				(1,360)	22,160
		31,200				
TWDV c/f		94,650		14,200	2,040	
						42,710

Expenditure eligible for IBAs

	£
Levelling the land	19,200
Architects fees	30,800
Factory	187,500
General offices (less than 25% of total)	62,500
	300,000

IBA @ 4% (building in use on 31 March 2007) £12,000

	FYA £	Pool £	Expensive car £	Short life assets £	Allowances £
Year ended 30.6.03					
WDV b/f		29,700			
WDA @ 25%		(7,425)			7,425
Additions	1,917			3,667	
FYA @ 40%	(767)			(1,467)	2,234
		1,150			9,659
		23,425		2,200	
Year ended 30.6.04					
WDA @ 25%		(5,856)		(550)	£6,406
		17,569		1,650	
Year ended 30.6.05					
Acquisitions			13,400		
WDA @ 25%		(4,392)	(3,000)	(413)	£7,805
		13,177	10,400	1,237	
Year ended 30.6.06					
Disposals		(340)		(2,000)	
		12,837		(763)	
Balancing charge				763	(763)
WDA @ 25%		(3,209)	(2,600)		5,809
		9,628	7,800		5,046
Period ended 31.12.06					
Disposals		(24,000)	(10,600)		
Balancing charge		(14,372)	(2,800)		£(17,172)

Tutorial note

1   There is never any private use restriction when calculating capital allowances for companies.

2   Since Dexter Ltd is a medium sized enterprise, 100% FYA for computers is not available (only small enterprises qualify). However, a 40% FYA is available.

Revision Companion – capital allowances: answers

6

	Pool £	Expensive car £	Short life assets £	Allowances £
WDV b/f	106,000	7,000	17,500	
Transfer	17,500		(17,500)	
	123,500		0	
Disposals	(5,000)	(6,000)		
Balancing allowance		1,000		1,000
	118,500			
Addition		14,000		
WDA	(29,625)	(3,000)		32,625
WDV c/f	88,875	11,000		33,625

Tutorial note. If a short life asset has not been disposed of within four years of the end of the accounting period in which it was acquired, it must be transferred to the general pool.

7 New factory

As Biswas Ltd is the second owner, it will write off the lower of the original cost (£100,000) or own cost (£80,000) ie £80,000.

The tax life of the building is 25 years from 1 September 1996. 15 years of the tax life remain.

The allowance for y/e 31 March 2007 is therefore:

$$\frac{£80,000}{15} = \underline{£5,333}$$

Original factory

Qualifying expenditure was:

	£
Tunnelling	10,000
Factory	85,000
	95,000

The cost of the land is not qualifying. The showroom is a non-qualifying part exceeding more than 25% of the expenditure so must be excluded.

The allowance for y/e 31 March 2007 is:

£95,000 × 4% = £3,800

Total allowances are therefore:

£(5,333 + 3,800) = £9,133

Answers to chapter 4: TAXING UNINCORPORATED BUSINESSES

(a) *Taxable profits*

Tax year	Basis period		Taxable profits £
2004/05	(1.7.04 – 5.4.05)	$\frac{9}{22} \times £33,000 =$	13,500
2005/06	(6.4.05 – 5.4.06)	$\frac{12}{22} \times £33,000 =$	18,000
2006/07	(1.5.05 – 30.4.06)	$\frac{12}{22} \times £33,000 =$	18,000

(b) *Overlap profits*

The profits taxed twice are those for the period 1.5.05 to 5.4.06:

$\frac{11}{22} \times £33,000 = £16,500$

Tutorial note. Overlap profits are the profits taxed twice in the early years.

	£
2004/05: Actual 1 July 2004 to 5 April 2005 (9/11 × £22,000)	18,000
2005/06: 1st 12 months (no CYB) 1 July 2004 to 30 June 2005 £22,000 + (1/12 × £18,000)	23,500
2006/07: (CYB) Year ended 31 May 2006	18,000
Overlap period is 1 July 2004 to 5 April 2005 and 1 June 2005 to 30 June 2005	18,000
(1/12 × £18,000)	1,500
	19,500

3

			£
2006/07	1 May 2005 to 31 December 2006 (16,000 + 4,000)		20,000
	Less: overlap relief		(9,000)
			11,000
2005/06	Year ended 30 April 2005		48,000
2004/05	Year ended 30 April 2004		36,000

4

	£	£
2002/03		
1st year – 1.5.02 to 5.4.03		
11/15 × £18,000		13,200
2003/04		
2nd year 12 months to 31.7.03 (1.8.02 – 31.7.03)		
12/15 × £18,000		14,400
2004/05		
3rd year y/e 31.7.04		11,700
2005/06		
y/e 31.7.05		8,640
2006/07		
y/e 31.7.06	4,800	
p/e 28.2.07	5,100	
	9,900	
Less: Overlap profits (W)	(9,600)	300

Working

Overlap profits

Overlap period is 1 August 2002 to 5 April 2003, ie 8/15 × £18,000 = £9,600

Tutorial note. It is very important to state the tax year to which you allocate profits, not just st that a year is the "first year", "second year" and so on.

5 Taxable trading profits

		£
2005/06	(1 February 2006 to 5 April 2006) 2/14 × £25,224 (W1)	3,603
2006/07	(1 April 2006 to 31 March 2007) 12/14 × £25,224 (W1)	21,621

There are no overlap profits

Workings

1

		£	£
Net profit per accounts			30,014
Add: depreciation		9,000	
office desk		1,800	
proprietor's salary		5,000	
legal expenses		950	
motor car expenses		360	
			17,110
Less: capital allowances (W2)			(21,900)
Taxable trading profits			25,224

2

	FYA @ 50% £	Pool £	Expensive car £	Allowances £
Addition			13,000	
WDA × £3,000 × 14/12			(3,500) × 80%	2,800
			9,500	
Addition	28,000			
FYA @ 50%	(14,000)			14,000
		14,000		
Addition	8,400			
FYA @ 50%	(4,200)			4,200
		4,200		
Office desk	1,800			
FYA @ 50%	(900)			900
		900		21,900
C/f		19,100	9,500	

6 (a)

	FYA @ 50% £	FYA @ 40% £	Pool £	Car (65%) £	Allowances £
1.1.04 – 30.4.05					
Car				6,600	
WDA @ 25% × 16/12				(2,200) × 65%	1,430
Desk and office furniture		940			
General plant		3,835			
Secondhand oven		1,200			
Delivery van		1,800			
Typewriter		425			
		8,200			
FYA @ 40%		(3,280)			3,280
			4,920	4,400	4,710
Year ended 30.4.06					
WDA @ 25%			(1,230)	(1,100) × 65%	1,945
			3,690	3,300	
General plant	1,000				
General plant	1,556				
	2,556				
FYA @ 50%	(1,278)		1,278		1,278
WDV c/f			4,968	3,300	3,223

(b) Profits are as follows.

Period	Profit £	Capital allowances £	Trading profits £
1.1.04 – 30.4.05	20,710	4,710	16,000
1.5.05 – 30.4.06	15,125	3,223	11,902

(c) The taxable profits are as follows.

Year	Basis period	Working	Taxable trading profits £
2003/04	1.1.04 – 5.4.04	£16,000 × 3/16	3,000
2004/05	6.4.04 – 5.4.05	£16,000 × 12/16	12,000
2005/06	1.5.04 – 30.4.05	£16,000 × 12/16	12,000
2006/07	1.5.05 – 30.4.06		11,902

The overlap profits are the profits from 1 May 2004 to 5 April 2005: £16,000 × 11/16 = £11,00(

Tutorial notes

1. Writing down allowances are time apportioned in a long period of account but first ye allowances are not.

2. As Miss Farrington's business is a small enterprise she is entitled to 50% FYAs on the pla purchased between 6.4.06 to 5.4.07. When different rates of FYA are available, as here, suggest that your computation deals with the different rates of FYA in different columns as have done here. The key to getting a capital allowance question correct is to set up proforma with the various columns that we have shown here.

3. Don't forget that the private use of an asset restricts the allowances available to a sole trad

Answers to chapter 5: RELIEVING TRADING LOSSES

	2004/05 £	2005/06 £	2006/07 £	2007/08 £
Trading profits	12,000	NIL	8,000	14,000
s385 relief			(3) (8,000)	(4) (3,600)
			–	10,400
Rental income	10,400	11,000	11,000	11,000
STI	22,400	11,000		
s380	(1) (22,400)	(2) (11,000)		
Revised STI	–	–	11,000	21,400

Loss Memo

	£
Loss in 2005/06	45,000
s380: 2004/05 (1)	(22,400)
s380: 2005/06 (2)	(11,000)
c/f under S385	11,600
s385: 2006/07 (3)	(8,000)
	3,600
s385: 2007/08 (4)	(3,600)
	–

Note. s385 relief is given against taxable trading profits only, whereas s380 relief is given against statutory total income.

(a) The loss of £11,000 is a loss for 2006/07.

Possible loss relief claims are:

(i) against total income for 2005/06

(ii) against total income for 2006/07

(iii) under (i) and then the remaining loss under (ii)

(iv) against the taxable trading profits of £14,000 in 2007/08

(b) (i) (and therefore (iii)) should be avoided, as loss relief in 2005/06 would cover income whi[ch] would in any case be covered by the personal allowance. Both (ii) and (iv) save tax at 22[%]. However, as (ii) saves tax more quickly it is more beneficial from a cashflow point of view.

	2005/06 £	2006/07 £	2007/08 £
Taxable trading profits	4,000	0	14,000
Rental income	0	19,000	12,000
	4,000	19,000	26,000
Less s 380 loss relief	0	(11,000)	0
	4,000	8,000	26,000
Less personal allowance	(5,035)	(5,035)	(5,035)
Taxable income	0	2,965	20,965

Tutorial note. If you set out the alternative loss relief claims clearly, the computation shou[ld] have been straightforward. It is important to practise giving finished answers to questio[ns] which require you to list alternative claims; do not assume that a scrappy note will do a[nd] that neatness and clarity will come naturally in the real examination.

Answers to chapter 6: Partnerships

First apportion profit to each partner based on the profit sharing agreement in force for each period of account:

	Fimbo £	Florrie £	Pom £	Total £
12 months to 31 December 2005				
Salary	5,000			5,000
Balance 60:40	3,000	2,000		5,000
	8,000	2,000		10,000
12 months to 31 December 2006				
Salary	5,000			5,000
Balance 60:40	9,000	6,000		15,000
	14,000	6,000		20,000
12 months to 31 December 2007				
Salary	6,500			6,500
Balance 1:1:1	6,167	6,167	6,166	18,500
	12,667	6,167	6,166	25,000

Assessments	Fimbo £	Florrie £	Pom £
2004/05			
Actual (1 January 2005 to 5 April 2005)			
3/12 × £(8,000)/(2,000)	2,000	500	N/A
2005/06			
CYB – year ended 31 December 2005	8,000	2,000	N/A
2006/07			
CYB – year ended 31 December 2006	14,000	6,000	
Year 1 for Pom = Actual			
(1 January 2007 to 5 April 2007)			
3/12 × £6,166			1,541
2007/08			
CYB – year ended 31 December 2007	12,667	6,167	6,166

Overlap profits for Pom = £1,541

Revision Companion – partnerships: answers

2 Allocation of Profits

	Total £	John £	Paul £	George £
Period ended 31 July 2004				
4:3:3	24,300	9,720	7,290	7,290
Year ended 31 July 2005				
4:3:3	16,200	6,480	4,860	4,860
Year ended 31 July 2006				
4:3:3	14,900	5,960	4,470	4,470

Assessments

	John £	Paul £	George £
2003/04			
1 January 2004 – 5 April 2004			
3/7 × £(9,720/7,290/7,290)	4,166	3,124	3,124
2004/05 (1 January 2004 to 31 December 2004)			
1 January 2004 to 31 July 2004	9,720	7,290	7,290
1 August 2004 to 31 December 2004			
5/12 × £(6,480/4,860/4,860)	2,700	2,025	2,025
	12,420	9,315	9,315
2005/06			
Year ended 31 July 2005	6,480	4,860	4,860
2006/07			
Year ended 31 July 2006	5,960	4,470	4,470
Overlap periods			
1 January 2004 to 5 April 2004	4,166	3,124	3,124
1 August 2004 to 31 December 2004	2,700	2,025	2,025
Overlap profits	6,866	5,149	5,149

3 Profit allocation

	Total £	Strange £	Pavin £	Lehman £
Year ended 31 December 2004				
Interest on capital				
£20,000 × 5%	1,000	1,000		
£10,000 × 5%	500		500	
	1,500			
Salaries	20,000	15,000	5,000	
	21,500			
3:2:1 (balance)	26,000	13,000	8,667	4,333
	47,500	29,000	14,167	4,333

	Total £	Strange £	Pavin £	Lehman £
Year ended 31 December 2005				
1 January 2005 – 31 July 2005				
Interest on capital				
£1,000/5,000 × 7/12	875	583	292	
Salaries				
£15,000/5,000 × 7/12	11,667	8,750	2,917	
	12,542			
3:2:1 (balance)	15,458	7,729	5,153	2,576
£48,000 × 7/12	28,000	17,062	8,362	2,576
1 August 2005 – 31 December 2005				
Salary (£20,000 × 5/12)	8,333	8,333		
2:2:1 (balance)	11,667	4,667	4,667	2,333
£48,000 × 5/12	20,000	13,000	4,667	2,333
Total	48,000	30,062	13,029	4,909
Year ended 31 December 2006				
Salary	20,000	20,000		
Profits (2:2:1) (balance)	40,000	16,000	16,000	8,000
	60,000	36,000	16,000	8,000

Assessments

	Strange £	Pavin £	Lehman £
2004/05			
Year ended 31 December 2004	29,000	14,167	4,333
2005/06			
Year ended 31 December 2005	30,062	13,029	4,909
2006/07			
Year ended 31 December 2006	36,000	16,000	8,000

4 Y/e 31.5.06

	Total £	Bob £	Annie £	John £
1.6.04 – 31.1.05				
Salaries				
£15,000 × 8/12	30,000	10,000	10,000	10,000
Balance				
£(90,000 × 8/12 – 30,000) = £30,000	30,000	15,000	7,500	7,500
1.2.06 – 31.5.06				
Salaries				
£15,000 × 4/12	10,000	n/a	5,000	5,000
Balance				
£(90,000 × 4/12 – 10,000) = £20,000	20,000	n/a	10,000	10,000
Totals	90,000	25,000	32,500	32,500

Y/e 31.5.07

	Total £	Annie £	John £
Salaries	30,000	15,000	15,000
Balance			
£(120,000 – 30,000) = £90,000 × 50%	90,000	45,000	45,000
Totals	120,000	60,000	60,000

Answers to chapter 7: CAPITAL GAINS TAX FOR SOLE TRADERS

	£	Total £
Asset A		
Proceeds	40,000	
Allowable cost	(7,500)	
Enhancement expenditure	(500)	
Unindexed gain	32,000	
Indexation allowance (0.626 × £7,500)	(4,695)	
None on enhancement (after April 1998)		
Indexed gain	27,305	
Gain after taper relief		
(6 April 1998 to 5 April 2006) (25% × £27,305)		6,826
Asset B		
Proceeds	18,000	
Allowable cost	(4,400)	
Unindexed gain	13,600	
Indexation allowance (0.171 × £4,400)	(752)	
Indexed gain	12,848	
Gain after taper relief		
(6 April 1998 to 5 April 2006) 25% × £12,848		3,212
Asset C		
Proceeds	16,000	
Less: cost	(7,500)	
Gain before taper relief	8,500	
Gain after taper relief		
(31 December 2005 to 31 December 2006 = 1 year)		
50% × £8,500		4,250
		14,288

	£
Net gains 2006/07	14,288
AE	(8,800)
Taxable gains	5,488

	£		£
Tax @ 20% (£33,300 – 30,700)	2,600 @ 20% =		520
Tax @ 40%	2,888 @ 40% =		1,155
	5,488	CGT due	1,675

2

	£
Gains	17,200
Losses	(7,000)
	10,200
Losses b/f £(10,200 – 8,800)	(1,400)
	8,800
CGT annual exemption	(8,800)
Taxable gains	NIL

Losses c/f (5,000 – 1,400) = £3,600

Taper relief is effectively lost on the business assets as it applies after losses are deducted.

3 Office block

	£
Sale proceeds	300,000
Less: cost	(100,000)
	200,000
Less: indexation (1.006 × £100,000)	(100,600)
Gain before taper relief	99,400

Factory

	£
Proceeds	400,000
Less: cost	(700,000)
Allowable loss	(300,000)

Shop

	£
Proceeds	500,000
Less: cost	(120,000)
Gain before taper relief	380,000

Note. The enhancement expenditure is not deductible as it is not reflected in the state and nature of the retail premises at the date of sale

The shop has been owned for one year, so 50% of the gain is chargeable after taper relief.

The office block has been owned for at least two years since 6 April 1998 so 25% of the gain chargeable after taper relief.

The allowable loss is set against the gain where the highest percentage of the gain remains chargeable, ie against the gain on the shop.

	£	£
Gain on shop	380,000	
Allowable loss	(300,000)	
	80,000	
Gain after taper relief (50%)		40,000
Gain after taper relief on office (25% × £99,400)		24,850
Gain after taper relief		64,850
Less: annual exemption		(8,800)
Taxable gain		56,050

As taxable income exceeds £33,300 all of the gain is taxed at 40%.

CGT payable 40% × £56,050 = £22,420

Land

	£
Proceeds	23,000
Less: cost	(26,000)
Allowable loss	(3,000)

Car

The car is an exempt asset.

Premises

	£
Proceeds	80,000
Less: cost	(20,000)
	60,000
Less: Indexation 0.708 × £20,000	(14,160)
Gain before taper relief	45,840

	£
Gain	45,840
Less: loss	(3,000)
	42,840
Less: loss b/f	(2,500)
	40,340

	£
Gain after taper relief	
25% × £40,340	10,085
Less: Annual Exemption	(8,800)
	1,285

Answers to chapter 8:
CHARGEABLE GAINS: ADDITIONAL ASPECTS

	£
Proceeds	45,000
Cost £8,000 × $\dfrac{45,000}{45,000+50,000}$	(3,789)
Unindexed gain	41,211
Indexation allowance 0.968 × £3,789	(3,668)
Indexed gain	37,543

	£
Gain after taper relief (6 April 1998 to 5 April 2005)	
25% × £37,543	9,386
Less: AE	(8,800)
Taxable gain	586

Summary of gains:

	Business assets £
Antique office desk (W1) (25%)	1,667
2 acres of land (W2) (25%)	1,819
Factory	–
Racehorse	–
Gains after taper relief	3,486

Workings

1 *Antique office desk*

	£
Gross proceeds	10,000
Less: fees (5% × £10,000)	(500)
	9,500
Less: probate value (January 1987)	(1,500)
	8,000
Less: indexation (0.626 × £1,500)	(939)
Gain before taper relief	7,061

Restricted to 5/3 × (10,000 – 6,000) = £6,667

For taper relief purposes the desk has been owned for at least two years (6 April 1998 to 5 April 2006).

		£
2	2 acres of land	
	Proceeds	12,000
	Less: cost $\left(£10,000 \times \dfrac{12,000}{12,000+40,000}\right)$	(2,308)
		9,692
	Less: indexation (1.047 × £2,308)	(2,416)
	Gain before taper relief	7,276

For taper relief purposes the land has been held for at least years.

3   The disposal to Ian's wife is made on a no gain/no loss basis. This means that no chargeable gain or allowable loss arises.

4   The racehorse is an exempt chattel so no gain/loss arises.

3   Hilary Spencer – CGT 2006/07

Summary

	Business £
Building (W1) – 2+ years taper (25%)	71,980
Plant (W2) – 2+ years taper (25%)	1,667
	73,647
Less: loss	(1,000)
Net gains before taper relief	72,647
Gains after taper relief	
25% × £72,647	18,162
Less: annual exemption	(8,800)
Gains chargeable to CGT 2006/07	9,362

Tutorial notes

1   As both assets are subject to the same amount of taper relief it does not matter how the loss is offset.

2   You are given an indexation factor in the question which is deliberately put in to test whether you know the rules, but is not actually needed in the correct solution. You must ensure you know which indexation factor to use.

Workings

1 Building

	£
Proceeds	106,000
Less: cost	(28,000)
Unindexed gain	78,000
Less: indexation allowance to 4.98 0.215 × £28,000	(6,020)
Gain before taper relief	71,980

Taper relief ownership period – 6.4.98 – 5.4.06 = 2+ years

2 Chattel

	£
Proceeds	7,000
Less: cost	(5,000)
Gain before taper relief	2,000
Restricted to 5/3 × £(7,000 – 6,000)	1,667

Taper relief ownership period – 18.10.99 – 17.10.06 = 2+ years

3 Chattel

	£
Proceeds [presumed]	6,000
Less: cost	(7,000)
Loss	(1,000)

Answers to chapter 9:
SHARES

Capital gains tax liability – 2006/07

	£
Gain on shares (W1)	18,597
Less: annual exemption	(8,800)
Chargeable gain	9,797

CGT thereon £9,797 @ 20% = £1,959

Note. Taxable income is £19,800. Thus £13,500 of basic rate band remains (£33,300 – £19,800).

Workings

1) Sale of shares

		£	£
a)	*May 2001 acquisition*		
	Sale proceeds (1,000 shares) $\left(\frac{1,000}{5,000} \times £90,000\right)$	18,000	
	Less: cost	(3,000)	
	Gain before taper relief	15,000	
	Gain after taper relief (2+ years)		
	25% × £15,000		3,750
b)	*FA 85 pool*		
	Sale proceeds (4,000 shares) $\left(\frac{4,000}{5,000} \times £90,000\right)$	72,000	
	Less: cost (W2)	(7,143)	
		64,857	
	Less: indexation allowance (W2)	(5,467)	
	Indexed gain	59,390	
	Gain after taper relief		
	(6 April 1998 – 5 April 2005)		
	25% × £59,390		14,847
			18,597

2) FA 1985 pool

	No of shares	Cost £	Indexed cost £
Purchase	2,000	3,000	3,000
Initial indexation to April 1985			
0.158 × £3,000			474
			3,474
Index to November 1985			
0.012 × £3,474			42
Purchase	5,000	9,500	9,500
	7,000	12,500	13,016
Index to October 1987			
0.073 × £13,016			950
			13,966
Sale	(3,000)	(5,357)	(5,985)
	4,000	7,143	7,981
Index to April 1998			
0.580 × £7,981			4,629
			12,610
Sale July 2006	(4,000)	(7,143)	(12,610)
	–	–	–

The indexation allowance on the July 2006 sale is £(12,610 – 7,143) = £5,467.

2 a) Gains

10 April 1999 Acquisition: match post 6 April 1998 acquisition first:

	No of shares	Cost £
10 April 1999 – purchase	8,000	29,000
20 September 1999 – bonus issue	2,000	–
	10,000	29,000
15 March 2007	(10,000)	(29,000)
C/f	NIL	NIL

10 April 1999 Acquisition

	£
Proceeds $\left(\dfrac{10,000}{12,000} \times £48,000\right)$	40,000
Less: cost	(29,000)
Gain before taper relief	11,000

Gain after taper relief (10 April 1999 to 9 April 2006)

25% × £11,000 = £2,750

FA 1985 pool

	No of shares	Cost £	Indexed cost £
10 February 1986	12,000	18,000	18,000
Index to April 1998			
0.683 × £18,000			12,294
	12,000	18,000	30,294
20 September 1999 – bonus	3,000	NIL	NIL
	15,000	18,000	30,294
15 March 2007 – sale	(2,000)	(2,400)	(4,039)
C/f	13,000	15,600	26,255

FA 1985 pool

	£
Proceeds $\left(\dfrac{2,000}{12,000} \times £48,000\right)$	8,000
Less: cost	(2,400)
Unindexed gain	5,600
Less: IA £(4,039 – 2,400)	(1,639)
Gain before taper relief	3,961

Gain after taper relief (6 April 1998 to 5 April 2005)

25% × £3,961 = £990

Total gains £(2,750 + 990) = £3,740

b) **Gains**

10 April 1999 Acquisition

	No of shares	Cost £
10 April 1999 – purchase	8,000	29,000
20 September 1999 – rights issue	2,000	6,000
	10,000	35,000
15 March 2007	(10,000)	(35,000)
C/f	NIL	NIL

	£
Proceeds $\left(\dfrac{10,000}{12,000} \times £48,000\right)$	40,000
Less: cost	(35,000)
Gain before taper relief	5,000

Gain after taper relief (10 April 1999 to 9 April 2006)

25% × £5,000 = £1,250

FA 1985 pool

	No of shares	Cost £	Indexed cost £
Pool at April 1998 (see part (a))	12,000	18,000	30,294
20 September 1999 – rights	3,000	9,000	9,000
	15,000	27,000	39,294
15 March 2007 – sale	(2,000)	(3,600)	(5,239)
C/f	13,000	23,400	34,055

FA 1985 pool

	£
Proceeds	8,000
Less: cost	(3,600)
Unindexed gain	4,400
Less: IA £(5,239 – 3,600)	(1,639)
Gain before taper relief	2,761

Gain after taper relief (2+ years)

25% × £2,761 = £690

Total gains £(1,250 + 690) = £1,940

3   Shares in JB Ltd

	£	Gains/(losses) £
Next 30 days		
Proceeds $\left(\frac{200}{4,000} \times £26,180\right)$	1,309	
Cost	(1,150)	
		159

No taper relief

1985 Pool

	£	
Proceeds $\left(\frac{3,800}{4,000} \times £26,180\right)$	24,871	
Cost (W)	(13,379)	
Unindexed gain	11,492	
Indexation (W1) (18,833 – 13,379)	(5,454)	
Chargeable gain	6,038	

Gain after taper relief
  (6 April 1998 to 5 April 2006)

25% × £6,038		1,509
Total gains		1,668

Working

1985 Pool

	No of shares	Cost £	Indexed cost £
9 December 1986 – purchase	3,600	10,900	10,900
Index to April 1998 (0.632 × £10,900)			6,889
	3,600	10,900	17,789
October 1998 rights (1:3)	1,200	6,000	6,000
	4,800	16,900	23,789
Disposal	(3,800)	(13,379)	(18,833)
	1,000	3,521	4,956

Summary

	£
Faltskog Ltd (see below)	3,095
Anderson Ltd (see below)	1,750
	4,845

The shares in Faltskog Ltd

	£
Proceeds	160,000
Less: cost (W1)	(75,000)
Unindexed gain	85,000
Less: indexation £(147,619 – 75,000) (W1)	(72,619)
Chargeable gain before taper relief	12,381

The shares have been held for at least two complete years since April 1998 so 25% of the gain is chargeable:

25% × £12,381 = £3,095

The shares in Anderson Ltd
1 January 2001 holding

	£
Proceeds: $\left(\dfrac{10,000}{25,000} \times £40,000\right)$	16,000
Less: cost	(9,000)
Gain	7,000

Chargeable gain after taper relief (2+ years)

25% × £7,000 = £1,750

FA 85 pool

	£
Proceeds $\left(\dfrac{15,000}{25,000} \times £40,000\right)$	24,000
Less: cost (W2)	(14,500)
Unindexed gain	9,500
Less: indexation allowance £(24,491 − 14,500) = 9,991*	(9,500)
Chargeable gain before taper relief	NIL

*Indexation cannot create a loss, so restricted to £9,500.

Workings

1) Faltskog Ltd

	No of shares	Original cost £	Indexed cost £
FA85 pool			
Shares at 6 April 1985	50,000	75,000	86,025
Index to April 1998			
0.716 × £86,025			61,594
	50,000	75,000	147,619
Disposal	(50,000)	(75,000)	(147,619)

2) Anderson Ltd

	No of shares	Original cost £	Indexed cost £
FA85 pool			
1 January 1986	15,000	14,500	14,500
Index to April 1998			
0.689 × £14,500			9,991
	15,000	14,500	24,491
Disposal	(15,000)	(14,500)	(24,491)

5   Post 6.4.98 acquisitions are treated as disposed of on a LIFO basis:

   a)   3.11.05 acquisition

	£
Proceeds (2,000/11,000) × £66,000)	12,000
Less: Cost	(12,800)
Allowable loss	(800)

   b)   29.6.04 acquisition

	£
Proceeds (3,000/11,000 × £66,000)	18,000
Less: Cost	(11,500)
Gain before taper relief	6,500

The shares are a business asset. They have been held for one complete year so taper relief available, but see below.

c) *The FA 1985 pool*

	Shares	Cost £	Indexed cost £
Acquisition 19.9.82	2,000	1,700	1,700
Indexation to April 1985			
0.158 × £1,700			269
Acquisition 17.1.85	2,000	6,000	6,000
Indexation to April 1985			
0.039 × £6,000			234
	4,000	7,700	8,203
Indexed rise to December 1985			
£8,203 × 0.013			107
Acquisition 12.12.85	2,000	5,500	5,500
	6,000	13,200	13,810
Indexed rise to April 1998			
£13,810 × 0.694			9,584
Value when pool closes (5.4.98)	6,000	13,200	23,394
Disposal 17.5.06	(6,000)	(13,200)	(23,394)
	0	0	0

	£
Proceeds $\frac{6,000}{11,000} \times £66,000$	36,000
Less cost	(13,200)
	22,800
Less indexation allowance £(23,394 − 13,200)	(10,194)
Chargeable gain	12,606

There are at least two complete years of post 5 April 1998 so the chargeable gain must be reduced by taper relief.

Losses may be set against gains in the most beneficial way before taper relief is applied:

	£	£
Gain on sale of 29.6.04 acquisition	6,500	
Less: loss on 3.11.05 acquisition	(800)	
Gain before taper relief	5,700	
Gain after taper relief (50%)		2,850
Gain on FA 1985 pool shares after taper relief (25%)		3,152
Gain after taper relief		6,002

Tutorial note. You should always set losses against gains with the lowest amount of taper relief attached.

Revision Companion – shares: answers

6   *FA 1985 pool*

	No of shares	Original cost £	Indexed cost £
September 1990			
Acquisition	5,000	10,000	10,000
October 2000			
Indexed rise 0.327 × £10,000			3,270
Rights 1:5 @ £5	1,000	5,000	5,000
	6,000	15,000	18,270
August 2001			
Indexed rise 0.014 × £18,270			256
Acquisition	14,000	84,000	84,000
	20,000	99,000	102,526
January 2006			
Indexed ruse 0.141 × £102,526			14,456
			116,982
Sale	(18,000)	(89,100)	(105,284)
C/f	2,000	9,900	11,698

Sale

	£
Proceeds	135,000
Less: cost	(89,100)
Unindexed gain	45,900
Less: indexed cost £(105,284 – 89,100)	(16,184)
Indexed gain	29,716

Note. Companies are not entitled to taper relief or the annual exemption.

7   Box plc: Chargeable gains y/e 31.3.2007

Summary of gains and losses

	£
Shares: last nine days (W1)	400
FA 1985 pool (W2)	3,200
	3,600

Workings

1) *Crate Ltd shares – acquisition in last nine days*

	£
Proceeds 11,000/22,000 × £136,400	68,200
Less: cost	(67,800)
Gain	400

2) Crate Ltd shares – FA 1985 pool

	No.	Cost £	Indexed cost £
26.5.92			
Acquisition	4,000	24,000	24,000
30.6.93 Bonus issue	2,000		
24.10.00			
IA			
0.232 × £24,000			5,568
			29,568
Acquisition	5,000	27,500	27,500
c/f	11,000	51,500	57,068
22.5.06			
IA 0.139 × £57,068			7,932
			65,000
Disposal	(11,000)	(51,500)	(65,000)
c/f	nil	nil	nil

Gain	£
Proceeds 11,000/22,000 × £136,400	68,200
Less: cost	(51,500)
Unindexed gain	16,700
Less: indexation allowance £(65,000 – 51,500)	(13,500)
Indexed gain	3,200

Tutorial notes

1   For companies, indexation is available to the date of disposal of an asset.

2   A bonus issue merely effects the number of shares in issue. As bonus shares have no cost there is no need to index the Finance Act 1985 pool to the date of the bonus issue.

Answers to chapter 10: DEFERRING TAXATION OF CAPITAL GAINS

	£	£
Proceeds		200,000
Less: cost	65,000	
Less: gain held over	(15,000)	
		(50,000)
Less: indexation		
£50,000 × 0.500		(25,000)
Chargeable gain before taper relief		125,000

	£
Gain after taper relief (25% × £125,000)	31,250
Less: annual exemption	(8,800)
Taxable gain	22,450

a) **Fran's gain**

	£
Proceeds (MV) June 2006	500,000
Less: cost	(75,000)
Unindexed gain	425,000
Indexation (0.179 × £75,000)	(13,425)
Gain heldover	411,575

b) **Anna's gain**

	£	£
Proceeds July 2008		520,000
Cost (MV)	500,000	
Less: gain held over (from part a)	(411,575)	
Base cost		(88,425)
Gain before taper relief		431,575

Gain after taper relief (1 June 2006 – 31 May 2008 = 2 years)

25% × £431,575 = £107,894

	£
Proceeds	125,000
Less: cost	(50,000)
	75,000
Less: IA (1.159 × £50,000)	(57,950)
	17,050

This gain qualifies for replacement of business assets (rollover) relief:

	£
Gain	17,050
Less: chargeable in 2005	
£(125,000 – 120,000)	(5,000)
Gain rolled over	12,050

Note. The amount chargeable in 2002 is equal to the proceeds not reinvested.

Base cost of new freehold = £120,000 – £12,050 = £107,950

Gain chargeable in 2003 = £5,000

Note. Companies are not entitled to taper relief.

4 The workshop

	£
Proceeds	125,000
Less: cost	(60,000)
Unindexed gain	65,000
Less: indexation allowance to April 1998	
£60,000 × 0.716	(42,960)
Indexed gain	22,040

Rollover relief available only to the extent that the sale proceeds are reinvested in another qualifying asset.

	£
Chargeable gain before rollover relief	22,040
Less: proceeds not reinvested (= the gain immediately chargeable before taper relief)	(1,500)
Gain rolled over against new premises	20,540

Gain after taper relief (6 April 1998 to 5 April 2006)

25% × £1,500 = £375

5 Rollover relief

The following conditions must be met for rollover relief to be claimed.

- The asset sold and the new asset must both be used in the trade or trades carried on by the person claiming rollover relief.

- The asset sold and the new asset must normally both fall within one (but not necessarily the same one) of the following classes of asset.

    1) Land and buildings used for the purpose of the trade
    2) Fixed plant and machinery
    3) Goodwill (not companies).

- Reinvestment of the proceeds must take place in a period beginning one year before and ending three years after the date of the disposal.

Deferral is obtained by carrying forward the chargeable gain and deducting it from the cost of the new asset. To obtain full relief, the whole of the consideration for the disposal must be reinvested. Where only part is reinvested, part or all of the gain will be liable to tax immediately.

For individuals, the gain rolled over is the gain before taper relief.

a) **Gain on disposal**

	£
Proceeds August 2006	120,000
Allowable cost	(25,000)
Unindexed gain	95,000
Indexation (1.006 × £25,000)	(25,150)
Indexed gain: all available for roll-over as all proceeds reinvested within three years	69,850

Deemed cost of new factory for future CGT computations:

	£
Actual cost	180,000
Gain rolled-over	(69,850)
Base cost	110,150

No taper relief applies to the gain rolled over.

b)

	£
Indexed gain on disposal as above	69,850
Less proceeds not reinvested £(120,000 − £85,000)	(35,000)
Indexed gain available for roll-over	34,850

Gain chargeable in August 2006 before taper relief = £35,000

Gain after taper relief (6 April 1998 – 5 April 2006)

25% × £35,000 = £8,750

Deemed cost of new factory for future CGT computations:

	£
Actual cost	85,000
Gain rolled-over	(34,850)
Base cost	50,150

7

1) The office block

	£	£
Proceeds		500,000
Less: November 1984 cost	120,000	
December 1985 enhancement expenditure	25,000	
August 1990 enhancement expenditure	30,000	
		(175,000)
		325,000
Less: indexation allowance:		
£120,000 × 1.170	140,400	
£25,000 × 1.055	26,375	
£30,000 × 0.541	16,230	
		(183,005)
Chargeable gain		141,995

2) The plot of land

	£	£
Proceeds October 2006		140,000
Less: base cost		
cost August 1990	60,000	
Less: rollover	(32,000)	
		(28,000)
Less: indexation allowance (£28,000 × 0.541)		(15,148)
Chargeable gain		96,852

3) The office building

The sale of first building November 1983:

	£
Proceeds November 1983	120,000
Less: cost May 1982	(50,000)
	70,000
Less: indexation allowance (£50,000 × 0.062)	(3,100)
Gain rolled over	66,900

The gain in November 2006 is as follows:

	£	£
Proceeds November 2006		210,000
Less: cost November 1983	120,000	
Less: gain rolled over (as above)	(66,900)	
Base cost November 1983		(53,100)
		156,900
Less: indexation allowance (£53,100 × 1.282)		(68,074)
Chargeable gain		88,826

Answers to chapter 11: COMPUTING PROFITS CHARGEABLE TO CORPORATION TAX

	£	£
Profit per accounts		656,980
Add: depreciation	83,420	
gift aid donation	1,900	
gifts to customers	900	
repairs	12,200	
		98,420
Less: debenture interest	24,700	
bank interest	4,800	
dividends	56,000	
capital allowances	13,200	
		(98,700)
Taxable trading profit (Schedule D Case I)		656,700

Notes

1) The costs of renewing a short lease and of obtaining loan finance for trading purposes are allowable.

2) The replacement of the wall is allowable since the whole structure is not being replaced. The repairs to the office building are not allowable, being capital in nature, as the building was not in a usable state when purchased and this was reflected in the purchase price.

3) The patent royalties were paid for trade purposes so the amount charged in the accounts is deductible.

a) **Taxable trading profits**

	£	£
Net profit per accounts		627,340
Less: dividends received	1,460	
profit on the sale of shares	780	
Bank interest	1,500	
Capital allowances	123,000	
		(126,740)
		500,600
Add: depreciation	150,000	
gift aid donation	1,500	
entertaining customers	750	
		152,250
Adjusted trading profit (Schedule D Case I)		652,850

b) **Chargeable profits computation for the year ended 31 December 2007**

	£
Adjusted Trading Income (Schedule D Case I) (part (a))	652,850
Chargeable gain	1,000
Interest (Schedule D Case III)	1,500
Less: Gift Aid donation	(1,500)
Profits chargeable to CT	653,850

Tutor's note. Dividends are not included in PCTCT

3 a) Capital allowances

	General pool £
Brought forward 1.4.06	15,000
WDA @ 25%	(3,750)
WDV Carried forward	11,250

b) **Taxable trading profits**

	£	£
Net profit per accounts		101,957
Add: disallowable items:		
depreciation	20,000	
entertaining suppliers	630	
legal fees: lease on new premises	100	
gift aid payment	200	
political donation	500	
		21,430
		123,387
Less: profit on sale of investment	5,770	
dividends received	750	
bank interest	1,875	
capital allowances (a)	3,750	
		(12,145)
Taxable trading profits (Schedule D Case I)		111,242

c) **Chargeable profits computation for the accounting period to 31 March 2007**

	£
Trading profits	111,242
Bank interest	1,875
Chargeable gain	2,356
Less: charges paid – Gift Aid donation	(200)
Profits chargeable to corporation tax	115,273

	Year to 31 December 2006 £	Five months to 31 May 2007 £
Trading profits (12:5)	352,941	147,059
Rental income	10,800	4,500
Chargeable gain	–	3,000
	363,741	154,559
Gift aid donation paid	(30,000)	(40,000)
PCTCT	333,741	114,559

Tutor's notes

1) Trading profits are time apportioned.
2) Rental income is allocated to the accounting period in which it accrued.
3) Chargeable gains are allocated to the period in which they are realised
4) Gift aid donations are allocated to the period in which they are paid.

Capital gains/losses

a) Factory – 14.4.06

	£
Proceeds	230,000
Less: cost	(140,000)
Unindexed gains	90,000
Less: 1.099 × £140,000 (restricted)	(90,000)
	nil

b) Warehouse – 18.7.06

	£
Proceeds	80,000
Less: cost	(100,000)
Loss	(20,000)

Indexation allowance cannot increase loss

c) Factory – 17.9.06

	£
Proceeds	280,000
Less: cost	(85,000)
Unindexed gains	195,000
Less: IA	
0.469 × £85,000	(39,865)
Indexed gains	155,135

d) *Offices – 14.11.04*

	£
Proceeds	140,000
Less: Cost £250,000 × $\frac{140,000}{320,000+140,000}$	(76,087)
Unindexed gain	63,913
Less: IA 0.320 × £76,087	(24,348)
Indexed gain	39,565

e) *Summary*

	£
i)	nil
ii)	(20,000)
iii)	155,135
iv)	39,565
Net gains for accounting period	174,700

Answers to chapter 12: COMPUTING CORPORATION TAX PAYABLE

	8 months to 31 August 2006 £
Taxable trading profit	35,000
Capital gain	6,000
Less: Gift Aid donation	(3,000)
PCTCT	38,000
Dividends (£6,750 × 100/90)	7,500
'Profits'	45,500

Small companies' lower limit = $\dfrac{£300,000}{5} \times \dfrac{8}{12} = £40,000$

Small companies' upper limit = $\dfrac{£1,500,000}{5} \times \dfrac{8}{12} = £200,000$

Therefore, small companies' marginal relief applies (FY05 and FY06).

	£
£38,000 × 30%	11,400
Less: small companies' marginal relief 11/400 £(200,000 – 45,500) × $\dfrac{38,000}{45,500}$	(3,548)
CT	7,852

	Year to 31 December 2006 £
Trading profit	10,000
Interest	5,000
Chargeable gains	6,000
Gift aid donation	(3,000)
PCTCT	18,000
Dividends (£5,400 × 100/90)	6,000
Profits ('P')	24,000

Therefore, starting rate marginal relief applies:

	FY05 3 months to 31.3.06 £	FY06 9 months to 31.12.06 £
PCTCT (dividend 3:9)	4,500	13,500
'Profits' (dividend 3:9)	6,000	18,000
Lower limit for starting rate (FY05 only)		
£10,000 × 3/12	2,500	
Upper limit for starting rate (FY05 only)		
£50,000 × 3/12	12,500	
Tax on PCTCT		
FY05 £4,500 × 19%	855	
Less: starting rate marginal relief		
£(12,500 − 6,000) × $\frac{4,500}{6,000}$ × $\frac{19}{400}$	(232)	
FY06 £13,500 × 19%		2,565
		623
CT payable y/e 31.12.06		3,188

3   SCR limits £1,500,000 × 10/12 = £250,000
    £300,000 × 10/12 = £1,250,000

	£
Trading profits	600,000
Rental income	300,000
PCTCT	900,000
Dividends received × 100/90	180,000
'Profits'	1,080,000

Small companies' marginal relief applies:

	£
Calculation: £900,000 × 30%	270,000
Less: MR	
11/400 × £(1,250,000 − 1,080,000) × $\frac{900,000}{1,080,000}$	(3,896)
	266,104

4

	£
Trading profits	2,000,000
Chargeable gain	600,000
PCTCT	2,600,000

As 'profits' are above the upper limit the full rate of tax applies:

£2,600,000 × 30% = £780,000

	Year ended 31 October 2006 £	2 months to 31 December 2006 £
Trading profits (12:2)	4,285,714	714,286
Interest (12:2)	120,000	20,000
Chargeable Gain	300,000	
PCTCT	4,705,714	734,286

The full rate of tax applies in both accounting periods.

CT @ 30%	£1,411,714	£220,286

Answers to chapter 13: CORPORATION TAX LOSSES

	Year ended 30 June			
	2003	2004	2005	2006
	£	£	£	£
Trading profits	6,000	12,000	2,000	–
Interest	1,200	1,200	600	1,200
	7,200	13,200	2,600	1,200
S393A – current	–	–	–	(1,200)
S393A – carried back	–	–	(2,600)	
	7,200	13,200	–	
Gift Aid donation	(100)	(100)		
PCTCT	7,100	13,100	–	–
Unrelieved Gift Aid donations			50	100

Loss memorandum

	£	£
Year ended 30 June 2006		13,000
S393A(1) – current	(1,200)	
c/b June 2005	(2,600)	
		(3,800)
c/f under s393(1)		9,200

	Year ended 31 December		
	2004	2005	2006
	£	£	£
Trading profits	10,000	–	11,000
S393(1)	–	–	(5,000)
	10,000	–	6,000
Interest	5,000	5,000	5,000
	15,000	5,000	11,000
S393A – current		(5,000)	–
	15,000	–	11,000
S393A – carry back	(15,000)	–	–
	–	–	11,000
Gift Aid donations	–	–	(1,000)
PCTCT	–	–	10,000
Unrelieved Gift Aid donations	1,000	1,000	

405

Revision Companion – corporation tax losses: answers

Loss memorandum

	£
Year ended 31 December 2005	25,000
S393A – current year	(5,000)
	20,000
S393A – carried back	(15,000)
	5,000
S393(1)	(5,000)
	–

3

	Year ended 31 December 2004 £	Nine months ended 30 September 2005 £	Year ended 30 September 2006 £
Trading profits	45,000	85,000	–
Interest	8,000	12,000	14,000
Chargeable gains	10,000	2,000	–
	63,000	99,000	14,000
Less: s393A – current	–	–	(14,000) (i)
	63,000	99,000	–
S393A – carry back	(15,750) (iii)	(99,000) (ii)	–
	47,250	–	–
Gift Aid donation	(1,000)	–	–
PCTCT	46,250	–	–
Unrelieved Gift Aid donations	–	1,000	1,000

Loss memorandum

	£
Loss year ended 30 September 2006	200,000
Less: s393A (i)	(14,000)
	186,000
Carried back to 30 September 2005 (ii)	(99,000)
Carried back to 30 September 2004 (£63,000 × 3/12) (iii)	(15,750)
Loss to carried forward	71,250

Carry forward amounts

A loss of £71,250 is available at 30 September 2006 to carry forward against future profits of the same trade.

There is also a capital loss of £2,000 to carry forward against future chargeable gains.

Corporation tax y/e 31.3.07

	£	£
Taxable trading profits	360,000	
Less: loss b/f	(10,000)	
		350,000
Interest – bank interest		6,000
Rental income		18,000
Capital gain	14,000	
Loss b/f	(14,000)	nil
Loss c/f £(15,000 – 14,000) = £1,000		
Total profits		374,000
Less: gift aid payment (charge)		(6,000)
PCTCT		368,000

	£
PCTCT	368,000
Dividends (10,800 × 100/90)	12,000
'Profits'	380,000

'Profits' are above £300,000 but below £1,500,000 so SCR marginal relief applies.

Tax payable

	£
Corporation tax on PCTCT	
£368,000 × 30%	110,400
Less: small companies' marginal relief	
£(1,500,000 – 380,000) × $\frac{368,000}{380,000}$ × $\frac{11}{400}$	(29,827)
Tax payable	80,573

Tutorial notes

1. The capital loss can only be set against the capital gain. The unrelieved loss must be carried forward.

2. Bought forward trading losses can only be set against taxable profits.

Answers to chapter 14: NATIONAL INSURANCE

a)
	£
Profits	12,830
Less: lower limit	(5,035)
Excess	7,795

Class 4 NICs (8% × £7,795) = £623.60

Class 2 NICs = £2.10 × 52 = £109.20

b)
	£
Upper limit	33,540
Less: lower limit	(5,035)
Excess	28,505

	£
Class 4 NICs (8% × £28,505)	2,280.40
+ 1% × £(35,000 − 33,540)	14.60
	2,295.00

Class 2 NICs = £2.10 × 52 = £109.20

c) As Raj's profits are below the lower limit, there is no liability to Class 4 NICs. He is also excepted from payment of Class 2 NICs.

Employers

To: A Colleague
From: Accounts assistant
Subject: Employers' NICs

Employers must pay two types of NICs:

Class 1A NICs
Class 1 Secondary NICs

Class 1A NICs

These are paid in respect of any taxable benefit paid to employees. They are calculated as 12.8% × the value of the taxable benefit.

Class 1 NICs

These are paid on earnings paid to employees. They are calculated as 12.8% of the amount by which earnings exceeds the earnings threshold (£5,035 for 2006/07).

Earnings include most vouchers and amounts paid that can be surrendered for cash.

NICs relate to an earnings period. This is the period to which earnings paid to an employee are deemed to relate. It is usually monthly or weekly. Only the earnings in the earnings period are considered.

3 **Earnings** for NICs

Class 1 secondary contributions – payable by employer

	£
12.8% × £(405 – 97) = £39.42 × 52	2,049.84

Class 1A contributions – payable by employer

£6,850 × 12.8%   £876.80

4 a) Class 2 = £2.10 × 52 = £109.20

	£
Class 4 £(33,540 – 5,035) × 8% (main)	2,280.40
£(80,000 – 33,540) × 1% (additional)	464.60
	2,745.00

b) A self employed person must notify HMRC that he or she is liable to Class 2 NICs within three months of the end of the month in which he or she becomes self employed.

5 a) Share of profits for y/e 31.12.07 is £120,000 × 20% = £24,000

2006/07

1.1.06 to 5.4.06
3/12 × £24,000 = £6,000

2007/08

1.1.07 to 31.12.07 = £24,000

Overlap period is 1.1.07 to 5.4.07 so overlap profits are £6,000.

b) Class 4 NICs for 2006/07

£(6,000 – 5,035) = £965 × 8% = £77.20

Answers to chapter 15: ADMINISTRATION AND PAYMENT OF INCOME TAX, CGT AND CLASS 4 NICs

To: Office Assistant
From: AN Accountant
Subject: Tax returns

Simon must submit his tax return to HMRC by 31 January 2008.

If Simon misses this deadline for submitting his return there is an automatic maximum penalty of £100. If the return is over six months late the maximum penalty rises to £200. If the return is over 12 months late there is a tax geared penalty equal to 100% of the tax due.

If either payment on account of Simon's 2006/07 income tax and Class 4 NIC is paid late, interest will run from the due date of payment. Similarly interest will be charged on any balancing payment paid late from the due date of payment.

In addition, a surcharge of 5% will be made on balancing payments paid more than 28 days after the due date. The surcharge rises to 10% on balancing payments that are paid more than six months late.

Savannah will not have to make payments on account of her 2006/07 tax liability since she had no income tax liability in 2005/06.

£12,000 for 2006/07 is therefore all due on 31 January 2008. Interest runs from this date if the payment is made late. In addition a surcharge of 5% will be charged if payment is over 28 days late. The surcharge will rise to 10% if the payment is over six months late.

Savahhan's 2007/08 liability will be due as follows:

	£
31 January 2008	6,000
31 July 2008	6,000
31 January 2009	2,000

Interest will be charged from the dates shown on any of these amounts paid late. In addition if the £2,000 due on 31 January 2009 will be subject to a surcharge if it is paid late. The surcharge will be 5% for payment more than 28 days but less than six months late. This rises to 10% if the payment is made more than six months late.

3 a) *Taxable trading profits 2006/07*

	£	£
Net profit per accounts		5,000
Add: wages of proprietor	15,000	
private motor 20% × £2,500	500	
depreciation	3,000	
entertaining suppliers	750	
legal costs re grant of lease	450	
		19,700
		24,700
Less: capital allowances		(1,600)
Taxable trading profit		23,100

b) *Class 2 NICs 2006/07*

£2.10 × 52 = **£109.20**

Class 4 NICs 2006/07

£(23,100 − 5,035) = £18,065 × 8% = **£1,445.20**

c)

Box 3.1	Martin's The Greengrocer		
Box 3.2	Retail greengrocer		
Box 3.4	01/04/06		
Box 3.5	31/03/07		
Box 3.16	£1,600		
Box 3.22	£1,600		
Box 3.29	£100,000		
Box 3.46	£40,000		
Box 3.49	£60,000		
Box 3.33	£15,000	Box 3.51	£35,000
		Box 3.52	£7,000
		Box 3.54	£1,000
Box 3.37	£500	Box 3.55	£2,500
Box 3.39	£750	Box 3.57	£1,000
Box 3.40	£450	Box 3.58	£1,250
		Box 3.60	£500
Box 3.44	£3,000	Box 3.62	£3,000
		Box 3.63	£3,750
Box 3.64	£55,000		
Box 3.65	£5,000		
Box 3.66	£19,700		
Box 3.69	£19,700		
Box 3.70	£1,600		
Box 3.72	£1,600		
Box 3.73	£23,100		

Answers to chapter 16: ADMINISTRATION AND PAYMENT OF CORPORATION TAX

	£
PCTCT	48,000
FII (× 100/90)	2,000
	50,000

Small companies' lower limit = $\dfrac{£300,000}{5} \times \dfrac{8}{12} = £40,000$

Small companies' upper limit = $\dfrac{£1,500,000}{5} \times \dfrac{8}{12} = £200,000$

Therefore, small companies' marginal relief applies.

	£
£48,000 × 30%	14,400
Less: small companies' marginal relief 11/400 £(200,000 – 50,000) × $\dfrac{48,000}{50,000}$	(3,960)
CT	10,440

£10,440 is due for payment on 1 September 2007.

The return covering this accounting period must be filed by 30 November 2007, or 3 months after the notice to deliver a return is issued, if later.

Note. Sims Ltd does not need to pay its corporation tax in instalments as it is not a large company.

PCTCT = £3,000,000

The full rate of corporation tax applies, so Port Ltd must pay its CT in instalments.

£3,000,000 × 30% = £900,000

£900,000 is due in initial instalments of 3/8 × £900,000 = £337,500

Therefore, 14 November 2006 = £337,500
              14 February 2007 = £337,500
              14 April 2007 = £225,000 (balance)

3

	Year ended 31 August 2006 £	4 months to 31 December 2006 £
Trading profits (12:4)	2,400,000	800,000
PCTCT	2,400,000	800,000

The full rate of tax applies in both accounting periods.

CT @ 30%	£720,000	£240,000

The tax for the year ended 31 August 2006 must be paid in instalments as follows:

£

14 March 2006 $\left(\dfrac{720,000}{4}\right)$ 180,000

14 June 2006   180,000
14 September 2006   180,000
14 December 2006   180,000

Tax for the 4 months to 31 December 2006 must be paid in instalments of:

$$\dfrac{3 \times 240,000}{4} = £180,000$$

14 March 2007 = £180,000
14 April 2007 = £60,000 (balance: 4th month after end of accounting period)

The returns for both accounting periods must be filed by 31 December 2007.

4 To: Office colleague
From: AN Accountant
Subject: Filing corporation tax returns

Corporation tax returns must normally be filed within twelve months of the end of the period account concerned.

There is a fixed penalty of £100 if a return is not filed on time. This rises to £200 if a return is fil more than three months late. The £100/£200 penalties increase to £500/£1,000 for the th consecutive late filing of a CT return.

Any enquiry into a tax return must be commenced by a year after the later of:

a) the due filing date

b) the 31 October, 31 January, 30 April or 31 July next following the actual delivery of return.

a)

	FYA £	Pool £	Exp. car £	Allowances £
TWDV b/f		12,000		
Additions		10,000	25,000	
		22,000	25,000	
WDA @ 25%		(5,500)	(3,000) (max)	8,500
		16,500	22,000	
Addition	5,000			
FYA @ 50%	(2,500)	2,500		2,500
TWDV c/f		19,000	22,000	
Allowances				11,000

b) *Corporation tax computation y/e 31.3.07*

	£
Taxable trading profits (£405,000 – £11,000)	394,000
Interest	3,000
Rental income	10,000
Other income	6,000
PCTCT	413,000

	£
£413,000 × 30%	123,900.00
Less: Small companies' marginal relief	
£(1,500,000 – 413,000) × 11/400	(29,892.50)
	94,007.50
Less: income tax deducted at source £6,000 × 22%	(1,320.00)
Corporation tax due	92,687.50

c) You should have made the following entries on the form CT 600.

Taxable trading profits (box 3): £394,000
Net trading profits (box 5): £394,000
Interest (box 6): £3,000
Rental income (box 12): £10,000
Other income (box 14): £6,000
Profits (box 21): £413,000
Profits chargeable to corporation tax (box 37): £413,000
Franked investment income (box 38): £0
Associated companies (box 39): 0
Marginal relief (box 42): X
Financial year (box 43): 2006
Amount of profit (box 44): £413,000
Rate of tax (box 45): 30.00
Tax (box 46): £123,900.00
Corporation tax (box 63): £123,900.00
Marginal rate relief (box 64): £29,892.50
Corporation tax net of marginal rate relief (box 65): £94,007.50
Corporation tax chargeable (box 70): £94,007.50
Income tax deducted (box 84): £1,320.00
Tax payable (box 86): £92,687.50
Corporation tax outstanding (box 92): £92,687.50

Capital allowances
Machinery and plant (box 107): £8,000
Cars (box 109): £3,000
FYA expenditure (box 118): £5,000
Other expenditure on plant and machinery (box 121): £35,000

PRACTICE EXAM 1
(DECEMBER 2003 PAPER)

UNIT 18

ANSWERS

practice exam 1 (December 2003 paper): answers

SECTION 1

Task 1.1

a) **Capital allowances**

	FYA @ 40% £	FYA @ 50% £	Pool £	Private use asset × 75% £	£
Period ended 30.9.05					
Addition				13,800	
WDA (£3,000 × 9/12)				(2,250) × 75%	1,688
Additions	12,750				
FYA @ 40%	(5,100)				5,100
			7,650		6,788
			7,650	11,550	
Year ended 30.9.06					
Addition			10,000		
Disposal			(5,050)		
			12,600	11,550	
WDA			(3,150)		3,150
Additions	8,050	16,902		(2,888) × 75%	2,166
FYA @ 40%	(3,220)				3,220
			4,830		
FYA @ 50%		(8,451)			8,451
			8,451		
			22,731	8,662	16,987

Tutorial notes

1. FYA are not pro-rated in a short period.
2. The key to getting a capital allowance question right is to set out the proforma as shown here
3. As the business is a small enterprise, 50% FYA are available on the acquisition December 2004 and May 2006.

b) **Industrial buildings**

Period ended 30 September 2005

IBAs £95,000 × 4% × 9/12 = £2,850

As the building was in industrial use on 30 September 2005, IBAs are available for the period. the period is only nine months long, time apportionment is needed.

Note that the date of purchase of the building does not effect the IBAs available.

Year ended 30 September 2006

IBAs £95,000 × 4% = £3,800

practice exam 1 (December 2003 paper): answers

Task 1.2

	Period to 30 September 2005 £	Year to 30 September 2006 £
Profits	14,363	38,114
Capital allowances (1.1)	(6,788)	(16,987)
IBAs	(2,850)	(3,800)
Taxable trading profits	4,725	17,327

Task 1.3

	Total £	James £	Linda £
2004/05			
1 January 2005 to 5 April 2005	1,575	1,050	525
2005/06			
12 months ended 31 December 2005	9,057	6,038	3,019
2006/07			
Year ended 30 September 2006	17,327	11,551	5,776
Overlap profits			
1 January 2005 to 5 April 2005	1,575	1,050	525
1 October 2005 to 31 December 2005	4,332	2,888	1,444
	5,907	3,938	1,969

Task 1.4

	James £	Linda £
2006/07		
Year to 30 September 2006	11,551	5,776

Task 1.5

James and Linda are self-employed they are required to pay Class 2 and Class 4 NICs.

NICs payable for 2006/07:

		James £	Linda £
Class 2	£2.10 × 52	109	109
Class 4	8% (£11,551 − £5,035)	521	
	8% (£5,776 − £5,035)		59
		630	168

Task 1.6

The £300 for the new tyres is a revenue expense as it is a cost of repair rather than improvement to the car.

This means that the £300 can be deducted in computing taxable trading profit.

As the £300 is not a capital expense, it is not eligible for capital allowances.

Task 1.7

If the industrial building bought in April 2005 was sold for more than its original cost a chargeable gain will arise on sale.

The gain may be deferred by claiming rollover relief. The gains is deferred by deducting it from the cost of the new building. The gain deferred is the gain before rollover relief.

If all of the disposal proceeds are invested in the new building, the full chargeable gain otherwise arising is deferred. If the disposal proceeds are not completely reinvested an amount of the gain equal to the proceeds not reinvested will remain chargeable. The remaining gain is deferred and deducted from the cost of the new building.

SECTION 2

Task 2.1

Capital gain

1985 pool

	No of shares	Cost £	Indexed cost £
February 1994	5,000	16,900	16,900
Indexation to November 1997			
0.123 × £16,900			2,079
	5,000	16,900	18,979
Rights issue	500	1,000	1,000
	5,500	17,900	19,979
Indexation to May 1999			
0.038 × £19,979			759
May 1999	5,000	21,600	21,600
	10,500	39,500	42,338
Index to August 2006			7,917
0.187 × £42,338	10,500	39,500	50,255

	£
Sale proceeds	72,300
Less indexed cost	(50,255)
Chargeable gain	22,045

Task 2.2

	£
Net profit	162,040
Add: entertaining	1,640
depreciation	98,320
Less: profit on sale of shares	(32,800)
bad debts recovered – non-trade	(1,500)
Capital allowances	(23,700)
Adjusted trading profit	204,000

practice exam 1 (December 2003 paper): answers

Task 2.3

	£
Trading profit (Schedule D Case I)	204,000
Chargeable gains (£22,045 – £2,353)	19,692
PCTCT	223,692

Task 2.4

As 'profits' are below the small companies' lower limit of £300,000 the small companies' rate of t applies in both FY 2005 and FY 2006.

CT Due: £223,692 × 19% = £42,501

CT of £42,501 is due for payment on 1 October 2007.

Task 2.5

If an associated company is acquired, the rate of tax that had to be paid by Quinten Ltd will chang This is because the companies must share the upper and lower profits limits. The upper limit for Quint Ltd would be £750,000 and the lower limit £150,000.

If Quinten Ltd had had an associated company in the year to 31 December 2006 tax would have be due at 30% less small companies marginal relief rather than at 19% as shown above.

PRACTICE EXAM 2 (JUNE 2004 PAPER)

UNIT 18

ANSWERS

practice exam 2 (June 2004 paper): answers

SECTION 1

Task 1.1

	£	£
Net profit per accounts		87,070
Add: gifts to customers	1,350	
cost of installing machinery	2,200	
increase in general bad debt provision	400	
motor expenses (25% × £4,680 + 15% × £3,200)	1,650	
depreciation	21,080	
		26,680
Adjusted trading profit before capital allowances		113,750

Tutorial note. Gifts of food are never allowable.

Task 1.2

a)

	FYA £	Pool £	George's car (75%) £	Carol's car (85%) £	Capital allowances £
		18,444	15,630	8,780	
WDA @ 25%		(4,611)			4,611
WDA @£3,000/25%			(3,000) × 75%	(2,195) × 85%	4,116
		13,833	12,630	6,585	
Addition	15,400				
Installation	2,200				
	17,600				
FYA @ 50%	(8,800)				8,800
		8,800			
		22,633	12,630	6,585	17,527

b) IBA = £88,000 × 4% = £3,520

Note. As the period of account is 12 months long, there is no need to time apportion the IBAs.

Task 1.3

	£	£
Trading profit before capital allowances (task 1.1)		113,750
Less: capital allowances (task 1.2)	17,527	
IBAs (task 1.2)	3,520	
		(21,047)
Net trading profit		92,703

Task 1.4

Payments on account of income tax for 2006/07 are due on 31 January 2007 and 31 July 2007. Any final balancing payment will be due on 31 January 2008.

Task 1.5

		£
Class 2	NICs (£2.10 × 52)	109.20
Class 4	£(33,540 – 5,035) × 8%	2,280.40
	£(46,352 (note) – 33,540) × 1%	128.12
		2,517.72

Note. As profits are shared equally Carol's profits are £46,352 (£92,703 × 50%)

Task 1.6

Gift relief would be available to defer any gain arising on the gift of the business to George's son, Elliot.

A claim would need to be made for this relief.

The gain deferred by gift relief is calculated assuming that the business is disposed of at market value to George's son.

George's son is then deemed to have acquired the business for the market value less the amount of the deferred gain.

The deferred gain will effectively become chargeable when Elliot disposes of the business.

Task 1.7

Taxable trading profits of the year to 31 January 2007 are taxed in 2006/07.

Profits of the four months to 31 May 2007 will be taxed in 2007/08.

Profits taxed in 2007/08 (the closing year) can be reduced by any overlap profits that arose at the start of the business.

SECTION 2

Task 2.1

FA 1985 pool

	No of shares	Cost £	Indexed cost £
April 1986	2,000	25,000	25,000
Index to June 1991			
0.373 × £25,000			9,325
	2,000	25,000	34,425
Addition	2,000	35,000	35,000
	4,000	60,000	69,325
Bonus issue	400	–	–
	4,400	60,000	69,325
Index to September 1999			
0.239 × £69,325			16,569
	4,400	60,000	85,894
Rights issue	880	8,800	8,800
	5,280	68,800	94,694
Index to May 2006 0.176 × £94,694			16,666
	5,280	68,800	111,360
Less: sale	(4,000)	(52,121)	(84,364)
	1,280	16,679	26,996

	£
Disposal proceeds	120,000
Less: cost	(52,121)
indexation (£84,364 – £52,121)	(32,243)
Chargeable gain	35,636

Notes

1. For companies, indexation runs to the date of disposal of an asset.
2. There is no need to compute indexation to the date of the bonus issue.

Task 2.2

	£
Sale proceeds	260,000
Less: cost	(150,000)
indexation (£150,000 × 0.182)	(27,300)
Chargeable gain	82,700

£30,000 of the gain is immediately chargeable, as this amount of the proceeds are not reinvested in the replacement factory.

£52,700 of the gain is rolled over. This amount of the gain is set against the base cost of the replacement factory.

Task 2.3

	£
Adjusted trading profit	623,024
Chargeable gain (task 2.1)	35,636
Chargeable gain (task 2.2)	30,000
PCTCT	688,660

There are two associated companies, so the small companies' lower and upper limits must be divided by 2:

Small companies' upper limit = £750,000

Small companies' lower limit = £150,000

Therefore, the small companies' marginal relief applies:

	£
£688,660 × 30%	206,598
Less: 11/400 × (£750,000 − £688,660)	(1,687)
	204,911

£204,911 must be paid by 1 January 2008.

Task 2.4

Box 3	£623,024
Box 5	£623,024
Box 16	£65,636
Box 18	£65,636
Box 21	£688,660
Box 37	£688,660
Box 39	1
Box 42	X
Box 43	2006
Box 44	£688,660
Box 45	30%
Box 46	£206,598.00
Box 63	£206,598.00
Box 64	£1,686.85
Box 65	£204,911.15
Box 70	£204,911.15
Box 86	£204,911.15

Task 2.5

Tell the friend politely that the ethical guideline of confidentiality means that it is not possible to disclose details of the company's profit.

PRACTICE EXAM 3
(DECEMBER 2004 PAPER)

UNIT 18

ANSWERS

practice exam 3 (December 2004 paper): answers

SECTION 1

Task 1.1

Capital allowances to the date of cessation

	Pool £	Private use car £	Allowances £
TWDV b/f	7,330	9,570	
Proceeds	(8,200)	(6,000)	
	(870)	3,570	
Balancing charge	870		(870)
Balancing allowance		(3,570) × 70%	2,499
Allowances			1,629

Task 1.2

Net taxable trading profits

Final tax year of business is 2006/07, basis period 1 January 2006 – 30 September 2006

	£
Trading profits	53,000
Less: capital allowances	(1,629)
	51,371
Overlap profits	(21,050)
Net taxable trading profits 2006/07	30,321

Task 1.3

Net gain chargeable to capital gains tax, before annual exemption

	£	£
Sale proceeds		225,000
Less: cost July 1995	82,500	
improvements February 2003	17,000	
		(99,500)
Unindexed gain		125,500
Less: indexation on cost July 1995 – April 1998		
£82,500 × 0.091		(7,508)
Indexed gain		117,992
Business asset owned at least two years: tapered gain £117,992 × 25%		29,498

430

practice exam 3 (December 2004 paper): answers

Task 1.4

To:	Angela Graham	Subject:	Various queries
From:	Accounting Technician	Date:	30 November 2006

The net taxable trading profits of a partnership are calculated in the same way as for a sole trader. They are then apportioned between the partners according to the profit sharing ratios in force during the period in which the profit was earned. Each partner is then taxed on her share of the profits as if she were a sole trader.

The tax payable by each partner is determined by adding up that partner's income, ie her share of taxable trading profits from the partnership plus any other income, such as interest and dividends. From this is deducted the personal allowance, and the tax is calculated using the tax rates and bands for the tax year.

You and your sister will need to pay Class 2 and Class 4 National Insurance Contributions.

Class 2 costs are paid at a flat weekly rate, currently £2.10, but contributions need not be paid if your share of profits are less than £4,465. Class 4 contributions are paid with income tax, and are calculated at 8% of profits between £5,035 and £33,540, and 1% on profits in excess of £32,760.

The records to be maintained will include all the details that you used to prepare accounts, such as copy invoices for income and expenses etc. The records must be kept for almost 6 years from the end of the tax year, and HMRC may charge a penalty of up to £3,000 for failing to keep adequate records.

Task 1.5

As Angela's final total tax liability for 2006/07 exceeds the £10,000 that she has already paid, the balance will be payable on 31 January 2008.

Box 3.4	1 January 2006
Box 3.5	30 September 2006
Box 3.8	30 September 2006
Box 3.14	870
Box 3.17	2,499
Box 3.22	870
Box 3.23	2,499
Box 3.29	257,200
Box 3.46	79,400
Box 3.49	177,800
Box 3.64	124,800
Box 3.65	53,000
Box 3.68	2,499
Box 3.69	2,499
Box 3.70	870
Box 3.72	870
Box 3.73	51,371

SECTION 2

Task 2.1

Chargeable gain from sale of shares in Yellow Ltd

	£
Proceeds	24,500
Less: cost November 2001	(11,650)
Unindexed gain	12,850
Less: indexation November 2001 to March 2007	
£11,650 × 0.149	(1,736)
Chargeable gain	11,114

Task 2.2

Adjusted trading profit, before capital allowances, for the 15 months to 31 March 2007

	£	£
Net profit		49,090
Add: gift aid donation	3,500	
entertaining customers	8,450	
depreciation	14,600	
		26,550
		75,640
Less: profit on sale of shares	12,850	
UK dividends received	4,500	
rental income	7,500	
		24,850
Adjusted trading profits		50,790

Task 2.3

a) PCTCT, 12 months to 31 December 2006

	£
Trading profits 12/15 x £50,790	40,632
Less: capital allowances	(8,750)
	31,882
Rental Income 12 x £500 = £6,000 – loss b/f £1,000	5,000
Gift aid	(3,500)
PCTCT	33,382

practice exam 3 (December 2004 paper): answers

PCTCT, 3 months to 31 March 2007

	£
Trading profits 3/15 × £50,790	10,158
Less: capital allowances	(2,600)
	7,558
Rental Income 3 × £500	1,500
Chargeable gain	11,114
PCTCT	20,172

Task 2.4

Corporation tax payable 12 months ended 31 December 2007

	£
PCTCT	33,382
FII £4,500 × 100/90	5,000
Profits	38,382

	FY05 3 months to 31.3.06 £	FY06 9 months to 31.12.06 £
PCTCT (dividend 3:9)	8,346	25,036
'Profits' (dividends 3:9)	9,596	28,786
Lower limit for starting rate (FY05 only) £10,000 × 3/12	2,500	
Upper limit for starting rate (FY05 only) £50,000 × 3/12	12,500	
Tax on PCTCT		
FY05 £8,346 × 19%	1,586	
Less: starting rate marginal relief £(12,500 − 9,596) × $\frac{8,346}{9,596}$ × $\frac{19}{400}$	(120)	1,466
FY06 £25,036 × 19%		4,757
Corporation tax payable for y/e 31.12.06		6,223

Corporation tax payable 3 months to 31 March 2007

The small companies limits are time apportioned for a three month accounting period:

Small companies lower limit £300,000 × 3/12 = £75,000

Corporation tax payable: £20,172 × 19% = £3,833

practice exam 3 (December 2004 paper): answers

Task 2.5

From: AAT@horatio.co.uk
To: MD@horatio.co.UK
Sent: 30 May 2007 15.55
Subject: Tax return

The corporation tax return for the year to 31 December 2005 should have been filed by 31 December 2005, and was therefore 9 months late.

The company will be liable to penalties of:

- £200 as the return was more than 6 months late, and
- 10% of the tax unpaid as the returns was between 6 and 12 months late. The tax unpaid £(19,600 – 15,000) = £4,600, so the penalty is £460.

The additional tax of £4,600 was payable by 30 September 2005. HM Revenue and Customs will charge interest from the due date until the date before the tax is paid, so the outstanding tax should be paid straight away to prevent further interest from accruing.

PRACTICE EXAM 4 (JUNE 2005 PAPER)

UNIT 18

ANSWERS

practice exam 4 (June 2005 paper): answers

SECTION 1

Task 1.1

	£	£
Net profit		2,326
Add: Salary – Philip	22,500	
Depreciation	8,780	
Increase in general bad debt provision	220	
Motor expenses (30% × £5,630)	1,689	
Entertaining customers	250	
		33,439
Less: profit on sale of equipment		(310)
Adjusted trading profit before capital allowances		35,455

Task 1.2

(a) 1.2.05 – 31.1.06

	FYA @ 40% £	FYA @ 50% £	Pool £	Private use (70%) £	Allowances £
Additions – FYAs					
February 2005		8,040			
March 2005		10,020			
		18,060			
		(9,030)	9,030		9,030
December 2005	2,130				
FYA @ 40%	(852)		1,278		852
TWDV c/f			10,308		
Allowances					9,882

436

b) 1.2.06 – 31.1.07

	FYA @ 50% £	Pool £	Private use (70%) £	Allowances £
TWDV b/f		10,308		
Addition – no FYA				
August 2006			10,000	
WDA @ 25%			(2,500) × 70%	1,750
Disposal – April 2006 (less than cost)		(2,800)		
		7,508		
WDA @ 25%		(1,877)		1,877
Additions – FYA		5,631		
November 2006	3,300			
FYA @ 50%	(1,650)	1,650		1,650
TWD V c/f		7,281	7,500	
Allowances				5,277

Tutorial notes

1   You need to take great care to identify the rates at which FYAs are available.

2   Vans are classified as plant and machinery and, therefore, should have been added to the general pool.

3   Full allowances are given in the private use asset column but then a percentage of the allowance is taken to deduct from taxable profits.

Task 1.3

	Adjusted Trading profit £	Capital Allowances £	Taxable trading profit £
y/e 31.1.06	14,556	9,882	4,674
y/e 31.1.07	35,455	5,277	30,178

Task 1.4

	£
2004/05 (1.2.05 – 5.4.05) 2/12 × £4,674	779
2005/06 (y/e 31.1.06)	4,674
2006/07 (y/e 31.1.07)	30,178
Overlap profits (1.2.05 – 5.4.05) =	779

practice exam 4 (June 2005 paper): answers

Task 1.5

	£
Class 2 NICs (£(52 × £2.10))	109.20
Class 4 NICs (£(30,178 – 5,035) × 8%)	2,011.44
	2,120.64

Task 1.6

It would only be possible to give Philip the information regarding his uncle if his uncle has specifically authorised the firm to do so. This authorisation would need to have been made in writing.

Task 1.7

Some expenditure on plant and machinery purchased between 6 April 2006 and 5 April 2007 gave rise to a 50% capital allowance, known as a first year allowance. However, first year allowances (FYA) are not normally available on the purchase of cars. The only exception is that 100% FYA are available on the purchase of certain low emission cars but this does not apply in your case.

As your car cost £10,000, your car will have its tax value written down by 25% a year. As you use your car for business purposes you will be entitled to 70% of the 25% allowance each year.

The motor car expenses shown in your profit and loss account are £5,630. As you use your car 30% for private purposes, 30% × £5,630 = £1,689 must be added back to your profits when calculating taxable trading profits.

Task 2.1

IBAs on lower of
(i)   £120,000 and
(ii) £80,000

ie £80,000

Over remaining tax life, (25 – 9 = 16 years) = £5,000

Task 2.2

	£
Trading profit	470,200
Less:	
Capital allowances	(37,110)
IBAs	(5,000)
Adjustable taxable trading profit	428,090

Task 2.3

FA 1985 POOL

	No	Cost £	Indexed Cost £
April 2001	10,000	95,000	95,000
Index to December 2003 95,000 × 0.060			5,700
	10,000	95,000	100,700
Rights issue 1 for 4	2,500	12,500	12,500
	12,500	107,500	113,200
Index to June 2006 113,200 × 0.067			7,584
	12,500	107,500	120,784
June 2006 disposal	(4,000)	(34,400)	(38,651)
	8,500	73,100	82,133

	£
Proceeds	58,000
Less: Cost	(34,400)
	23,600
Less: Indexation (£38,651 − £34,400)	(4,251)
Chargeable gain	19,349

Tutorial notes

It is very important to get the layout of the share pool correct.

Remember that, for companies, the share pool must be indexed to the date of disposal of the shares.

Task 2.4

	£
Taxable trading profit	428,090
Chargeable gain	19,349
PCTCT	447,439

practice exam 4 (June 2005 paper): answers

(b) As Woodpecker Ltd has one associated company the upper and lower limits for small companies rate purposes for both FY 2005 and FY 2006 are:

	£
Upper limit £1,500,000 ÷ 2	750,000
Lower limit £300,000 ÷ 2	150,000

Therefore, small companies' marginal relief applies.

	£
£447,439 × 30%	134,232
Less: 11/400 (750,000 – 447,439)	(8,320)
CT payable on 1 August 2007	125,912

Task 2.5

Woodpecker Ltd must file its corporation tax return 12 months after the end of the accounting period concerned, ie by 31 October 2007. If this return is late the penalties will be:

Up to 3 months late	£500
Over 3 months late	£1,000

These levels of penalties apply because this would be the third successive late filing of the corporation tax return. There is an additional tax geared penalty of 10% of the unpaid tax if the return is filed more than six months late but less than twelve months late. This rises to 20% of that tax if the return is over twelve months late.

Task 2.6

	y/e 31.12.03 £	y/e 31.12.04 £	y/e 31.12.05 £	y/e 31.12.06 £
Adjusted trading profit	320,000	175,000	–	48,000
Rental income/loss	5,000	(4,000)	3,000	(1,500)
Capital gain	14,500	–	–	11,000
	339,500	171,000	3,000	57,500
Less: S393A	–	(92,000)	(3,000)	–
	339,500	79,000	–	57,500

Notes

1. Trading losses can be set against other income in the year of the loss and in the previous 12 months
2. Rental losses can be set against all other income in the year of loss.
3. Capital losses can only be set against capital gains in the year they are made and subsequent years. Therefore, £6,000 of the capital loss in y/e 31.12.04 is set off against the gain of £6,000 in y/e 31.12.05 and the remaining £(12,000 – 6,000) = 6,000 is set off against the gain of £17,000 y/e 31.12.06, leaving £11,000 left in charge.

PRACTICE EXAM 5
(DECEMBER 2005 PAPER)

UNIT 18

ANSWERS

practice exam 5 (December 2005 paper): answers

SECTION 1

Task 1.1

The 2005/06 tax return should have been filed by 31 January 2007, or three months after the issue the return, if that was later. As the return is between six and twelve months late a fixed penalty of £20 will be charged.

Task 1.2

Page 1

Name: Andrena Milburn

Box 3.1: Andrena Milburn   Box 3.2 Footwear manufacturer

                                                        Box 3.4 1/12/04   Box 3.5 30/11/0

Box3.22 3,560

Page 2

				Box 3.29	87,435
				Box 3.46	25,335
				Box 3.49	62,100
		Box 3.52	2,500		
Box 3.37	1,760	Box 3.55	4,400		
Box 3.44	1,200	Box 3.62	1,200		
				Box 3.64	8,100
				Box 3.65	54,000
		Box 3.66	2,960		
				Box 3.69	2,960
		Box3.70	3,560		
				Box 3.72	3,560
				Box 3.73	53,400

practice exam 5 (December 2005 paper): answers

Task 1.3

	£	£
Net profit		46,400
Add:		
Depreciation	1,200	
Motor expenses (60%)	2,160	
		3,360
		49,760
Less: capital allowances		(2,840)
Taxable trading profit		46,920

Task 1.4

1.12.05 – 28.2.06

$\frac{3}{12}$ x £46,920   £11,730

£11,730 arose whilst Andrena was a sole trader.

1.3.06 – 30.11.06

$\frac{9}{12}$ x £46,920   £35,190

£35,190 was allocated to the partnership.

Task 1.5

2006/2007 (y/e 30.11.06)

	£
1.12.05 – 28.2.06	11,730
1.3.06 – 30.11.06	
(£35,190 x $\frac{1}{2}$)	17,595
	29,325

443

Task 1.6

	£
Class 2 NIC (£2.10 × 52)	109.20
Class 4 NIC (8% (29,325 − 5,035))	1,943.20
	2,052.40

Task 1.7

Thank you for your recent e-mail concerning your proposed purchase of a new building. Industr[ial] Buildings Allowance (IBA) applies to both new and used buildings, but in slightly different ways.

An industrial building has a tax life of 25 years. This means that if you own the building for 25 years, t[he] whole cost of the building can be written off for tax purposes. For a new building, this done by givi[ng] an IBA of 4% of its cost per year. Therefore, if you buy the new building you will be able to deduct IBA of £50,000 × 4% = £2,000 each year for each year you own the building up to a maximum of [25] years.

If you buy the used building, its tax life remaining is (25 − 9) = 16 years. The amount on which you [get] tax relief is the lower of the original cost to the current owner (£40,000) and the purchase cost to y[ou] (£50,000). This amount is then divided by the remaining tax life of the building, giving you an annu[al] allowance of £40,000 ÷ 16 = £2,500 for each year of your ownership for a maximum of 16 years.

In the short term, therefore, the used building would attract faster tax relief but if you intend to stay [in] the building for a long period the new building would give more tax relief overall.

Please let me know if you have any further queries.

A Technician

practice exam 5 (December 2005 paper): answers

SECTION 2

Task 2.1

	FYA £	General Pool £	Expensive Car £	Allowances £
Addition – no FYA				
Managing director's car			25,000	
WDA (car £3,000 x $\frac{9}{12}$)			(2,250)	2,250
Additions – FYA				
May 2006	7,500			
November 2006	10,000			
	17,500			
FYA @ 50%	(8,750)			8,750
		8,750		
TWDV c/f		8,750	22,750	
Allowances				11,000

Notes

1. The WDA is pro-rated in a short period of account but FYAs are not.

2. There is no adjustment to a **company's** capital allowances as a result of the private use of an asset.

	£
Adjusted trading profit	25,000
Less: capital allowances	(11,000)
Taxable trading profit	14,000

Task 2.2

	£
Disposal proceeds	25,000
Less: cost	(10,000)
	15,000
Less: Indexation	
10,000 × 0.019	(190)
Capital gain	14,810

445

practice exam 5 (December 2005 paper): answers

Task 2.3

	£
Taxable trading profits	14,000
Capital gain	14,810
Rental income (£500 × 12)	4,500
PCTCT	33,310

Task 2.4

The accounting period to 30 September 2006 straddles two financial years:

	FY 2005 ($\frac{3}{9}$)	FY 2006 ($\frac{6}{9}$)
	£	£
PCTCT	11,103	22,207
Starting rate upper limit £50,000 × 3/12	12,500	–
Starting rate lower limit £10,000 × 3/12	2,500	–
	Starting rate marginal relief applies	
Small companies lower limit		150,000
		Small companies rate applies

Therefore:

	£	£
FY 2005		
£11,103 × 19%	2,110	
Less: $\frac{19}{400}$ × (12,500 – 11,103)	(66)	
		2,044
FY 2006		
£22,207 × 19%		4,219
		6,263

Task 2.5

I understand that consideration is being given to acquire an associated company for Harrison Ltd during 2007.

The main tax effect of such an acquisition would be in the calculation of the limits for the rates at which corporation tax is charged. The full rate is 30%. The small companies rate is 19%.

If Harrison Ltd does not have an associated company for y/e 31 December 2007 and its profits chargeable to corporation tax are £200,000, it will be within the small companies rate of tax as the lower limit for this rate is £300,000.

However, if Harrison Ltd has an associated company for any part of y/e 31 December 2007, the lower limit will be divided equally between the two companies. Therefore the lower limit will be £150,000. Harrison Ltd would be liable to corporation tax at 19% on its PCTCT up to £150,000 and the excess (about £50,000) at the marginal rate of 32.75%.

I hope this explanation is clear, but please let me know if you need any further information.

Technician

Task 2.6

If Harrison Ltd fails to notify HMRC that trading has commenced, an initial penalty of £300 can be imposed.

INDEX

Administration and payment of corporation tax 171
Allowable costs 79
Annual exemption 81
Assets used partly for private purposes 35
Associated companies 137

Badges of trade 12
Balancing allowance 33
Balancing charge 33
Basis period 48
Bonus and rights issues 102

Capital losses 148
Chargeable assets 77
Chargeable disposals 77
Chargeable persons 77
Charitable donations 16
Class 1A NICs 155
Class 2 contributions 154
Class 4 contributions 154
Client confidentiality 166
Computing capital gains tax payable 84
Computing the corporation tax liability 130
Current year basis of assessment 48

Determining the rate of corporation tax 130
Disallowable expenditure 14

Enhancement expenditure 79
Enquiries 165, 174

Filing date 172
Filing tax returns 160
Financial Year 140
First year allowances 30

Gift relief 112

Income tax suffered or withheld 177
Industrial Buildings Allowance (IBA) 38
Interest 164

Large companies 175
Long periods of account 124
Losses arising from the rental of property 148

Methods of operating a business 4

Operative events 99
Overlap profits 52

Partnerships 63
Payment of tax and interest 175
Payments of tax 162
Penalties 173
Penalties for late filing 160
Plant 28
Profits chargeable to corporation tax 117, 118

Quarterly instalments 175

Records 173
Relevant legislation and guidance from HMRC 5
Repayment of tax and repayment supplement 165
Revenue expenditure 15
Rollover relief 110

S380 relief 59
S385 relief 58
S393(1) relief 144
S393A relief 145
Secondary Class 1 NICs 155
Shares 95
Short accounting periods 136
Short life assets 36
Small and medium sized companies 177
Statutory total income 5
Surcharges 164

Taper relief 82
Tax returns and keeping records 160
Tax year, fiscal year or year of assessment 48
Taxable income 5

449

The FA 1985 pool 98
The indexation allowance 79
Trading losses 144
Trading profits 14

Writing Down Allowance (WDA) 28